Dear Reader:

The book you are about to read is the latest bestseller from the St. Martin's True Crime Library, the imprint *The New York Times* calls "the leader in true crime!" Each month, we offer you a fascinating account of the latest, most sensational crime that has captured the national attention. St. Martin's is the publisher of bestselling true crime author and crime journalist Kieran Crowley, who explores the dark, deadly links between a prominent Manhattan surgeon and the disappearance of his wife fifteen years earlier in THE SURGEON'S WIFE. Suzy Spencer's BREAKING POINT guides readers through the tortuous twists and turns in the case of Andrea Yates, the Houston mother who drowned her five young children in the family's bathtub. In Edgar Award-nominated DARK DREAMS, legendary FBI profiler Roy Hazelwood and bestselling crime author Stephen G. Michaud shine light on the inner workings of America's most violent and depraved murderers. In the book you now hold, THE PASTOR'S WIFE, acclaimed author Diane Fanning digs into the mysterious murder of a pastor.

St. Martin's True Crime Library gives you the stories behind the headlines. Our authors take you right to the scene of the crime and into the minds of the most notorious murderers to show you what really makes them tick. St. Martin's True Crime Library paperbacks are better than the most terrifying thriller, because it's all true! The next time you want a crackling good read, make sure it's got the St. Martin's True Crime Library logo on the spine—you'll be up all night!

Charles E. Spicer, Jr.

Charles E. Spicer, Jr.
Executive Editor, St. Martin's True Crime Library

OTHER TRUE CRIME ACCOUNTS
BY DIANE FANNING

Out There

Under the Knife

Baby Be Mine

Gone Forever

Through the Window

Into the Water

Written in Blood

THE PASTOR'S WIFE

*The True Story of a Minister
and the Shocking Death that Divided a Family*

Diane Fanning

THE PASTOR'S WIFE

For information address St. Martin's Press, 175 Fifth Avenue, New York, NY 10010.

ISBN: 978-1-60751-328-5

Printed in the United States of America

St. Martin's Paperbacks are published by St. Martin's Press, 175 Fifth Avenue, New York, NY 10010.

ACKNOWLEDGMENTS

It is always useful when a true crime writer can count a private investigator among her friends. Dan Phillips of Mission Investigations in New Braunfels is mine. He's terrific at digging up obscure information for me, but the best thing about Dan is that he is a diehard Dallas Cowboys fan.

There are so many people in Selmer, Tennessee, who have been wonderful to me. I can't say enough about Russell Ingle, reporter for the *Independent Appeal* in Selmer. He welcomed me warmly to his hometown and offered every professional courtesy. But Russell went beyond that. He didn't just help me when I asked him; he offered his assistance at every opportunity. He's a great guy and a dedicated journalist. Thank you, Russell, for everything.

In the McNairy County Court Clerk's Office, I always found a smiling face and willing assistance. Y'all are a great bunch of folks—you made me laugh and you kept me from crying. Thanks to everyone there including Court Clerk Ronnie Brooks, Jackie Cox, LeAnn Knight, Dana Seigler and Pam West.

The state of Tennessee sent Sue Allison, public information officer for the Tennessee Supreme Court, down to Selmer, where she bridged the gap between the court and the media with stunning professionalism and cordiality. Thank you, Sue. And thanks to Judge Weber McCraw for creating a reporter-friendly environment, and to Judge Van McMahan, who gave up his courtroom for the use of hordes of journalists who landed in town for the trial. And thanks to District Attorney General Michael Dunavant for the post-trial interview.

Thanks to all the law enforcement folks who added to my information base and my understanding, including Investigator Roger Rickman and Police Chief Neal Burks of the Selmer Police Department, Rodney Weaver of the West Tennessee Task Force and Theresa Hockabee and Sheriff Rick Roten of the McNairy County Sheriff's Department.

Around town, there were a lot of people who made my visits memorable or helped me with information, but I especially want to thank Patricia Templeton of The Book Shop, Pam Killingsworth and Dorothy Weatherford. And thanks to Fourth Street Church of Christ Elder Drew Eason who discussed theology with me on a Sunday evening after the service.

And thanks to Pat's Place, now I know what a Slug-Burger is, and actually ate one—and enjoyed it, too.

In McMinnville, thanks to Alice Weddington of the McMinnville–Warren County Chamber of Commerce, for an overview of the community, and Mary Robbins, head librarian at the Magness Library, for historical background.

Thanks to all the other people in McMinnville who spent a little time with me including Paul Pillow of Cleaners Express, Robert Harper, principal of Boyd Christian School, Evon Dennis and JoAn Cantrell.

Thanks to all the members of the media I met while at that trial, but especially Emanuella Grinberg of Court TV, Tonya Smith-King with *The Jackson Sun* and *It's Your Call* with Lynn Doyle. And thanks to Kerry Cobb and reference librarian Sharon Hoyt for answering far more questions than it was reasonable for me to ask.

If you've read any of my books before, you'll know what's coming next—an expression of my gratitude to the two anchors in my writing life, my peerless agent Jane Dystel and St. Martin's Press executive editor Charles Spicer.

And I would be lost without my partner in crime, my talented and fantastic editor, Yaniv Soha.

Finally, I send a bucketful of appreciation to my partner in life, Wayne Fanning. He's stuck with me through every page of every book and he promised he will never leave— unless I buy a shotgun.

THE DISCOVERY

"A good name is better than precious ointment; and the day of death than the day of one's birth."

—*Ecclesiastes* 7:1

CHAPTER 1

By 6:45 on the evening of Wednesday, March 22, 2006, uneasiness crept like a surreptitious fog over the leaders of Fourth Street Church of Christ in Selmer, Tennessee. The bulk of the congregation at the mid-week Bible Study was oblivious to their concerns. The adult church members sat in pews or stood in aisles chatting with friends and unwinding before the service. The children were in classrooms in the lower level of the building, participating in age-appropriate classes.

The preacher, Matthew Winkler, and his wife, Mary, should have been among those chatting in the sanctuary, and their three daughters should have been with the other children. But they were not. And Matthew had not called any one of the elders or deacons, or the church secretary to explain his family's absence, or give a reason for their delay.

An elder telephoned the church-owned parsonage about a mile away, but no one answered. *He must be on his way*, one elder assured another. They checked the parking lot and looked up the street—no sign of the Winkler family.

Five minutes passed. They placed another call to the parsonage—still no answer. *A family emergency?* another elder wondered. "Maybe Matthew went to visit Mary Anne in the hospital in Memphis and got caught up in bad traffic," Elder Ashe suggested. They all knew, though, that Matthew Winkler was responsible. If he had to leave town—even under the direst circumstances—he would have called someone.

Another five minutes crawled by. Even if the Winklers had stepped out the door just as the first call rang in their home—or even if they were still inside, but had decided not to answer it, since they were running late—they would have reached the church by now.

The elder called the parsonage again. No answer.

Pam Killingsworth, vice principal at Selmer Elementary, where two of the Winkler girls attended school, was in the church nursery caring for babies and toddlers that night. Her brother Wayne stuck his head in the door checking to see if the littlest Winkler was there. She wasn't. He asked Pam if the older daughters had been in school that day.

"No," she said. "And the girls didn't come to their music classes after school, either. What's wrong?"

Wayne shook his head and left. The church leaders' anxiety now had a foothold in the nursery.

Seven o'clock. Time for Bible Study to begin. One last call to the Winklers. Nothing. The elders decided to start the service. *He'll still come*, they hoped and prayed.

The assigned song leader, a worried Wilburn Ashe, stepped in front of the congregation, and the buzz of conversation ceased. He said that they would sing until Pastor Winkler arrived to teach, and then announced the page number of the first hymn. *A capella* voices rose in unison from the pew—no instruments were allowed in the church.

After opening prayer, the service continued with scripture reading and the Wednesday night devotional. On this night, they lifted up their voices in song and made a more joyful noise unto the Lord than usual, to fill the gap where the preacher's Bible Study would have been.

Wilburn and another church elder, Dr. Drew Eason, took a trip to the parsonage during the service, but found no one at home. They slipped back into the sanctuary while the service was in progress.

At the end of the service, Matthew Winkler's whereabouts were still unknown. Wilburn wondered aloud again about the possibility that Matthew was visiting Mary Anne Wilson in Memphis. Church secretary Betty Wilkerson expressed her concern that Matthew did not pick up his office mail that day.

Drew, James Turner, Randy Smith, Kevin Redmon and Drew's 15-year-old son went back to the parsonage on Mollie Drive and checked all the doors and windows. Everything was locked up tight. The television set was on in the living room. They heard the telephone ringing inside the home, but no one answered. They returned to Fourth Street.

At the church, leaders called the parsonage yet again. They called Matthew's and Mary's cell numbers. They prayed while the phones rang, but they did not receive the answer they devoutly desired.

Something's wrong. The potential dangers that waited outside their sanctuary swarmed like agitated demons through their thoughts—the tenets of their religion painted society as a sinful place full of temptation and evil. They were urged to be "in the world" but not "of the world"—and now that world threatened theirs. Calls went out to members of Matthew's and Mary's families and neighbors. No one knew where they were.

With the help of the secretary, the elders searched the church office for keys. As they looked, they reassured each other that it was just a big mix-up—Matthew had told someone he'd be out of town, and that person dropped the ball. They would find nothing at the preacher's house, and later they would laugh with him about their fears.

They located a ring of unmarked keys, and headed back out the church doors, hoping one would open the house where maybe—hopefully—they'd find answers.

They hung a left at West Court Avenue and continued to the fork in the road, bearing left onto East Poplar Avenue. Just past the sprawling fifties-era Selmer Elementary School, they turn left on lovely, serene Mollie Drive. Headlights brushed the branches of the tall winter-stark trees and illuminated the green of the budding new leaves. The promise of another glorious spring mocked their fears as they drove to the brick ranch parsonage.

The home sat off the road on a small rise. Pulling into the driveway, headlights scanned across its windows and doors, revealing no signs of any turmoil inside its walls. The absence of the family mini-van was cause for relief. *The Winklers must have left town.*

They tried all the keys in the front door lock and then moved to the back, but none of them worked. Drew stepped into the unlocked storage room on the carport, hoping to find a key tucked away in case the Winklers accidentally locked themselves out of the house. He found a small handful in a tackle box. One of those slipped into the back door and clicked as the bolt released. They entered the den of the tidy home around 9 P.M.

"Matthew, Mary! Is anyone home?" they called out. Their voices echoed in the silence of the quiet home.

A light burned in the den, but most of the rest of the house lay in darkness. They flipped switches on as they walked past the kitchen on their right, past the bathroom on their left and out into the hallway. Stepping through the doorway, they split up. Some turned toward the living room; the rest moved down the hall, checking out the three bedrooms. They saw no one or nothing to cause alarm. Then Randy Smith entered the glow of the light issuing from the master bedroom.

Sprawled on the floor beside the bed was the body of Matthew Winkler—their charismatic, dynamic preacher—lying on his back in a dried circle of blood, the covers from the bed lumped under his body. Clad in the T-shirt and old shorts he wore to sleep, it was apparent Matthew had not started his day that morning.

Randy shouted to Drew, the medical doctor of the group. Drew knelt by Matthew's side. Blood-tinged froth crusted the preacher's mouth and nostrils. His skin was ashen and cold. Drew felt his neck for a pulse and found nothing. Drew's shoulders sagged. He looked up at Randy with a grimace and shook his head. Matthew Winkler, a mere 31 years old, was dead. Drew and Randy returned to the den, where Drew picked up the phone and punched in 9-1-1. He reported the death of Matthew Winkler and the disappearance of his family.

The hearts of all four men filled with dread: *If someone had the strength and stealth to kill their tall, athletic preacher, what hope was there for his wife and three little girls?* They joined hands and lifted their voices in prayer.

While waiting for officials to arrive, they searched the basement in case a family member had sought refuge there and needed their help. They feared finding Mary Winkler's body—or even worse, the tiny bodies of 8-year-old Patricia, 6-year-old Allie or 1-year-old Breanna. While looking, they prayed that all of them were still alive.

The group explored every closet, the underside of each bed, every inch of the basement and main floor. There was no one else—dead or alive—inside the parsonage walls. *But where were they?*

CHAPTER 2

The men found no answers to their questions about Mary and the girls.

Across the street, Sharyn Everitt's adult daughter looked out the front window and said, "What in the world is going on at the preacher's house?"

Sharyn herself looked out and saw four cars parked at the neighbors' house, then heard the first siren. A police cruiser and an ambulance turned onto Mollie Drive with flashing lights and shrieking wails, disrupting the peace of the quiet neighborhood. They drove up to the parsonage less than ten minutes after receiving the call from Drew.

Officers Tony Westbanks and Tony Miller of the Selmer Police Department made a quick assessment of the situation inside the master bedroom. They ushered the church members out into the front yard and called Police Chief Neal Burks.

The chief wanted twenty-year veteran detective Roger Rickman on the scene, but Roger had spent the day at home sick in bed, so miserable that he'd turned off his cell phone. When Burks called his detective and was routed straight to voicemail, he sent a police car to the Rickman house. An officer woke Roger, who rose, dressed, and arrived on Mollie Drive before 10 o'clock.

He entered the parsonage's master bedroom and saw Matthew Winkler on the floor beside the bed with bloody saliva coming from his mouth and nose. On the bed, he saw another splotch of blood. A telephone drew his eyes away from the body. It sat on the floor out of Matthew's reach. The cord was not attached to the receiver—it would have been useless, even if the victim had been able to crawl and pick it up.

Roger photographed the room and the body, and reported the obvious signs of foul play to the police chief. Burks called for support from the Tennessee Bureau of Investigation (TBI). He knew a homicide investigation required experienced, expert forensic technicians. There simply wasn't enough violent crime in his town for his department to staff a team and a lab for forensic analysis. Less than half an hour after his arrival, Roger exited the home to await the state crime-scene investigators and technicians.

Questions arose in every mind. *Where was Mary Winkler? Where were the three little girls?* The members of law enforcement on the scene asked each other: *Was Mary a perpetrator or a victim?* Although an abduction scenario was possible, there were no signs of forced entry, and only the master bedroom showed any signs of disarray.

The church members who knew Mary could not imagine that she was responsible. All four members of Matthew's family had to have been kidnapped. Their thoughts turned to the many people who called to the preacher for help in times of need. Many were decent folks down on their luck. Others were drug users or worse, trying to take advantage of Matthew's compassion. Perhaps he denied assistance to someone who shot him in anger and abducted the family in a state of panic or a paroxysm of greed. The congregation waited for the ransom call.

Whether or not Mary played a role in her husband's death, one fact was apparent: Danger hung heavy over the three missing children. There was a long history of parents killing their progeny before committing suicide in similar situations.

Roger talked to Rodney Weaver, director of the West Tennessee Task Force. Weaver immediately got busy. His "number one concern" was finding the wife and children alive. But in the back of his mind, he had "a feeling that Mary Winkler was a suspect."

Sharyn Everitt and her daughter kept returning to the window to gaze out at the commotion across Mollie Drive. Within an hour, the street was lined with police vehicles.

Sharyn's mind flashed on a paranoid possibility: *What if someone is targeting preachers?* She called her pastor and told him what had happened, sharing her concern and urging him to be careful.

At 11 P.M., Special Agent Donna Nelson, forensic scientist for the Tennessee Bureau of Investigation, was called to duty at her home in Memphis. She phoned her team members, Lauren James, Erica Catherine and Francesca Sanders. They met at the Memphis Regional Crime Lab, loaded the Violent Crime Response Team truck and drove to Selmer.

Agent Chris Carpenter of the Tennessee Bureau of Investigation walked into the house at 11:55 P.M. Carpenter observed the body and lifted up the front of Matthew's shirt. There he found a single shotgun pellet. After photographing it in place, he sealed it in an evidence bag. He rolled the victim over and saw a gunshot wound in the middle of the preacher's back.

Carpenter collected items he thought might prove useful for finding the children: the victim's cell phone, billfold and personal items, as well as a family portrait. The photograph he selected was less than a year old. It displayed a happy family of five, all with brown eyes and brown hair. Matthew, the 30-year-old father, was tall, robust, with a strong jaw line, forceful chin and an engaging smile. By his side was his petite 31-year-old wife with a pixie-like face stretched wide with an infectious grin. In her arms she held the newest family addition, infant Breanna. In front of them, the two other daughters stood wearing identical sailor-styled dresses. The oldest girl, 8-year-old Patricia, had darker shoulder-length hair, a mischievous smile and a broad face that resembled her father's. The middle child, Allie, had a lighter shade of hair and wore a thoughtful expression on a tiny face with pointed chin that looked just like her mother's. Carpenter headed out to scan the photo onto a computer and issue an AMBER Alert.

When the forensic team first arrived at the scene, Nelson spoke to Chief Burks and then entered the home to perform a walk-through with Agent Carpenter. She briefed her team and all four went inside to thoroughly sketch, photograph and videotape the crime scene.

Documentation complete, they located, marked and collected evidence—keeping it, for the time, inside the home. In Patricia and Allie's bedroom, testing revealed the presence of bloodstains on a pillow on each of the twin beds. The investigators confiscated both.

In the master bedroom, they took swabs from under Matthew's body and from the sheet on the bed. They bagged the sheet from the floor beside the victim.

In the kitchen, they identified a smear of blood in the trash can and took a swab as evidence. They tagged three computers and various papers in other parts of the home for collection. They hoped to locate a possible murder weapon, but none was found.

CHAPTER 3

One of the church elders placed a phone call to the Freeman home in Knoxville. Mary's father Clark woke to answer the beckoning ring. "Matthew's been shot. He's dead. Your daughter and the three girls are missing." Clark was immediately certain they'd been kidnapped.

Dan and Diane Winkler, Matthew's parents, did not receive the frantic calls to their residence. They were vacationing in a rented cabin near Gatlinburg, a small town surrounded on three sides by the natural beauty of the Great Smoky Mountains National Park.

They had awoken that Wednesday morning to a wispy, smoke-like fog winding its tendrils around the ridges on the border of Tennessee and North Carolina. Dan and Diane spent the day basking in the glory of God's creation—a peaceful interlude of contemplation, spiritual renewal and celebration. Today, March 22, was Dan Winkler's birthday.

In the last hour of that lovely day, the shrill ring of the telephone jarred them out of their contentment. For Dan and Diane, like most everyone, a late-night call stirred up dread. No one would call at this time of night unless it was bad news.

Their youngest son, Jacob, carried the burden of delivering the news of his brother's death to his father. Dan had no time to absorb that horrific reality before Jacob hit him with another. Their son's wife and their three little grand-daughters were missing.

Diane knew the news was bad by the expression on her husband's face. When he hung up the phone, he turned to her. "Diane, you need to sit down."

"I don't want to sit down. I want to know what's going on."

"Matthew's been shot."

"Is he okay? Where was he?" Diane asked in a panicked voice.

"He's at home. He's been shot in the back."

"Danny, he's okay, right? He's okay?"

Dan did not want to answer. He did not want to inflict pain on the woman who'd been by his side for so many years. The moment the words escaped his mouth, he couldn't deny the truth to himself. "No. No, he's not," Dan said. "He's dead."

Diane tried to call Mary's cell phone, but got no answer. The two packed their bags as they made a series of calls to family members and friends. They did not want anyone to learn of this tragedy on television or in the newspaper over their first cup of morning coffee.

They drove north to Interstate 40 and then headed west. They journeyed through the night, across the state on three hundred miles of tedious highway, their speeding car enveloped in darkness. When they reached the exit for State Route 22, they turned off and made the twenty-minute drive north to their home in Huntingdon.

They stopped at the house just long enough to change from their mountain resort clothing to more somber and befitting attire. Then, they made the hour-and-a-half trip south to the police station in Selmer. If they hoped to find news of fresh developments, they were disappointed. The whereabouts of their grandchildren and daughter-in-law were still unknown. The Tennessee Bureau of Investigation continued to occupy their son's home in a search for answers. And Matthew still lay bloody and lifeless on the floor of his own bedroom.

Officers encouraged them to go home and wait, promising to call them if there was any news at all. Dazed, Dan and Diane drove back to Huntingdon to simmer in a stew of private agony, fear and prayer.

Russell Ingle, staff writer for the *Independent Appeal*, a weekly newspaper published since 1902, and the oldest existing business in McNairy County, received a phone call about the murder early in the morning of Thursday, March 23, while he was driving to work. He headed over to Mollie Drive, where yellow crime-scene tape surrounded the home. When he arrived, the only other media presence was a satellite uplink truck from a television station in Memphis. Soon, the number of press on the scene would be legion.

Russell spotted six marked and unmarked cars from the Selmer Police Department and TBI, as well as a white van from the State Medical Examiner's Office. Inside the house, the local, part-time medical examiner, a physician in the PrimeCare office in nearby Adamsville, determined that a large-caliber weapon—possibly a shotgun—caused the wound in Matthew's back. Russell watched from outside as the doctor supervised the removal of Matthew's body from the home and into the van. The vehicle backed down the driveway, heading northeast to Nashville for an autopsy.

Sharyn Everitt, unable to sleep, thought long and hard about what could have happened in the parsonage. By 2 A.M., she was convinced that Mary Winkler killed her husband and fled with the girls. Seconds after that epiphany, there was a knock on her front door. She greeted the first of many reporters.

That morning, law enforcement filed a search warrant in McNairy County General Sessions Court. The judge authorized the seizure of computers and any other evidence from the Winkler home that could help investigators find Matthew's missing family.

Donna Nelson and her forensic team loaded three computers, a black binder filled with family budget information, pillows, pillowcases, a sheet, shotgun pellets, swabs from the garbage can, a box of unused checks, various letters and bills and a copy of a check found in a trash can in the backyard.

All the serology evidence was taken to the lab in Memphis for further testing by team member Sanders. The computers headed to Nashville, where they were turned over to George Elliot for analysis in the lab there.

TBI left a copy of the search warrant and a list of items removed from the home on the kitchen counter with a note from TBI Agent Brent Booth:

The above described computers were found in the family home and found to have been used by someone in the home to communicate by e-mail with a person or persons unknown. The computers may hold information that could lead to the location of the missing Mary Winkler (mother) and the three children.

A large check written from the Winkler account sent TBI investigators to Regions Bank in Selmer. They confirmed financial irregularities involving counterfeit checks. Mary's status as a victim showed its first signs of fracture.

TBI also obtained authorization for cell phone records and for a pen register—a tracking system that could pinpoint the general location of Mary's device. Unless she turned it off, authorities could use her cell to sniff out her whereabouts.

As law enforcement plunged into their investigation, the news flashed across the nation. Major networks and cable news channel sent reporters. Every local television station out of Memphis, Nashville and Jackson arrived in Selmer in their ponderous uplink trucks. The circus was in full swing.

At 1 P.M., Selmer police blockaded Mollie Drive.

Deprived of even a small glimpse of the Winkler home, the reporters and cameramen swarmed to the City Hall building that housed the police department on Second Street, downtown.

Half an hour later, John Mehr of the Tennessee Bureau of Investigation and Selmer Police Chief Neal Burks held their first press conference in front of City Hall. Mehr announced the joint operation to find Mary and the children. Working together, to this end, were members of the TBI, the local police department, the United States Marshals Service, the FBI, the postal inspector's office and the Secret Service.

Mehr and Burks provided the media with AMBER Alert information and computer links, urging them to inform the public that anyone who spotted the vehicle in question should call the local police department. "Do not approach the vehicle," they cautioned. Investigators did not know if Mary and the girls were traveling alone or if they were the captives of an armed kidnapper. They promised the reporters regular briefings on the situation.

After the news conference, an Atlanta journalist stirred up hostility when he stood on the front steps of City Hall bad-mouthing the victim. "He probably slapped her around," he said.

When he took it a step further by suggesting that Matthew's relationship with his daughters may have been inappropriate, a local resident took umbrage. "You're not from here, you didn't know them!" he shouted. "How can you question someone you don't even know?"

The offices of the *Independent Appeal* sat catty-corner from City Hall, giving Russell Ingle a bird's-eye view of the pandemonium. He knew the death of Matthew Winkler was a big story for his paper—he had no idea it would be that big for the world outside of Selmer. The first reporter to come knocking at his door worked for CNBC. Soon, a number of journalists were going in and out of the *Appeal*'s offices seeking professional courtesies like the use of the Internet to file stories.

The demise of Matthew Winkler was not the only loss suffered by the Fourth Street Church of Christ on March 22, 2006. Another parishioner, Mary Anne Wilson King, a 49-year-old retired social worker and mother of two grown boys, passed away that day at the Methodist University Hospital in Memphis. She needed a bone marrow transplant to combat leukemia, but never got well enough to receive one. The church members' grief at her passage at such a young age was only compounded by the discovery of the body of their young minister.

News of the preacher's death rippled through Selmer the old-fashioned way—by word of mouth. The sadness that took hold of the town came hand-in-hand with stark fear. *Were Mary and the girls alive? Would they still be alive when they were found?*

At the Fourth Street Church of Christ, black ribbons hung from the front door. All day the church remained open, filled with a never-ending parade of parishioners and friends seeking solace with each other and peace in the sanctuary itself. Prayers for the safety of Mary and the girls rose from their hearts in a steady stream.

In front of City Hall late that afternoon, officials again spoke to the media throng. It was a short press conference. There were no new developments. They reiterated their concern for the safety of Mary and her children, and their worry that someone else could be with them, holding them against their will. They still would not answer reporters' questions about how Matthew died.

Then the pen register that traced the activity on cell phones scored a hit. Mary—or at least her phone—was in the vicinity of Orange Beach, Alabama, a coastal city nearly 400 miles from Selmer.

CHAPTER 4

Brilliant white-sand beaches grace the Alabama seashore resort town of Orange Beach. It sits on a jutting peninsula where turquoise waters lap the sand with gentle waves.

Although a small city of only 5,500 residents, it has experienced record growth in the last decade. In March of each year, the population swells with the addition of a steadily growing influx of spring breakers. The 2006 Surf & Turf Jet Ski event scheduled to begin on Friday added to the charged atmosphere in the resort town that week.

Officer Jason Whitlock of the Orange Beach Police Department traveled the roads with Reserve Officer Stephen Jerkins. They received the AMBER Alert notice and the known details of the murder in the middle of their shift on Thursday, March 23. Whitlock didn't know if he was looking for three children accompanied by a woman who shot her husband, or for a kidnapper with four victims. He did, however, know the precise vehicle he sought, including its license plate number.

Near the end of the shift, Whitlock and Jerkins spotted a vehicle matching the description of the Winkler minivan traveling westbound on Perdido Beach Boulevard. The driver made an illegal U-turn right in front of them, and they realized it bore the right license plate number. Whitlock followed it while Jerkins called in for back-up. Whitlock could not determine the presence of the children, nor could he tell with any certainty if the driver was the only adult inside.

At 7:30 P.M., Officers Woodruff, Beaman and Long responded to the call for back-up and three marked police cars with flashing blue lights joined Whitlock and Jerkins. Whitlock pulled the mini-van over in the parking lot of the Winn-Dixie grocery store and they approached it with drawn guns. One officer knocked on the window and Mary rolled it down. The officers screamed at her, "Get out of the van! Get out of the van!"

At the sound of raised voices, the two K-9 dogs on the scene barked and strained at their leashes. The three frightened little girls burst into tears. The officers shouted again, ordering Mary to step out of her vehicle, hold her hands up in the air and walk backwards toward them.

She complied with hesitation, as if fearful she would do the wrong thing. Her flip-flops slapped the pavement as she approached the officers in her pink sweat suit. Whitlock snapped handcuffs on Mary's wrists and Officer Travis Long put her in the back of his patrol car. He recited Miranda warnings. As Mary listened, she demonstrated no signs of distress. In fact, she appeared relieved.

While Long secured Mary, Whitlock approached the Sienna van with caution and saw the three girls—they were alone. He tried to comfort and calm them.

Allie said, "Our daddy is in the hospital. A bad man had robbed us in our house and hit our daddy. And Mommy and us ran from the man." Then she added, "Mommy took a gun to protect us from the bad man."

Patricia repeated the same story. Long unfastened the restraining buckles on the seat belts of the two littlest girls, speaking to them in a soft, soothing voice and removed all three from the mini-van, placing them in the back seat of a patrol car.

In another police vehicle, Officer Long asked Mary if she had any relatives in the area who could take care of the children while she went to the police station for questioning. She said she did not, but gave him the names and telephone numbers of her in-laws in Huntingdon, Tennessee. Throughout the conversation, Mary never asked why he detained her. She never mentioned a thing about her husband. There were no signs of sadness or dread. Long found her lack of emotion odd as he transported her to the city jail.

Lieutenant Investigator Steve Brown arrived on the scene and gave the authorization to detain Mary, and Whitlock and Jerkins climbed back into their patrol car. Whitlock looked back at Mary and saw her blank stare—a face devoid of emotion. He thought Mary appeared exhausted and maybe even relieved that her flight was now over. When he drove off to transport her to the city jail, Mary lay down in the back seat and immediately fell asleep. She did not say a word along the way. Of the $500 she had when she left home, just $123 remained.

Learning that the girls had been on their way to the Waffle House for dinner when the van was stopped, the officers took them to McDonald's to eat. Afterwards, at the station house, they gave the children stuffed animals to cuddle. Officers' wives came in and kept the children busy watching movies and playing games.

Informed that Mary was in the custody of the Orange Beach police, Corporal Stan Stabler, agent with the Alabama Bureau of Investigation, arrived at the police station around 10 P.M. First, he spoke with 8-year-old Patricia and 6-year-old Allie.

Patricia told him that she heard a loud noise and went to her parents' bedroom. "I thought Daddy fell and knocked over the night stand." She saw her father lying face down on the floor and heard him say, "Call 9-1-1."

As Stabler was leaving the room, Patricia stopped him and asked his name, saying that she wanted to put him on "my list of people I talk to." Stabler stifled the surge of emotion he felt, and promised to return a little later and help her with the spelling.

CHAPTER 5

Back in Selmer, Agent John Mehr and Police Chief Neal Burks stepped out of the station to speak with the media. Mehr said, "Just in the last few minutes, we've gotten news that they've been stopped in Orange Beach, Alabama, by the Orange Beach Police Department. The wife and the three children are okay, and we are sending a team of agents to Alabama at this time, and working with the Orange Beach Police Department to go through the van and see what the other details are." He offered no answers to reporters' questions, but said, "We're happy that the children and her are alive and well."

The word quickly traveled to the church members gathered in the sanctuary for a special service they'd called to pray for the safe return of the preacher's wife and his daughters.

With Special Agent Steve Stuesher from the Federal Bureau of Investigation, Stabler entered the interrogation room, starting the tape recorder and beginning his interview with Mary Winkler at 9:55 P.M. He observed his subject carefully, looking for any signs of intoxication. Seeing none, he read the waiver of rights form to her. Mary agreed to sign it.

After getting basic biographical information, he assured Mary that her children were fine. "They've had McDonald's, they ate and they're wrapped up in blankets, warm, watching a movie."

"Thank you," Mary said with a smile.

"They're concerned about Mom. I told them you were fine, and we were fixing to come in here and talk with you, too." Stabler moved on with the questioning. "How long have you been married?"

"Nine years, eleven months," Mary said.

"How was your marriage?"

"Good."

Noticing Mary's mouth appeared dry, he inquired about her thirst and got her water, at her request. He gave her time to stand and stretch, then resumed in earnest. "Is that a little better?"

"Yes."

"Okay, great. All right. We'll kind of pick up from where we left off, okay? So you've been married nine years and eleven months? Okay, and, now, I've been married seventeen years myself, and it's not my first marriage. Is this your first marriage?"

"Yes," Mary said.

"Okay. First and only, huh?"

"Right."

"Now, I know couples are going to have squabbles, that's typical, that's normal, but y'all didn't have any major, major problems going on?"

"No."

"None whatsoever?" Stabler asked. "Okay, anybody else involved with either party?"

"Oh, no."

"Okay. How were y'all financially?"

"Um, getting through," Mary said.

Stabler asked a few questions about their income and her schooling, and then asked, "When's the last time you talked to him?"

"Yesterday morning."

"Where was that at?"

"Home."

"Home? Okay. What did y'all discuss?"

"No real conversation," Mary said, fumbling for an answer. "Um, just no comment. I don't know."

Stabler spoke to Mary about her inability to change the past, and the possibility of controlling her future by making the right decisions today. As he talked, he studied Mary, looking for any emotion other than the eerie calm that seemed to possess her. "I'm just going to be frank with you. You need to talk with us. We need to work all this out, okay? You need to think about your girls, the baby, yourself. Okay? What, what was going on? What was the problem? I want to hear your side. I want you to tell me what was troubling you so much."

Mary was not able or willing to reveal anything. "I feel like you have genuine concern, and I do appreciate you, uh, I'm just not to that right now."

Stabler said, "I know that, you know, a lot of things can happen between people. I know, a lot of times, mental state, emotions, everything comes into play. And it's tough. It is tough being married sometimes these days. I mean, society itself has made it tough. I think there's a reason, I mean, I know there's got to be a reason that all of this had happened. I just, you know, we're kind of tasked with trying to figure this stuff out, but, there's only one person that really knows why, and it's you. We want to help you, but I don't know where to start, because I don't know what's going on. It's your life."

"I just . . ." Mary began.

"I mean, I don't even know. I didn't know exactly what or how to even talk to your little girls a little bit, you know?"

"I appreciate it," Mary said, turning the conversation to her girls. "I was sitting in there, and at first, I thought, *Who in the world would have children down here at this hour?* And I thought, *Well, they're getting paperwork done and they had their kids with them.* And then at some point, I heard or understood the voices coming that way. And those men were very nice, and, you know, I felt like, I thought I was chained to one particular area and I about did a back-flip to get out of—because I was in the line of sight, and so I really appreciated we took care of that before they saw me, but, anyway, I heard their voices. I heard Allie going on about something. That is, uh, right now, just shock and whatever emotion, I don't know, but that those three right there are my only concern right now."

"I know. I know," Stabler reassured her.

"When can Nana and Poppa get here?"

"They told me they were in the mountains, and they're our concern, too."

"Nana can take care of them, but I do appreciate that."

"Okay, all right. Will you do this for me? When you're ready to tell me why, what's troubling you, will you do that? Without telling me why, or the troubles that were going on, would you tell me what happened?"

"I haven't been told really anything myself. I don't know," Mary said, denying her knowledge of the events that occurred in her home the day before.

"Mary?"

"Hmm?"

"I talked with the girls a little bit, okay?"

"Hmm."

"And they told me what they've seen and heard."

"Right," Mary acknowledged without giving an inch.

"Okay. I need you to fill in those gaps a little bit. Well, all three know, to an extent, what's taken place."

"What did you ask me?"

"To tell me what happened," Stabler answered.

"Uh-huh, just not right now."

Stabler reminded her again of her children, of her unconditional love for the girls and her willingness to sacrifice for them. Special Agent Stuesher added, "You can tell by just the few minutes that we spent with them that you've taught them well."

"Yeah, you'd be proud of them," Stabler offered. "They're very fine young ladies."

"Very polite. Have manners," Stuesher said.

"They've got a lot they're going to have to go through, too, okay? We're going to have to talk about this, got to, for their sake," Stabler said.

"I just don't understand," Mary claimed. "Um, with all due respect, newspapers and, you know, whatever, this comes to pass. No matter what in the end, I don't want it, um, I don't want him smeared."

Stabler agreed with her that the media could be a problem, and griped about the bad image often given to law enforcement on television. "You'd probably feel more comfortable if I was down here beating on a desk yelling and screaming at you. That's what they make us look like on TV. Okay. But that's not— I'm just sitting here talking to you as a parent to parent, you know."

Stuesher spoke up again. "Are you concerned that the media's going to say a lot of negative things about you or your family or your husband or . . ."

"Yeah, what's your concerns?" Stabler asked.

Mary stammered about court cases and public records, unable to effectively verbalize her thoughts. "I don't even know the words to say."

"Just go step to step and tell me what happened," Stabler urged.

"I just can't right now. Sometimes I think something might have happened, and then, there's no way . . ."

"Just seems like it's not real, right?"

"Just not right now."

"Seems like a blur, I'm sure. Has he ever hurt you?"

"Not physically," Mary insisted.

"Not physically? Okay. What about mentally? Verbally? Any kind of abuse that way?"

"No comment. I just don't know if— Just trying to think this through some more myself. There's no sense in blaming . . . somebody else, but . . ."

Stabler pushed, but Mary offered no more. He switched his questions back to the crime scene. Mary denied knowing whether or not her husband was still alive. Then he asked her, "Why'd you shoot him?"

"Um . . ."

"I mean, like I said, we can't change the past, okay? You agree with me on that?"

"Agree."

"And we know some facts already. Had you planned ahead of time to shoot him, or did it happen just spur of the moment?"

"Not planned."

"It wasn't planned? It just happened? Were you scared or something when it happened?"

"I don't even know right now . . ."

"Were you arguing? What was going on?" he asked, then attempted to get her to define the time frame before pointing to the weapon confiscated from the mini-van. "Is that his shotgun?"

"Um . . ."

"Did he normally keep it loaded?"

"Um, I don't know . . ."

"Or did you load it? You don't remember if you loaded it or not, if it was already loaded?"

"I might have messed it up and then put it back. I don't know."

"Where was it?"

"We keep it in the top of the closet and out of reach."

Stabler turned the discussion to hunting, and Mary told him Matthew liked to hunt turkey and enjoyed fishing. Then Stabler switched back to the crime scene. "What was going on when you shot him? Was he lying in the bed, sitting in a chair, walking around? Hmmm?"

"I don't remember."

Stuesher offered her more water, then Stabler asked, "How many times did you shoot? You remember that? More than once?"

Mary and Stabler engaged in a discordant and confusing exchange that finally led to Mary's denial of more than one shot, and her admission that she never shot a gun before. Then, Stabler turned the conversation back to the three girls. "Mary, they're going through a lot. You're going through a lot. You're gonna have to . . ."

Stuesher interrupted. "You said he wasn't physically abusing you. We know how people can be abused emotionally and mentally. Was that pretty serious? What was happening?"

Getting unintelligible responses from Mary, they kept applying pressure, urging her to tell the truth about her marriage for her own sake as well as her daughters'. "Tell me why a mother of three, a wife of over nine years, almost ten years, going to college, you look like, you know, a nice well-to-do family, what would make you do this?" Stabler asked. "Why? That's what we've got to answer."

"Still no comment," was Mary's only response.

"Well, we know you shot him," Stabler continued. "You've told us that much. I just need to know why. And this is your opportunity, this is your chance, Mary, to shed some light on all this and to help yourself, okay? Do you want to help yourself? Why, why, why can't you talk to us? Is it me?"

"No."

"You just don't like me? Just don't want to tell me? Do I need to get someone else in here to talk to you?"

"Unh-uh," Mary said with a shake of her head.

"The best thing that we could do in a situation like this to stop the media from speculating and doing all the crap that they do is to find out what happened. We could put an end to all that speculation now, and that's up to you," Stabler said. He hinted at the wild stories the press could make up in the absence of the truth, but, in a seeming contradiction, assured her, "We're not going to make this public, what you tell us, okay? I don't think you're a cold-blooded killer. I wouldn't be sitting this close to you. I'd be scared of you. Something's happened. Something's bad went wrong. Now, I know you're hurting."

"I really don't mean this selfish[ly], but . . ." Mary began.

"I know you're not selfish, I know . . ."

"Driving down the road, I'd think, something would go in my head and I'd thought, *There is no way what had just happened*— And then, I hadn't really seen anything or heard anything. I've used my name everywhere I went, I just thought, you know, I possibly could, you know, whatever. And this just was my last time to be with them, and we were just going to have some fun. I just wanted to be with them before they had bad days, have a happy day."

"Okay, I think I understand a little bit about what you're telling me now," Stabler said, encouraging her to continue.

"And, uh, that's why, you know, the storyline was absent. Why there was an absence, but they could be happy and enjoy themselves. And as it's going, I just . . ."

"So you felt like that because of what you'd done, that you had to take some time to spend with them?"

"Yeah, that was it, yeah. I wasn't going to Mexico or, I just, I had five hundred dollars and . . ."

"You know that they had a happy day, too."

"Yeah, yesterday, we found an indoor swimming pool, was the goal of yesterday. And then, when I thought about going to Louisiana— We used to live in Baton Rouge, and I thought, *I know those streets*, and, I don't know, and I thought, *There's nothing to do there*," Mary said with a sigh.

"Right. Louisiana's pretty messed up."

"And so I thought, *They've— They don't ever— They've never been to a beach that they remembered*, and uh, so that, that was that."

"How long were you . . . ?"

"I planned to go home tomorrow."

"What were you going to do, go back up there and turn yourself in to . . . ?"

"I hadn't thought it through exactly, um. The Winklers live in West Tennessee, and I was trying to think of a scenario to get the girls to them."

"Before you . . ."

"And I didn't know where to go from there."

When Stabler asked her if she had any worries about leaving her daughters with Matthew's parents, she said, "Oh, no. Gosh, no."

"Good people?"

"Yeah. They're the family."

"Mary, we're making progress, okay? We can do that, and I can understand what's going through your mind as far as you being away from the kids. What were your thoughts? Just be honest with me. Are you going to be locked up the rest of your life, or were you afraid you were going to be . . . ?"

"Oh, yeah. Uh . . ."

"You just . . ."

"But I guess my not wanting to be selfish is: I'm just still thinking about him. And I probably deserve a slap in the face for that. I don't know. I just don't know."

"I'm battling back and forth with this *why* thing," Stabler said. "I mean, you seem like such a nice person. I know something had to happen."

"I was just lying there tonight and I fell asleep, after all this. They woke me up to come in here. It's just the thought of stupid stuff."

"Like what?" Stabler asked.

"Like schedules, and this, in this certain order . . . I love him dearly, but, gosh, he just nailed me in the ground, and uh, I was real good for quite some time. My problem was, I got a job at the post office a couple of years ago, and the first of our marriage, I just took it like a mouse. Didn't think anything different. My mom just took it from my dad, and that stupid scenario. And I got a job where I had to have nerve and high self-esteem, and I have been battling this for years, and I don't know when, but for some time, it was really good. Then, I don't know. We moved over a year ago, February oh-five, and it just came back out for some reason."

"He would knock your self-esteem down?"

"Uh, no. Just chewing, whatever. And that's the problem, I have nerve now and I have self-esteem, so my ugly came out."

"So you were more or less standing up for yourself more now than you did in the past?"

Mary veered off to talking about her children; Stabler brought her back on point when he asked, "Just fussing at you, nagging all the time?"

"Just mistakes. And some well deserved, by all means."

"Did he pick on the little things a lot, though?"

"Yeah."

"That gets old."

"And I— But gosh, I don't want to talk about that now."

"I know you don't want to."

"But that's just, yeah. I didn't just get up and say, *Hey, let's see how this thing works.* I've been battling not to do that forever, and I don't know why."

"Was he chewing on you when it happened?"

"I don't even know," Mary said. "It was this and that and, I can't even, I can't imagine pulling anything, I'll tell you that," she said, referring to the trigger on the shotgun. "I don't, I just, I really don't know that one still."

"Just kind of got to a boiling point and just boiled over?"

"But he was so good, so good, too. It was just a weakness. I think a lot of times— He had high blood pressure, but he'd never go enough to the doctor to get medicine for it. He was a mighty fine person, and that's the thing. There's no sense, you know, Fox News saying some hicktown lady did this because he was a mean— You know? No sense in that. *Just say the lady was a moron evil woman and let's go on with it.*"

Both men objected, saying that they did not believe that was true. Mary turned her thoughts to her girls again. "My thing there is, their Nana will get them through this. Their Nana will take care of them, for however long it takes. And if they never want to see me again, but I don't want them hearing that, and . . . I don't know— Patricia's too old, it's too late. I can't imagine Bren not knowing him."

"I'm sure it's tough living with a situation like that. I know . . ."

"Even . . . But my dad called. I checked the voicemail the other day and sometimes I just want to go through the phone and rip his head off. There you go, I opened up. And then, 'cause I thought, *I do not want him to even ever come and visit me*, and I know that he'll want to live wherever I am, and visit every day, but I am not wanting to see him."

"Your dad, what'd your dad say on the voice message?"

"Um, something, just, uh, calling. I guess some stuff had started happening, I couldn't really tell if it was— But he never calls me, so I'm sure— But, uh, I just don't know. There's some of it. There's no *Poor me*. I'm in control."

"There's no major event that took place? There's just kind of an accumulation over the years?"

Mary talked about her nerves and then moved on. "I just never know what's coming next. I think we're having a good day and then, bam! I'm nervous about something and he's aloof about it. But it's just no excuse for anything. But, you know, it wasn't just out of the blue, either. I don't know."

"Have you thought about doing it before?" Stabler asked her.

"Uh, it's crossed minds," Mary said; "threats have been made, to me as well, but, I mean, that's hearsay, you know."

"Everybody's probably thought about it," Stabler empathized. "I've picked at my wife before. You know when you got some serious problems going on, that thoughts run through your mind. You said he's threatened you before, too?"

Mary mentioned an incident from six years earlier when she and Matthew lived in Pegram, and things were at their worst, describing it as "a life-threatening situation."

"Was it getting that way again?"

"In the past year and a half, it had."

Stabler and Stuesher attempted to get her to re-create

the events of the morning she shot Matthew, but Mary balked, stumbled around with her words and got weepy. She blamed her tears on allergies.

After providing a tissue for her, the men tried to establish where she and Matthew were at the time she pulled the trigger. She was vague about her husband's location, but said she kept losing her balance because she was standing on the decorative pillows that lay on the floor beside the bed.

"What did you think had happened," Stabler pressed, "or did you know?"

"I thought something shot," Mary babbled, "the smell and there was a little bang, wasn't near what I thought."

"Did he ask you to call 9-1-1? Or did you just tell the girls that?"

"I was trying to ease them," she explained. "I lied a lot yesterday, then and today."

Mary insisted that she did not know whether Matthew was dead or alive—

"Now, Mary, I'm going to tell you what you probably don't want me to tell you. He didn't survive it, okay?"

"Has anybody told them?" she asked.

"Huh?"

"Has anybody told them?"

Stuester caught on first. "Your daughters? No."

"Nobody's told the kids," Stabler emphasized. "Nobody's told them."

"Thank you."

Agent Stabler thought he turned off the tape recorder when they left the room to give Mary a few moments to herself. They hoped with some time to reflect, she would open up to them a bit more.

But Mary disappointed them in that. She didn't want to talk about the reasons she shot Matthew. She simply said, "Y'all are so kind. Y'all are very kind, but I just— There's no reason for him to have anything ugly, because I have obviously done something very bad, so let me just, you know, be the, get the bad. That would be my request."

They objected, but it was futile. Mary's mind was made up. The only thing she wanted to talk about now was making sure no obstacles stood in the way of her girls being with Matthew's mother.

CHAPTER 6

Dan and Diane Winkler spent Thursday afternoon in earnest and anguished prayer for the safety of their daughter-in-law and their three precious grandchildren. That evening, the phone rang, and their prayers were answered. Patricia, Allie, Breanna and Mary were all alive—and safe.

The next piece of news was something they did not want to hear. Their daughter-in-law Mary was being questioned for her role in Matthew's death. They were needed in Alabama to take responsibility for their grandchildren.

They attempted to get a flight out from Nashville to Orange Beach that night, but it wasn't possible. They booked a flight in the morning and spent the next hours in fitful and restless sleep before rising to drive to the airport.

In Selmer, on Friday, March 24, the grapevine hummed with news of the discovery of Mary and her girls. The community breathed a sigh of relief. There would be tears and sorrow at the funeral of the young, charismatic preacher, but they'd been spared the agony of tiny coffins enclosing three innocent little girls. Soon, however, the communal rejoicing turned to astonishment and dread. *Mary killed Matthew?* It didn't seem possible.

Life in the small town no longer bore its peaceful appearance. Satellite trucks from local, regional and national media outlets filled Second Street and the surrounding neighborhood. Any resident with business at City Hall or the police station put it off for another day if they could. There was no place to park, and when they walked in from a distant space, they were besieged by hungry journalists.

Every downtown store and office faced herds of roaming reporters seeking news and gossip—anything to pump up a headline or spark a sound bite. It felt like an invasion to the local population—but the press was just doing their job, nothing more. Selmer Police Chief Neal Burks gave regular press briefings in front of City Hall to apprise the journalists of the latest developments. But, as with every breaking story, it was never enough to satiate the media.

That Friday morning was no exception. The police chief introduced Investigator Roger Rickman to read the official statement.

> *"On March twenty-second, 2006, the body of Matthew Winkler was found in his home in Selmer, Tennessee. Mr. Winkler had been shot. On March twenty-third, 2006, the deceased's wife, Mary Carol Winkler, was apprehended by law enforcement officers in Orange Beach, Alabama. According to agents of the Alabama Bureau of Investigation, Mary Winkler confessed to the murder of her husband, Matthew Winkler, shooting him on March the twenty-second, 2006, and leaving Selmer with her three daughters.*

"These warrants," he said, holding them up in one hand, "have been faxed down to the TBI and the West Tennessee Drug Task Force and Violent Crimes, who are down there right now, and we anticipate this warrant being served within the next hour. And they're in the process now of getting her extradited back to Tennessee."

Rickman would not answer any questions about Mary's interviews with law enforcement, the murder weapon, the motive, the means of death, the contents of the van or Mary's state of mind. He did tell them that they anticipated

Mary's return to McNairy County this weekend and a hearing next week.

After seven minutes of back-and-forth, Neal Burks interrupted and announced, "This will be the last news conference that we have."

Reporter Russell Ingle stood in the lobby of City Hall talking to a couple of police officers about the impact the Winkler story had on their town, when a 9-1-1 call came in reporting the possible discovery of a bazooka.

The weapon was transported back to the National Guard armory in Selmer. It was missing its warhead, but the booster charge remained alive. The Jackson Police Department dispatched their bomb disposal unit to Selmer, where they blew it up and eliminated the threat.

As the only full-time staff writer at the *Independent Appeal*, Russell covered the bazooka story as well as other developing news in the area during the week. He wrote half of the ten pieces about the Winkler tragedy in the first issue after Matthew's death.

He and his local colleagues were under pressure unknown to the out-of-town reporters. When the story played itself out to the end, they would still be here. They would be judged by their neighbors for what they wrote.

"We tried not to hurt the people in the churches. They are our friends. They are our advertisers," Tom Evans, managing editor of the *Appeal*, said. "We didn't want the church to take a hit for the story. We wanted them treated with respect." At the same time, they knew they needed to be objective, truthful, and tell the whole story. It was a precarious tightrope.

There were no services or events planned at the Fourth Street Church of Christ on Friday, but the traffic in and out of the sanctuary never ended, with journalists and photographers keeping watch outside. A steady flow of church members knocked on the locked door and slipped inside. Out of sight of the cameras, they greeted one another, embraced, offered words of support and prayed for strength and resolution.

Mid-afternoon, a member ducked out the front door and hung up a handwritten sign reading, "No more interviews today." In the lobby outside of the sanctuary, photographs of the children and their mother were stapled to a bulletin board. In another room, an easel held a more extensive display of pictures: Patricia and Allie in costumes, playing basketball, posing with kittens and sitting with Santa Claus, one of Mary holding up her youngest daughter and laughing. A shot of Matthew flashing a big smile at a church social as he balanced brimming plates of food in each hand.

That morning, Dan and Diane Winkler flew from Nashville to Alabama to take care of their son's daughters. Throughout the flight, they prayed for the strength and grace to handle the situation in a manner befitting Christians who loved the Lord. They drove straight from the airport to the Baldwin County Courthouse.

There, they learned that Mary was "a person of interest" in the murder of their son, and asked to speak with their daughter-in-law. They were allowed to visit, one at a time, under the watchful eye of an officer. The atmosphere was tense. Law enforcement had no indication that the elder Winklers intended to harm the prisoner. But, after all, it appeared as if she killed their son.

Dan entered the holding area first. "Mary, I am so sorry for all of this."

Mary hung her head and did not respond.

"I wish we could take the handcuffs off so I could give you a big bear hug."

Mary reached toward him with her bound hands and a soft, slight smile on her face. He gave her an awkward embrace and said, "I love you, Mary."

Dan left with a heavy heart. He wanted Mary to ask for forgiveness. And he wanted to forgive her, but he knew he couldn't. The tenets of his faith demanded that the sinner ask for forgiveness in a state of penitence and contrition before it could be granted. Mary did not ask. She did not utter a single word of remorse.

Diane stepped up to Mary and folded her in a heartfelt embrace.

"I'm sorry I'm putting y'all out with the girls," Mary said.

"There's no problem with that, Mary. We love you and we love the girls. We'll take good care of them."

"Thank you."

"Don't worry about the girls," Diane assured her before she left.

Right after their visit, Agent Chris Carpenter of the Tennessee Bureau of Investigation arrived in Alabama bearing an arrest warrant issued that morning charging Mary Winkler with first-degree murder.

Carpenter led the interview with Mary. Also present at the interrogation were Lieutenant Kim Holley and Officer Byron Maxedon of the Selmer Police Department, and additional officers with the state law enforcement agency who'd rushed to the Alabama coast. TBI policy prohibited recording the event. Carpenter summarized her words in his handwriting. Mary signed the statement, putting her initials on each page.

In the interview, Mary admitted that she was there when her husband died.

He had a shotgun he kept in the closet in a case. I don't remember going to the closet or getting the gun. The next thing I remember was hearing a loud boom and I remember thinking that it wasn't as loud as I thought it would be. I heard the boom, and he rolled out of the bed onto the floor and I saw some blood on the floor and some bleeding around his mouth. I went over and wiped his mouth off with a sheet. I told him I was sorry and that I loved him and I went and ran.

I do remember me holding the shotgun, hearing the boom, and then a smell. He asked me why and I

*just said I was sorry. I was scared, sad, and wanted
to get out of the house.*

The statement ended with a pathetically thin answer to
the reason for the shooting.

*I was upset at him because he had really been on me
lately, criticising [sic] me for things, the way I walk,
what I eat, everything. It was just building up to this
point. I was just tired of it. I guess I just got to a
point and snapped.*

CHAPTER 7

After their visit with Mary, Dan and Diane Winkler followed representatives from social services to the foster home where the three girls spent the previous night. They hugged and kissed their granddaughters, gave vague answers to their questions and assured them that they were loved.

They all traveled to the courthouse in Foley, Alabama, for a hearing before a juvenile judge. Baldwin County officials transported Mary to the hearing as well, where she indicated her approval of her in-laws as guardians of her daughters. Dan and Diane spoke to her again, telling her once more that they loved her. The judge awarded custody of the children to the grandparents.

Upon leaving court, Dan spoke to the media, thanking supporters for their prayers. "Now we want to turn our attention to remembering our son and to the care of three young children."

In Selmer, members of the police department parked their vehicle in the lot behind the Fourth Street Church of Christ. They emerged from the building carrying a computer tower.

Authorities transported Mary from the courthouse to the Baldwin County Corrections Center in the county seat of Bay Minette, Alabama, more than an hour's drive away, the coastal town where police took her into custody.

Back in Orange Beach, TBI Agent Chris Carpenter searched through the passenger area of Mary's mini-van. Special Agent Brent Booth went through the contents of the rear compartment looking for any relevant evidence. He spotted an orange tackle box, but did not open it or confiscate it.

The Winklers spent the night in a hotel with their granddaughters. They were joined by both of their sons, and friends Eddie and Sheryl Thompson. They had the hard task of telling the two older girls that their father had passed away.

"Patricia, something terrible's happened to your daddy."

"I know someone hurt him," she said.

Then, they delivered the news that she would never see him alive again. They repeated the heart-wrenching scene with Allie. Breanna was too young to know or understand.

In the morning, the authorities released Mary's mini-van to the Winklers, who used it to make the long drive with the three girls to their home in Huntingdon. Their granddaughters behaved beautifully. The only unpleasant incident was when Patricia had a bout of car sickness. At one meal stop, a stranger recognized them and paid for their food. They arrived home very late, but Matthew's Aunt Linda and his maternal grandmother were there to greet them.

The girls were fearful and full of questions. Aunt Linda held her two great-nieces tightly to her side as they sobbed out the worries. They wanted someone they knew with them at all times—preferably Nana and Poppa. Lights had to be left on at night, or they were too afraid to sleep.

In Selmer, church members gathered to plant annuals in honor of their fallen minister on Saturday, pausing to share memories of him. Before his death, Matthew planned a spring clean-up of the church grounds that included planting flower beds. "We're doing this because Matthew wanted us to," James Turner said.

Retired psychiatric nurse Jimmie Smith said, "It keeps

us busy. We don't understand all of this, but God's with us, and we're working for Him, planting His flowers." Then she was back digging in the dirt.

In Bay Minette, Mary waived her right to an extradition hearing, clearing the way for her transfer back to Tennessee. Saturday morning, Baldwin County sheriff's deputies outfitted Mary with handcuffs, a belly chain and shackles. She climbed into the back seat of the McNairy County vehicle. Sheriff Rick Roten and Officer Byron Maxedon of the Selmer Police Department made the trip back to Tennessee with her.

Mary asked no questions and made no comments. She only spoke when asked if she needed a restroom break or if she was hungry or thirsty. At one of the two stops for gas, Mary was escorted to the service station lavatory. She went inside alone while Maxedon stood guard outside the door.

They pulled up to the back of the McNairy County Justice Center at the jail entrance around 4:30 that afternoon. She entered still wearing the pink sweat suit she had on when she was stopped by the Orange Beach police two days earlier.

The sheriff spoke briefly to the gathered media. "She's fine. She had no emotion whatsoever. She was quiet and cooperative," he said. "She didn't ask any questions, didn't talk about anything. She had good behavior. We've had no problems whatsoever."

Officials walked her through the standard booking procedures. She was fingerprinted, photographed and searched by a female guard, and placed in a holding cell alone for eight to ten hours. There she dressed in a prison uniform before being transferred to a cell in the female block.

Mary Winkler, preacher's wife, mother of three, college student, was now an inmate charged with first-degree murder of the man she claimed she loved.

THE LIVES

"Who can find a virtuous woman? For her price is far above rubies. The heart of her husband doth safely trust in her, so that he shall have no need of spoil. She will do him good and not evil all the days of her life."

—*Proverbs* 31: 10-12

CHAPTER 8

No one saw it coming. Nothing in Mary Winkler's history foreshadowed this horrendous event—the ultimate act of domestic violence. No one ever looked at Mary and believed she was capable of taking another person's life.

Clark Freeman and Mary Nell Hackney married on July 20, 1968. More than five years later, on December 10, 1973, Mary Nell gave birth to their first child, Mary Carol Freeman, in Knoxville, Tennessee.

At the time of Mary's birth, Knoxville was home to approximately 175,000 people, making it the third-largest city in the state.

Knoxville is situated in eastern Tennessee, in former Cherokee country, embraced by the Cumberland Plateau of the Appalachian mountain chain on one side and the Great Smoky Mountains National Park on the other. Growing up, Mary often visited the park and explored the 510,030 acres of ridges, hollows, river gorges, the most diversified plant life in the country and the largest stand of virgin timber east of the Mississippi, authorized by the federal government in 1934 and dedicated by President Franklin Delano Roosevelt in 1940.

The city began its life as a fort named after George Washington's secretary of war, Henry Knox. That structure still stands in the central business district of the city. In 1796, when Tennessee became a state, Knoxville was its first capital.

The Freeman lifestyle owed a lot to the Tennessee Valley Authority, a New Deal project under Franklin Roosevelt's administration, that transformed the Tennessee River and brought modern conveniences to the city. The program, beginning in 1933, built large dams, and purchased smaller existing private dams, and created a network of fifty that operated as a single system, generating power and enhancing the region's economic development. The Tennessee Valley Authority is still one of the two largest employers in Knoxville. The other is the University of Tennessee.

This institution of higher education began in 1794 as Blount College and gained its current status in 1879. It now leads a statewide university system that is a pivotal part of the Knoxville community, serving as a national leader in energy research and the cultural center of the city as well as providing a nationally recognized athletic program closely followed by local citizens.

After World War II, Knoxville felt the impact of the United States government again when the village of Oak Ridge—twenty miles west of the city—became the site of the Manhattan Project, a secret federal nuclear installation. The city benefited from another federal project in the fifties—the development of the interstate highway system during Dwight D. Eisenhower's administration. The city lies on U.S. Route 40, the long and winding highway that connects Wilmington, North Carolina, on the east coast, to Barstow, California, in the west. All these government programs boosted the economic growth of Knoxville, which positively impacted the standard of living enjoyed by Freeman family decades later.

Knoxville is a place of unquestionable beauty. The great debate is whether the most glorious season is spring or fall. The blooming of a great profusion of dogwoods and azaleas announces the arrival of the warm weather with a breathtaking display of whites and reds, highlighted by the intense, fresh green of new growth. Every autumn, the brilliance of the golds and reds racing down streets

and over mountaintops make the area glow like an exquisite work of art.

Mary grew up on Frontier Trail in a predominately
white, modestly affluent neighborhood in southwest
Knoxville. Her family attended the Laurel Church of
Christ, a 200-family congregation known for its ministry
at the University of Tennessee. Her father Clark served as
deacon. They lived the life dictated by the guidelines and
prohibitions of the Church. The man was the literal head
of the household in every way. Clark's word was law. He
made all the decisions for his family.

When Mary was 2 years old, her sister Patricia was
born. Patricia's life did not get off to an easy start. She was
born with cerebral palsy and developed spinal meningitis
and encephalitis as an infant. She suffered from significant
mental retardation and physical disability. Eventually, she
was capable of reading words off of a page, but she had no
comprehension of the meaning behind them.

Mary was close to and very protective of her little sister. Even though Mary had a room of her own, she usually
slept in Patricia's bed with her. She put a pillow between
them to keep from being banged up in her sleep by the
metal braces Patricia often had to wear.

Mary attended Mount Olive Elementary School. At
home she had a strict upbringing, where rules were made
to be followed without question. She learned to mind her
manners and respect her elders. She was a quiet and obedi-
ent child—reserved and soft-spoken, just like her mother.

When Mary was in middle school, her parents took in a
child named Shannon as a foster daughter. Shannon's four
siblings were spread out in other homes. When the Freemans submitted a request to serve as foster parents for all
five of them, they were denied. The state insisted that each
child have his own bedroom.

Mary offered to sleep on the sofa and give up hers, since
there were no rules requiring a biological child to have her
own space. Instead, Clark Freeman, a home improvement
contractor by trade, built an addition to his home. He hoped

that all of the kids could live with his family—but, if that still wasn't the case, at least the siblings would have a place to come together for visits on weekends and holidays.

By the time Clark finished the project, the five children were reunited with their biological parents. Once again, the Freemans were a family of four. Clark bought homes from individuals and from the U.S. Department of Housing and Urban Development, renovated them and sold them. He earned his living "flipping houses." Mary Nell was a teacher for the Knox County Schools. Although certified for the classroom, she chose instead to go to homes and instruct those children temporarily unable to attend school for medical reasons.

On April 15, 1987, tragedy struck the Freeman home. Mary Nell was giving her youngest daughter Patricia a bath. One minute, Patricia was singing in the tub, the next she had a heart attack. She never recovered. She was only 11 years old.

Reeling with grief, 13-year-old Mary turned to the counselor at school for help in dealing with her loss. Clark intervened. He called the school and insisted that the counselor not talk to his daughter. This was a matter for the family, the Church and God. No secular professionals were needed.

Decades later, fingers would point back to this period as the genesis of Mary's post-traumatic stress disorder. Mary, it was said, never recovered from the death of her sister.

Meanwhile, in Shannon's home, the abuse and neglect that had led to her temporary foster care by the Freemans began anew. The state stepped in and removed her and her siblings permanently from their biological home. The parental rights of her mother and father were revoked. The five children were placed in foster care and available for adoption.

The Freemans adopted 11-year-old Shannon and her siblings, 8-year-old Tabatha, 7-year-old Amanda, 6-year-

old Eric and 5-year-old Chase. The kids moved into the
new rooms constructed by Clark. Mary Nell purchased a
mini-van to transport her newly expanded brood. Amanda
later said, "When we all became a family, Mary was so loving, and, like my sister likes to say, kind of like our other
mom. She took us everywhere."

Mary reveled in the role of big sister and back-up care-
taker. She taught her new siblings to play tennis in the
summer and built gingerbread houses for them at Christmas time. Mothering them filled some of the void left in
Mary's heart after the death of her sister Patricia.

At Doyle High School, Mary went by her middle name,
Carol, since her mother's name was Mary Nell. It was a
typical act of a teenager seeking separation and indepen-
dence from her parents. She demonstrated an interest in
singing, first discovered when she joined her eighth-grade
chorus. Mary sang in the girls' and mixed choruses and
then competed for and earned a spot on the school's elite
madrigal group. She also played tennis, volunteered as a
peer tutor with the physically and mentally handicapped
students in the special education classes, and was active in
Young Life, a religious organization for high school and
college students, and in Y-Teens, a youth leadership group.

Her classmates described her as reserved, studious and
quiet, with a good sense of humor, a genuine interest in
others and a constant smile on her face. They didn't know
that behind that happy façade was a troubled girl, one who
would hide behind the clothing in her closet when she
couldn't cope. They only knew that sweet, nice girl who
brightened their day.

Her loving nature embraced more than just her immediate family and classmates. Long-time family friend
Christine Henderson remembered her as "a well-behaved,
adorable child, always courteous and thoughtful," who
grew into an "unselfish and compassionate" teenager. She
recalled Mary visiting the nursing home where Christine's
elderly bedridden mother was recuperating from a broken

hip. "I'll never forget the way my mother smiled when she told me about Mary's visit."

In Mary's senior year, Doyle and South–Young High Schools merged, forming South–Doyle High. Mary graduated from there in 1992.

In the fall, she attended Lipscomb University in Nashville, the flagship college for the churches of Christ, a form of worship that is prevalent throughout Tennessee. Even though she was living away from home, she was actively involved in family life. Every Tuesday night was Bible-reading night in the Freeman house and Mary joined in by telephone. She continued her musical interests with the University Singers and worked on the staff of the weekly newspaper, *The Lipscomb Babbler*. While there, she stopped using "Carol" and reverted to using her first name, Mary.

After two years of study, she transferred to a school offering a degree in special education, Freed-Hardeman University in Henderson, Tennessee—twenty miles north of Selmer.

During orientation, Mary, a tiny woman with long brown hair and an easy smile, met another transfer student, Elizabeth Gentle. They got to know each other better as they sat side-by-side in Bible class. "She was easy to get along with," Elizabeth said. "She just had a sweet spirit about her."

Mary was active in Phi Kappa Alpha, one of the six campus social clubs, and was a member of the campus Evangelism Forum, where she met a handsome, athletic student named Matthew Winkler.

CHAPTER 9

Matthew Winkler was born on November 21, 1974, when older brother Daniel was sixteen months old. At that time, the Winklers lived in Fort Worth, Texas, a major industrial city dominated by aviation producers, and grain and oil merchants. Its historical role as cattle marketers and meat-packers earned the city its nickname, "Cowtown." It was also where Matthew's grandfather, Wendell Winkler, a native of Port Arthur, Texas, made his mark with the churches of Christ.

Matthew's family had deep and substantial roots in this faith. By the time Matthew was born, his grandfather Wendell Winkler, a third generation Church of Christ pulpit minister, was director of the Brown Trail School of Preaching in Fort Worth. He had been spreading the word for thirty years in at least twenty-six states. He'd published nine books on biblical theology, among them the first five books in his "Sound Doctrine for Everyday Living" series and authored several smaller works, including one about the role of the preacher's wife.

Matthew's ancestors were pioneers in the movement that established the churches of Christ. Its history began in the early 1800s when preacher Alexander Campbell proposed a separation from the Presbyterian Church and a return to the primitivism of the first century Church, embracing the fundamental beliefs and fervor of the early

Christians. A new Christian denomination, the Disciples of Christ, was born.

In the early 1900s, another split erupted, led by those who felt that any denomination was wrong in God's eyes because it created divisions in the body of Christians, and that the existence of an umbrella organization over any individual congregation undermined the authority of Christ.

The new branch of the churches of Christ—unlike the United Church of Christ, a more liberal Protestant denomination—were all independent, autonomous congregations that reported to no headquarters or convention. Each Church of Christ, then as now, is governed by an all-male group of elders.

Wendell Winkler wrote that "the New Testament speaks only of local congregations . . . or the church embracing all of the saved." He insisted that "Our Lord was undenominational so must his church be." Winkler considered denominations to be unholy, man-made constructs and advocated for the end of them all:

> Unity exists because of allegiance to a single objective authority. In like manner, when all men will lay down their creeds, disciplines, manuals, confessions of faith, catechisms, think-so's, maybe's, and subjective feelings and each with an unprejudiced and receptive heart turns to the word of God, then, and only then, will unity result. Such will constitute the death knell to denominationalism. We must be committed to being nothing, calling ourselves nothing, obeying nothing, saying nothing except that which is authorized by the word of God.

Any name—Methodist, Baptist, or Lutheran—was wrong, he argued, because it was not contained in the scripture. Any rule of discipline—like the Presbyterian's Westminster Confession of Faith—was wrong because it set itself above and apart from the Gospel. Other churches said that denouncing denominations was itself destructive, in that it divided and excluded other Christians.

Nonetheless, this philosophy drove the growth of churches of Christ in a broad swath of this country—from Pittsburgh to El Paso—in the twentieth century. There are congregations in all fifty states and in eighty foreign countries, with 3,500,000 adherents. The majority are in Tennessee and Texas, with Tennessee having the largest per capita membership.

Despite the lack of an over-arching human authority, the churches do have consistencies in their doctrine. All congregations sing *a capella*—no instruments are allowed in worship services, since they are not described in the New Testament. Critics of this policy point to numerous mentions of harps and lyres in the Old Testament.

Another universal belief is that the role of women in the church and the home is secondary to that of men. Women are not allowed to serve in any leadership position in the worship service—not even as song leader. This belief is validated by a verse in the Bible that exhorts women to be quiet in church. Many theological historians believe that this biblical admonition was nothing more than the reflection of a society where women were not educated, and that it is irrelevant in today's world.

In the churches of Christ, however, that verse is law. Each congregation decides where to draw the line. In some, a woman is allowed to teach children's Sunday School classes; in others, putting a woman in charge of the church nursery is considered an affront to God.

Young women raised in the Church were urged to willingly choose submission to the authority of men as a way of life. Pulpit preachers told the girls that women are treasured and uplifted in the churches of Christ and that the acceptance of submission was a gift from God to be cherished and embraced by every woman. Their mandated purpose on earth was to care for their children and support their men.

Another sharp distinction between the doctrine of the

churches of Christ and the Christian denominations centers on the rite of baptism. Most protestant and Catholic churches practice infant christening. In this ceremony, the parents present their baby to be anointed on the forehead with water from a baptismal font or basin. Like the Baptists, the churches of Christ do not perform this service, and believe, instead, in full immersion baptism. A participant in this rite walks into waist-deep water in a river or small pool designed for this purpose in the front of the church. The minister lowers the celebrant backward until the head is completely submersed. But the purpose behind this act differs greatly. Baptists believe that once children reach the age of accountability, in other words, achieve an understanding about the difference between right and wrong, they can be saved by accepting Jesus into their hearts and asking for forgiveness of their sins. They are then eligible for baptism, a prerequisite for membership in the Church. To the Baptists, this ritual is one that follows the example set by Christ. It is a public affirmation of faith and a symbolic resurrection to a new life.

In the churches of Christ, however, full immersion baptism is an essential ingredient for salvation. It literally washes away sin. Without it, a soul is doomed to hell. Because of their belief that this form of baptism is the only way to avoid eternal damnation, many Baptist ministers have labeled churches of Christ a "sect" or "cult."

The churches of Christ provide an inflexible outline for living life, worshiping and raising children. Some Christians are turned off by this rigidity. Others find their black-and-white approach comforting.

The Winkler family emerged from the churches of Christ as a multi-generational dynasty. Matthew's father, Dan, began his ministerial career five years before Matthew's birth. As a high school student, Dan preached at a little church in the country. He continued delivering sermons through his college years. After graduating, he stepped into the pulpit full-time at the age of 21.

Dan met Diane while they were in college. They married in August of 1970. After graduation, Diane became a school teacher. During Matthew's childhood, the family moved from state to state, following a trail of pulpit positions. They moved from Fort Worth to Greenville, Texas, a small city northeast of Dallas, in the Blackland Prairie. Then to Woodbury, Tennessee, a small town southeast of Nashville, situated halfway between Murfreesboro and McMinnville. When Matthew was 5 years old, the family grew by one more boy, Jacob.

Then Dan moved on to the Huntingdon Church of Christ—in a town a little more than an hour's drive from Selmer. Matthew attended sixth and seventh grades, and played football at Huntingdon Middle School before Dan accepted a position at the Beltline Church of Christ, and the family moved to Decatur, Alabama, the seat of Montgomery County, on October 6, 1988.

Decatur is perched on a hill overlooking the Tennessee River. It began its life as Rhodes Ferry, named after the crossing established in the 1810s. Incorporated as Albany in 1821, a directive issued by President James Monroe changed its name to honor Stephen Decatur, renowned United States Navy commander, who was killed in a duel.

During the civil war, Yankee troops burned the city to the ground—only three buildings survived the conflagration. The city rose from the ashes despite the additional decimation caused by two yellow fever plagues. From that building spurt, the town now boasts the most intact Victorian-era neighborhood in Alabama.

Like Mary's hometown of Knoxville, Decatur was nestled on the Tennessee River, and benefited from President Roosevelt's creation of the Tennessee Valley Authority.

Dan assumed his new position as pulpit minister for Beltline Church of Christ, a well-established congregation—they had their first service under a big oak tree in 1931. Under Dan's leadership, the church grew, reaching 425 members, and built a new activity center with offices, workrooms, fellowship rooms, a benevolent area and several classrooms.

Matthew enrolled at Austin High School and played on the football team as an outside linebacker on defense, and fullback on offense. All three of the Winkler boys played football. Dan and Diane told each one of them to exercise their force on the field, but to always remember there were different expectations elsewhere. "Be nothing but a gentleman off the field." They believed all of their sons lived up to this ideal. They never saw any evidence that Matthew was emotionally or physically abusive to anyone.

His football coach, Dyer Carlisle, told reporter Tonya Smith-King of *The Jackson Sun* that the two older brothers were both hard-nosed players. Matt trained all summer long lifting weights to be the best player he could be. "The only difference between Daniel and Matthew, Matthew was more, probably more spirited. Daniel was even-keeled. And I mean this in a positive way, but Matthew, he would really get fired up. I mean, he really got into the game, he was very emotional . . .

"He was very passionate. As coaches, that was a good thing . . . Matthew was one of our best hitters. He was just pretty much a coach's dream to work with . . . I could see him maybe having a temper, but the only time I ever saw it was in relation to getting fired up about a game. He was a really tough-minded kid on the football field . . ." but ". . . he left it all on the field. He didn't bring it into the locker room or the community."

The coach also appreciated his star player's parents. "Even when things weren't going well with the team, let's say, they were always positive and always supportive. They were just the ideal parents to work with."

In addition to football, Matthew liked swimming, going to movies and playing Nintendo. He was active in the Lads to Leaders program at his church. He got involved in the puppet teams—putting on shows designed to tell the story of the Gospel to children—public speaking and Bible reading, and traveled to Nashville for competition with teenagers from other churches. He took to speaking in public as if he'd been born for the pulpit.

Matthew's charismatic personality came to the fore-front in these years. He was well-liked by fellow students, but he never had a steady girlfriend. His high school friend and football teammate Scott Fuller told *The Jackson Sun*, "I think more than anything I remember about Matthew was his love for life. He was always a comedian. He never got down about anything."

His universal popularity compelled his classmates to elect him "Mr. Austin" in his senior year. He received another honor when he was named one of the escorts for the school's Miss Bruin Pageant. He wasn't as intense academically as his older brother. Daniel usually received straight A's. Matthew was a solid A and B student, though. He graduated in 1993.

After graduation, Matthew felt a call to the ministry. Although Dan and Diane were careful not to pressure any of their children to take this path, they were delighted. Dan said, "We told all three of our sons if they wanted to preach, we would help them any way we can, and if you do not, we will help you any way we can."

Matthew followed his older brother to Freed-Hardeman University in Henderson, Tennessee, a small town of 5,600 located between Selmer and Huntingdon. It was a pretty, compact campus sitting on a hilltop, the clusters of converted old houses and newer brick buildings broken up by green space and trees.

The church's influence over campus life was apparent. "Modesty and appropriateness" were mandated in clothing and hair styles. Unless actively engaged in athletic activity, students were prohibited from wearing shorts in public. Attendance at chapel was a daily requirement. There were separate dormitories for male and female students. Only once during the school year were students allowed to go into the dorms of the opposite sex. That was on Halloween, where they were allowed to trick-or-treat at each other's residences.

In 1994, Matthew's parents moved from Georgia to Nashville, where Dan served eleven years as the pulpit

preacher of the 1,300-member Crieve Hall Church of
Christ. One year later, Matthew met and fell for another
student, a year older than he was. After dating her for three
months, Matthew knew it was serious. In October 1995,
she placed a call to her mother and father saying she was
coming home for a visit, and bringing along someone she
wanted them to meet. Before the weekend was over, Matt
asked Clark Freeman for his daughter's hand in marriage.
Six months later, wearing her mother's satin wedding
gown, and preceded by nine pink-gowned bridesmaids, she
walked down the aisle. Matthew sealed his fate on April
20, 1996, when he recited his wedding vows in Knoxville,
marrying Mary Carol Freeman.

CHAPTER 10

At the end of the academic year, the newlyweds both dropped out of school to save up money. They moved to the Knoxville area and into a tiny apartment in Louisville, a small town outside of the city. Matthew got a construction job working for his new father-in-law.

That summer, Matthew started shouting and yelling at his wife on a regular basis. Mary never understood what she did to provoke that behavior. Perhaps he was uncomfortable being dependent on Mary's father for his paycheck. Perhaps he was bitter about terminating his schooling. Whatever the cause, an angry Matthew was intimidating. At 6'1", he was still built like the linebacker he once was. Riled up, he paced the floor and waved his arms around—seeming to be everywhere at once. When making a point, he'd poke his fingers inches from Mary's nose. If she stood up for herself, he'd say, "That's your ugly coming out."

On one occasion, he sat her down and shouted, "You are my wife and we are a family now! Quit inviting your brothers and sisters over, and stop going over there all the time!"

They eventually returned to Henderson, where Matthew continued his education and Mary became the family breadwinner. She got a full-time job in the deli at Piggly Wiggly. Their first child, Patricia Diane Winkler—named for Mary's deceased sister and Matthew's mother—was born in the Jackson–Madison County General Hospital at 3 o'clock in the afternoon of September 30, 1997.

Matthew graduated with a degree in Biblical Studies in 1998 and accepted a job as youth minister at the Goodwood Boulevard Church of Christ in Baton Rouge, Louisiana. It was the first time Mary ever lived outside of Tennessee and she grew more homesick with each passing day. Matthew was not happy, either, being so far from his family. He searched for a new opportunity in his home state.

Mary's feelings of separation grew even more intense when her mother's life began to fade with the onset of cancer. Mary was pregnant with her second child when her mother passed away on April 10, 1999. With the death of Mary Nell, Mary's adopted siblings turned to her for help, guidance and comfort even more than before.

Matthew found a new youth minister position at the Bellevue Church of Christ in Nashville in June of 1999. He and Mary purchased a 1,300-square-foot home, still under construction, for $132,350 in Pegram, a town of 2,100 residents just nine miles from the church.

They moved back to Tennessee just in time for the birth of their second daughter. On Saturday, July 10, the furniture arrived at their new apartment and Mary began unpacking her household. On Tuesday, she went into labor. Mary Alice—named for Mary's mother and Matthew's great-grandmother—was born on Wednesday, July 14, five weeks premature. They nicknamed the baby girl Allie.

Their new home in the quiet hilltop neighborhood on Elkmont Place in the Grandview Heights subdivision was ready in September. It was not a good time for Mary. She was still grieving for her mother, suffering from a case of post-partum blues and caring for a toddler and an infant. Soon after, Matthew invited Mary's sisters and brothers for a visit at their new home.

Mary's family griped a lot about their infrequent visits with their sister. They were not pleased with Matthew's answer to their complaints: "Mary is not your sister like she was your sister when you were growing up. She is married now. She has two children now. Her responsibility is here, with her new family."

He was angry at their demands on Mary. The passion he brought to the football field and to the pulpit felt over-sized when it was revealed in a small roomful of people. The Freeman clan left Pegram with the feeling that Matthew was controlling, domineering and mean. Where did Mary stand in this confrontation? Did she resent Matthew's interference with her family? In later years, she would agree with her siblings' view, but, at the time, she appeared to side with her husband; friends recalled the negative comments she made about her family at the time.

Parishioners at Bellevue Church of Christ developed contradictory impressions of their new youth minister and his wife. One would say that Mary was the friendlier of the two. Another would insist that Mary was an odd person with poorly developed social skills.

The conflicting opinions may have been the result of Mary's unsettled state of mind, which led to dramatic mood swings. She was again coping with the childhood loss of her sister—feelings resurrected when her mother died. Two back-to-back pregnancies exacted an emotional toll. Adjusting to two new neighborhoods and two new congregations in a short span of time created additional strain.

To complicate her life even further, soon after they moved into their new home, Matthew invited his college roommate, Glenn Jones and his wife, Brandy, to live with them while construction took place on their house next door. Four adults and two children crowded the Winklers' small home.

Mary wasn't the only one under the gun. Matthew felt driven by an intense, self-imposed pressure to further his career, to have his own church, to be something more than a youth minister. It was a matter of living up to his father's example, as well as earning a sufficient salary to support his growing family.

Committed to monogamy and the sanctity of marriage,

Matthew also discovered an uncomfortable fact—he and Mary were sexually incompatible. Matthew wanted to experiment. Mary was more traditional. When they were outside of the bedroom discussing various practices, Mary spoke her mind about acts that she did not want to do— that she didn't feel were natural.

Matthew agreed not to do anything that made her uncomfortable during sex but in the throes of passion, he often went back on his word. Nonetheless, Mary said that if she pushed him away or even made the smallest involuntary flinch, he always backed off. However, on those occasions that she gave no indication that she wanted him to stop, he continued.

Later, they rehashed the problem. Mary re-stated her objections. Matthew once again agreed to abstain from practices she didn't like—and then he'd lose sight of it in the heat of the moment. It was a never-ending cycle of disparate desires and expectations.

A scary event rocked the Winkler home in the spring of 2001. Matthew had tooth trouble and his dentist prescribed pain medication. The drug did not interact well with Matthew's system, and it resulted in ugly side effects. Matthew grew paranoid, convinced that someone— perhaps Mary—was out to kill him. He threatened to cut her brake lines. Then, in a fit of rage, he picked up a recliner and tossed it on its side. Mary called Matt's younger brother Jacob, but he was a thirty- to forty-minute drive away. Matt was ranting and raving, and Mary knew something had to be done immediately.

She slipped out of the house and heard Matthew lock the door behind her. With curlers in her hair, she ran across lawns to Glenn and Brandy's home. Brandy said Mary arrived laughing about Matt's behavior. Mary would say that she was ashamed by Matt and was "blowing it off" for the sake of her own pride.

The Joneses had a spare key to the Winklers' home. Glenn grabbed it and walked back over with Mary. He unlocked the door, ready to confront a violent Matthew. By the time they arrived, though, Matt's rage had dissipated and he was stumbling around in a daze. Jacob arrived a short while later. Both men spent the night watching over Matthew, making sure he would be okay.

Mary said that her husband was angry and threatening during their years in Pegram, but, she insisted, he was never physically violent with her—that didn't happen, she said, until they moved to McMinnville. Still, years later, Mary recalled McMinnville with great fondness, but described Pegram as a "hard place."

CHAPTER 11

Matthew believed he'd made an advancement in his career when he secured a position as youth minister at the Central Church of Christ in McMinnville, Tennessee, in 2002. When he applied for the job, a church elder informed him that they expected he'd step up to the pulpit minister position when their current preacher left in two or three years. Matthew accepted the offer with his eye on the ultimate prize—one day in the near future, having his own church.

McMinnville, heralded as the Nursery Capital of the World for its vast plant and tree industry, and hometown of country and western star Dottie West, had a population of more than 13,000 when Matthew and Mary moved there with their two little girls. Matthew's new employer, the Central Church of Christ, was housed in a building constructed in 1928 on the grounds of the original old courthouse at the corner of Morford and College Streets. Just a short walk away, down sidewalks lined with old brick buildings, a small city park stood, filled with century-old stately maples, graceful elms, a sparkling fountain and an abundance of flowers in the spring and summer.

They bought an $85,000 home on Franklin Street. Once again, when they moved, Mary was pregnant. This time, however, she was not as far along and the pregnancy ended in miscarriage late in the first trimester.

They quickly became friends with an older couple across the street, Bob and Evon Dennis. Bob and Evon were Baptists, but that never interfered with the relationship between the two couples. In fact, Bob and Matt engaged in frequent, friendly debates on theological issues.

Evon enjoyed the energetic and perky Mary Winkler, but was especially drawn to the two little girls. She had her own grandchildren, but they were all boys. Patricia and Allie became surrogate granddaughters. Evon doted on them, remembering them with gifts every Christmas and birthday.

She loved watching them at play outside the house. When they spotted her, they'd stop, wave and yell greetings across the street. "They were both sweet girls—small and adorable. Patricia was very talkative. Allie was quieter."

Matthew and Mary were always on the run. Matt's position as youth minister required him to be away from home quite often in the summer as he took trips with the teenagers in his care. Year round, he had evening and weekend activities with them, and frequently entertained groups in his home.

Matthew faced a big challenge at Central Church of Christ. His predecessor had had a very lax demeanor, more interested in being friends with the teenagers than their mentor. He'd made no rules, set no boundaries and provided no structure. Matthew got the kids and the program back into shape.

Matthew could be stern and authoritative at times, but he kept them from losing control without being bossy. The teens appreciated always knowing where they stood with him and what he expected of them. Most of them looked up to him as an energizing and inspiring Christian leader. There were two or three teens who bumped heads with him, but that was to be expected when working with adolescents.

Mary pitched in with Matt's meetings and activities, and often ran errands for the youth group. She found the energy to visit with the housebound elderly church members and to sit with the sick. She made birthday cards on the computer and sent them out to all the church members.

She cared for two children and her home as well as working part-time, first at Super D drug store, and later at the post office, where she was a valued employee. The pharmacy owner, Donald Sullivan, wrote, "She was a very reliable and dependable employee that worked well with other employees and was well liked by our customers."

Bob and Evon, like many of the neighbors on Franklin Street, saw Mary and Matthew as loving and hard-working, and excellent role models for the other married couples. But Mary recalled it as a challenging time.

In August that first summer, Mary played catcher on the church softball team. At one point, a ball careened off a bat and hit her in the face, leaving a distinct bruise. She didn't go to the doctor.

Later that week, according to Mary, Matthew was shouting at her for some perceived wrong-doing when he knocked something off a table. Mary bent down to pick it up, and, she would later allege, Matthew kicked her in the face. She said that was when her face really started to hurt.

A week later, the lightest touch caused excruciating pain. Finally, Mary visited her physician. In his office, Mary explained the softball injury. She never mentioned any physical abuse from her husband. The doctor never suspected anything was amiss with Mary's story.

Soon after that incident, Mary confronted Matthew. "I want a divorce," she said.

"Absolutely not."

"I can't take it anymore, Matthew."

"A divorce will not be allowed."

"You tell me I'm fat, my hair isn't right. If something goes wrong with the girls, it's my fault. If it rains, it's my fault. I've got to get out of here."

"If you leave, I'll come and get you."

CHAPTER 12

In 2003, Matthew got the opportunity to earn additional money by teaching Bible classes at the Boyd Christian School. This private institution covered all levels of lower education from pre-kindergarten through the twelfth grade. Students received Bible instruction each school day.

The goal of the state-accredited school was to provide a quality education with more course offerings than available in public schools, and to do so in a more disciplined and safer environment. All high-schoolers studied a college preparatory curriculum. The school did not offer alternative paths, like technical or business, for a diploma. In addition to their education, the faculty fostered the students' spiritual development and growth.

Matthew was a welcome addition to the school. His students called him "Wink" and, although they knew he demanded that they study hard and behave, he also brought a lot of fun into the classroom. He was a creative and engaging teacher.

He got along well with the staff, too. Linda Love, an English, Journalism and foreign language teacher, said that he was a charismatic man, and a loving and doting father. She told *The Jackson Sun*, "Every time he talked, he had something positive to say about the kids, something positive to say about his family. He often commented on the girls, Patricia and Allie. He would tell about cute things they did." She added that he was always true to himself and never put on airs. "He had such a young heart, but an old soul."

She believed the Winkler couple had a wonderful relationship. She recalled Matthew and Mary trading affectionate looks on the General Jackson Showboat on the Cumberland River at a Christmas party sponsored by Super D drug store. "They seemed very loving, very close. It was a chilly night and I saw him wrap his coat around her."

Robert Jefferies, minister of the Smyrna Church of Christ in McMinnville, had a high opinion of Matthew and his relationship with his wife, too. Matthew worked with his congregation on several occasions, earning their affection and respect. He remembered once arriving at the Winkler home with Matthew. "We had come over just as she was getting ready to head back out to work," he told reporter Tonya Smith-King. "They hugged and kissed one another goodbye."

The older congregants at Central Church of Christ didn't have as much contact with Matthew as the younger ones did. Nonetheless, many had fond memories of his years at the church. Unlike some youth ministers, Matthew had time and a kind word for everyone.

Some people, though, saw another side of Matthew. Lori Boyd, the church secretary for part of Matthew's tenure at Central, worked at the main desk. Matthew's office was down a narrow hallway. At first, she felt he was extremely nice, but as time went by, she said, he became "mentally and emotionally berating and demanding, and hard to work with." She felt he looked down on her.

Matthew obviously was not satisfied with her job performance. He'd order her to do certain tasks. When she made excuses, he said, "You will have this done when I say so."

Lori was also aware of a "strained tension" in the office when Mary dropped by the church. Most of the time, she could not hear the words spoken between the two, but she could hear the sound of a deep rumbling voice echoing up the hall and she thought that it was filled with anger.

Mary frequently brought a fast food lunch to share with Matthew. Lori noticed a number of times that when Mary left the building, her lunch remained untouched on Matthew's desk. On one occasion, she heard Matthew say, "You're getting a little larger than you need to be. You don't need to have this food, Mary."

Lori was appalled. She confronted Matthew after Mary left. "Those are things I was hoping you wouldn't say to your wife. You're a man of God. You are supposed to be a leader of us. And you are supposed to lead by example."

There was another thing about Matthew that bothered Lori. As with many married working couples, Matthew and Mary's employment schedules overlapped from time to time. When that happened, Matthew brought Patricia and Allie to the church with him. If he had to leave on business, he locked the two girls in his office. Lori thought that the girls should go downstairs to the day care center to play with children there, or be allowed to roam the offices spending time with her and the pulpit minister. But Matthew justified locking them in by saying, "I want my kids to be safe."

Jonathan Allen, a member of Matthew's youth group, had nothing but praise for Matthew in his ministerial role. He did, however, recall Matthew yelling at Mary, but never heard Mary yell back at him. He noticed that Mary always seemed to do everything Matthew told her to do.

Congregant Rudy Thomsen said that his respect for Matthew faded one Sunday. He and his wife Kathy were sitting in the pews waiting for the start of morning worship service when Matthew, Mary and the girls entered the sanctuary. Mary had a black eye. This concerned Rudy enough that he asked Mary about it.

Mary said, "I was horsing around with the girls and one of them jabbed me in the eye with her elbow."

Rudy was skeptical of her response, but gave her the benefit of the doubt until one day at a church supper. Mary was in the fellowship hall flitting from table to table, smiling and chatting with everyone she met. Then, Matthew entered the room. Mary stopped talking, hung her head and took her seat, Rudy said. From that moment on, he no longer believed Mary's explanation for her black eye. He wondered just what was going on behind the preacher's closed doors.

Another person wondering was Paul Pillow, one of the owners of Cleaners Express, a business patronized by Mary. He said that in doing business together, his friendship grew with Mary over time, as it did with many of his regular customers. Although he enjoyed his interactions with her, he said that there was an unsettling nervousness about Mary. "She always seemed to be looking over her shoulder."

Mary often brought in the comforter from her bed with blood on it. She blamed her part-poodle, part-Maltese dog for the stain. He told her that she was going to have to keep the dog off of the bed. "Mary, you're going to wear this thing out cleaning it so much."

Mary chuckled and Paul laughed along with her. In retrospect, he wondered if there was a more sinister explanation. But at the time, the thought never crossed his mind.

He was privy to one family secret unbecoming of a minister and his wife. Mary was a secret smoker. Matthew dipped and chewed. Mary picked up her cigarettes and Matt's Skoal at a store where she thought she wouldn't be recognized.

Another person who didn't share in the admiration most had for Matthew was Sergeant Jimmy Jones of the Tennessee Highway Patrol. He moved into the neighborhood when his grandmother, a sixty-year resident of Franklin Street, was in poor health.

On August 19, 2003, it appeared that the end was near. Family started gathering at her home. Mary came over to check on his 92-year-old grandmother, as she often did. Later, he was standing outside with some family members, when he noticed Matthew moving in their direction. He thought, at first, that this man of the cloth was coming over to inquire about his grandmother, too. But, as Matthew crossed the street, he appeared upset.

Matthew stepped into the yard, but did not approach the group. He stood at a distance, waving his arms and shouting about the barking of a small dog that was keeping him awake. Jimmy was distressed by Matthew's behavior at this delicate time. He later nicknamed him "the Tasmanian Devil." Jimmy's grandmother passed away the next day.

But Evon and Bob, who saw a lot of the Winklers, never sensed that anything was amiss. Even looking back, they can't spot a single red flag.

CHAPTER 13

In March of 2004, Matthew's plan for the future fizzled out. Despite assurances made to him when he came to McMinnville, he was not promoted to the pulpit minister position. The church elders hired Timothy Parish to fill that vacancy. Matthew was disappointed and angry. He started the hunt for a pastoral position elsewhere in Tennessee.

That summer, an opportunity arose at the Fourth Street Church of Christ in Selmer. After an initial interview, the church invited him back for a second one and asked him to bring his wife. The elders talked to the two of them together and liked them both. Matthew's name made it to the short list for consideration.

Despite Matthew's bitterness over the recent developments at Central Church of Christ, he and Mary continued to invite members of the church to their children's parties. For Allie's fifth birthday in July and Patricia's seventh in September, church members, young and old, packed their house and spilled out into the yard.

That year, Evon and Bob decided to downsize from their huge, tall Christmas tree to a more manageable tabletop model with built-in lights. They gave their old tree and lights to Matthew and Mary. Bob drove it over in the back of his pick-up truck, dropping it on the carport when no one was at home.

A few days before Christmas, Bob and Evon looked out their window to the other side of the street. To their delight, they saw their old tree festooned with lights, on display in the picture window of the Winklers' home. They spent a lot of time that holiday season pausing to look over at it, reminiscing about Christmases past.

This holiday, the neighbors gave both Patricia and Allie big stuffed dogs. The girls weren't home when they were delivered, but as soon as they saw Evon and Bob, they ran across the street to thank them for the presents.

The extended Winkler family planned to celebrate Christmas Day in mountain cabins in Gatlinburg. To make it affordable for Matthew and his family, Dan and Diane paid for half the cost of their cabin.

One evening as they sat before a blazing fire playing checkers, Matthew and Mary told the others about Matthew's adverse reactions to a prescription for tooth pain in Pegram and another caused by a drug for his stomach in McMinnville.

Mary laughed about it, saying, "We sure don't want to be giving him them anymore."

Matthew received an offer to serve as pulpit minister from Fourth Street Church of Christ in Selmer, Tennessee. At last, he was going to have his own congregation. He tendered his resignation at Central Church of Christ and Boyd Christian School. To add to the good news, Mary was pregnant again.

Matthew talked with his fellow school faculty members about the exciting new developments in his life. He pointed to his Nissan Maxima in the parking lot and said, "Well, I'm going to have to trade in my car for a mini-van. It's finally happened. I've become one of *those* dads," he laughed.

According to Mary, though, a visit to the doctor's office took away his joyful anticipation. Matthew, Patricia and Allie crowded into the examination room for Mary's ultrasound. The results dashed Matthew's hopes. "The Winklers always had boys. Here I am with girls."

Mary knew by the way he looked at her that he placed

the blame for this predicament on her. She fought off tears.

Evon went to the jewelry store two weeks before the Winklers' scheduled departure to Selmer and bought a gold ring with a birthstone for each of the two girls. The night before the move, she invited the family over for dinner. They gave the girls the rings and told them to "remember us when you wear them." They presented Matthew a book of Bible commentary and Mary a night gown and a baby gift. Mary was now eight months pregnant—once again, just in time for a move.

The next day, two trucks sent by Fourth Street Church of Christ pulled up to the Winklers' house. Movers packed and loaded the family's possessions. When they pulled out of Franklin Street, one of the trucks towed one of the family cars. Matthew, Mary, the two girls and two dogs climbed into the other car. Before they drove off, Evon stopped them, handing over a bag filled with peanut butter crackers, hunks of cake, and other snacks for the road. She was going to miss those girls.

The Winklers drove southwest, passing through Lynchburg, Tennessee, and its Jack Daniel's distillery. Then in Fayetteville, they headed due west past the town of McBurg and Chicken Creek Road. All along the drive, they passed one Church of Christ after another—a reminder of the obvious presence of that form of worship in Tennessee.

They went up and down hills, past rolling fields and thick clusters of tall trees. They crossed into Lawrence County and into Lawrenceburg. Just outside of the city limits, they drove past David Crockett State Park, on the land where Crockett once operated a water-powered grist mill, powder mill and distillery.

Then, they zoomed onward to the Tennessee River. Soon after crossing it, they entered McNairy County and headed to their new home in the county seat of Selmer.

CHAPTER 14

The General Assembly of Tennessee formed McNairy County in 1823 when it cut 560 square miles out of Hardin County to create it. They named the new jurisdiction on the border of Mississippi after Federal Judge John McNairy, appointed to the bench by President George Washington. In 1838, history marked the county with pain, sorrow and national disgrace as one route of the Cherokee Trail of Tears.

When the Civil War ripped the nation apart, McNairy County was marked for disaster. Shiloh, where Union and Confederate soldiers clashed in the second largest battle of the war, was just miles away. Lieutenant Colonel Fielding Hurst, Tennessee-born and McNairy County–raised, led the Union forces on a path of destruction through western Tennessee. In the town of Purdy, he sang songs and prayed while his troops burned down all of the churches and most of the homes. Confederate General Nathan Bedford Forrest wrote: "From Tupelo to Purdy, the country has been laid waste."

The residents of the town struggled to recover, but the final blow brought an end to their dreams—their fifty-year-old brick courthouse was burned to the ground in 1881. By 1897, Purdy lay in ruins. The county seat moved by the railroad tracks in the recently incorporated town of New South, later renamed "Selma." However, when the documents were submitted, the applicant spelled the name phonetically, according to the local pronunciation, and the town of Selmer was born.

With its new county seat, McNairy County grew into a thriving area of industrial development dominated by textile plants. But in the 1970s, the factories began closing their doors—either going out of business or moving operations to foreign countries. The economic downturn placed it on the national list of impoverished counties. Its 22,000 predominantly white citizens remained in that condition until 2003 when an upsurge began in the area's fiscal health.

The annals of crime in McNairy County include the death of United States Post Office Inspector Elbert Lamberth in Stantonville on August 17, 1917. Long before "going postal" crept into the common vernacular, a postal carrier gunned down the inspector in front of the Elam Hotel.

It was another law enforcement official, though, who gained the greater prominence in crime lore for the county. His name was Sheriff Buford Pusser. His exploits inspired a cinematic depiction in the *Walking Tall* series of movies and a short-lived television show.

The 6'6", 250-pound man attended morticians' school in Chicago and earned a living wrestling as Buford the Bull—once defeating a grizzly bear.

In 1962, when his father Carl's health took a turn for the worse, Buford, his new wife and her children from a previous marriage moved back to McNairy County. He entered law enforcement working for his father. When Carl's medical problems forced him to resign as the town's police chief, the town council hired Buford to take his place.

It was a wild and wooly era in McNairy County and the adjoining Alcorn County across the Mississippi line. The Dixie Mafia and the State Line Mob ran successful bordellos, gambling dens and bootlegging operations on both sides of the border between the two states. Buford wanted to bring all of that to an end.

To accomplish that goal, he ran for sheriff in 1964. Two weeks after his predecessor, James Dickey, died in an automobile accident, Buford Pusser, at the age of 26, became the youngest sheriff in the history of Tennessee.

He got busy making enemies out of all the vice merchants in the area. In 1965 alone, he destroyed eighty-seven whiskey stills. A lot of people wanted him dead.

At 4:30 A.M. on August 12, 1967, he responded to a disturbance call on the state line. His wife, Pauline, rode with him in what was expected to be a routine call. But a black Cadillac pulled up beside them and a shot rang out. It hit Pauline in the head.

Buford raced away from the vehicle and came to a stop two miles down the road to care for his wife. The black car returned. He came under fire once again—one bullet lodged in Pauline's head, another hit Buford in the face, literally knocking off the left side of his jaw. Buford fell to the floorboard. Eleven additional bullets riddled his car.

Pauline died that night. But Buford, although disfigured, survived, and stepped into the national consciousness as a great American hero. By the time term limits pushed him out of office in 1970, he'd been shot eight times; knifed seven times; single-handedly fought off six men at once, sending three to jail and three to the hospital; and killed two people in self-defense. The *Walking Tall* legend was born.

On August 20, 1974, a year after the first movie hit theaters, Buford Pusser faced the media in Memphis at a press conference called to announce that he would play the lead in a new movie titled *Buford*. He then drove a hundred miles to Adamsville, where he changed clothes and got into his maroon Corvette to drive to the McNairy County Fair. There, he signed autographs and spoke to his 13-year-old daughter, Dawna, who arrived earlier with a family member. He left the fair around midnight.

He raced home alone up Highway 64. Six miles down the road, he lost control of his car and smashed into an embankment and was thrown from the vehicle. Dawna was in

the first car on the scene after the accident. She knelt in the
dirt by her father's side, begging him not to die.

The funeral cortege numbered in the thousands, including luminaries Joe Don Baker, Tammy Wynette and
George Jones. Even Elvis Presley showed up to pay his respects, but he did not want to steal Buford's moment of
glory, so he waited in the Pusser home during the funeral
and sat in his limousine and viewed the interment from a
distance. Buford was laid to rest beside his wife Pauline at
the Adamsville Cemetery.

As often happens with larger-than-life figures, Buford's
death gave birth to a cottage industry of rumors, conspir-
acy theories and innuendo.

Many, including Buford's mother and daughter, believed he was murdered, even though officials ruled his
death an accident caused by excessive speed. There were
those who claimed he was a player in the vice operations
in the county and his crime-fighting was only a thinly dis-
guised attack on his rivals in criminal enterprise. No one,
though, has offered any proof of this accusation.

A little more than a year after Matthew Winkler's arrival in McNairy County, his death would draw the country's attention back to this quiet, rural area. The rumors
spawned would again tarnish the reputation of a victim
of a violent death. Lines would be drawn, and life in
McNairy County would not be the same.

CHAPTER 15

As pulpit minister, Matthew earned an annual salary of $50,000 and the use of the church parsonage. The Winkler family moved into the three-bedroom brick ranch house, set high on a hill on Mollie Drive. Selmer Elementary, where Patricia and Allie would attend school, was only a couple of blocks away.

Mary's advanced pregnancy that early February 2005 made unpacking and settling into a new home a difficult and demanding task. It all had to be done while caring for two little girls. Mary, normally very energetic, had to struggle to keep in motion and get things done.

Allie had a hard time adjusting to kindergarten in her new school, and was anxious about being supplanted by the baby whose birth was just a month away. She cried every day in class, prompting the assistant principal, Pam Killingsworth, to schedule a meeting. Since Pam was also a member of Fourth Street Church of Christ, she was doubly pleased when her new pastor and his wife both showed up for the conference and displayed genuine concern for their little girl's distress.

Not everyone had a good first impression of Matthew Winkler. It took only two weeks until he had a run-in with one of his neighbors. The conflict arose over a 15-year-old rottweiler named Madison.

The dog's owners, Sharyn and Dan Everitt, lived across the street and two doors down. Since the Everitts' biological children grew up and left the house, the couple welcomed foster children into their home. In February 2006, they had six of them living there, ages 2 to 13.

In the Everitts' front yard, a 500-foot driveway formed a half-circle on the property. The children were outside one day writing on it with sidewalk chalk. Madison sat on the front porch watching over them while they played.

Sharyn was in the back rooms of the house when she heard two sharp warning barks. She walked to the front of the house, looked out the window and saw Matthew Winkler leaving her property and crossing the street.

The 8-year-old boy in her care raced into the house. "There's a man out there and he says he's going to kill Madison."

"You must have misunderstood," Sharyn said. "That man's not going to kill Madison. He's the new preacher. You don't need to be afraid."

But he was, and so were the rest of the kids. *They must have misunderstood what he said. He's a preacher*, Sharyn thought. She decided she needed to talk to him right away and clear up the misunderstanding.

The distance to the parsonage property was very short, but the incline up the driveway was quite steep. Unwilling to labor up the hill on foot, Sharyn drove over to the Winklers'. Matthew and Mary were outside with their girls, Patricia and Allie, who were bouncing a ball. She pulled up, rolled down the window and introduced herself.

"Matt Winkler," he said in response.

Sharyn nodded and said, "I thought I'd come over 'cause my kids were upset and I thought they must have misunderstood what you said."

"I think I made myself really clear," Matthew said.

Sharyn was still certain the children were alarmed over nothing and Matthew didn't realize what they thought he told them. She clarified, "The children said that you were going to shoot our dog."

"Yes. That's a rottweiler. Rottweilers kill people." Matthew's voice sounded etched with acid. "I have two children here. If your dog ever came after one of my kids, I'd kill it."

As he spoke, Mary stepped back to stand beside the two girls as if she wanted to put distance between herself and Matthew's words.

Fear, it's just a matter of fear. I need to reassure him, Sharyn thought. "My dog won't do that. She's used to children. You could break into our house and she would let you, but she wouldn't let you leave. You could come in with a gun in your hand and she'd grab that hand in her mouth. She's protection-trained. But since you're not going to break into my house, we don't have a problem."

"Look, lady. If I see that dog out of your yard, I'll shoot it."

Matthew wasn't budging an inch. Talking to him seemed fruitless, so Sharyn changed the subject, turning her attention to Mary. "When's your baby due?"

"April," Mary told her.

"Do you know the sex?"

"It's a little girl," Mary said.

"I bet you're excited."

Matthew chimed in, "You can't have too many princesses."

What an odd thing to say. "Well, it was nice meeting you," Sharyn said as she put her car in reverse and made her getaway.

"Don't you forget," Matthew hollered after her. "You keep that dog in your yard."

"I'll try," Sharyn said, but she wasn't sure how she'd make that happen. The neighbors across the street adored Madison. They often called her across to play ball. As long as Madison stayed out of the Winklers' yard, there wouldn't be a problem, Sharyn assured herself. Madison never roamed the neighborhood, so we have no cause for concern.

On the short drive back, Sharyn wondered about the addition to their neighborhood. *This is not new neighbor behavior. This is not preacher behavior. What is this aggression?* She put those thoughts aside and summoned up far more confidence than she felt as she comforted the children and promised them that everything would be fine. She calmed them for the moment, but she didn't really convince them. They harbored a permanent fear of their new neighbor. They wouldn't go over to the Winklers' yard to play with the girls unless Matthew was away from home.

When her husband Dan returned from work, she told him about her encounter with Matthew Winkler—about his threats, his tone of voice, his severe body language. She said, "Any man who talks like that to another man's wife is a man who abuses his own wife."

Dan laughed off her concerns.

"I'm serious, Dan," she said. "If he would say what he said and act that way with me, a neighbor, who knows what he'd do or say to his family?"

Two months later, Dan was mowing the front lawn when he spotted Matthew standing at the edge of the yard in the spot he just cut. Dan got off the mower and stepped over to Matthew and stuck out his hand.

The preacher wouldn't accept his greeting—he kept his hands on his hips. "Your dog is in a neighbor's yard. I've warned your wife. I'll shoot that dog."

"Sorry, I didn't know. We have small foster children, sometimes they let the dog out." Dan looked around, but didn't see Madison. "Do you know where the dog is now?"

Matt said "No," turned around and left.

Dan went into the house and discovered that Madison was inside. Matthew couldn't have seen their dog, but there were two other rottweilers living on the street. It must have been one of them. "You're right," Dan told Sharyn as he related his experience with Matthew. "I bet he is an abuser."

Not everyone in the community believed that the Everitts' version of events was accurate. Despite Sharyn's protestations that Madison was harmless, Vice Principal Pam Killingsworth thought otherwise. She said that a number of men on Mollie Drive had threatened to shoot that dog.

She recalled one day when Sharyn, whose granddaughter attended Selmer Elementary, came into the school office heavily bandaged. When Pam asked what happened, Sharyn said, "The dog bit me. I think I'm going to have to start chaining her up."

CHAPTER 16

Breanna Eloise Winkler was born on March 9, 2005, but something appeared to be wrong with her. Doctors held her in the hospital for an evaluation for a suspected liver malfunction. That proved to be a false alarm, but during the stay, respiratory problems became evident. They felt she would outgrow the problem, but made the parents aware of their need to monitor the situation.

Finally, Mary and the baby were home. In no time, Mary jumped into the fray of a busy life as a mother of three and wife of a preacher. The newborn was a happy baby who seemed to love the world and everyone in it. She never fussed as her mother happily passed her around before services to be admired by the congregation while Matthew joyfully welcomed members to what he called "the best place to be on the best day of the week."

Mary barely had time to adjust to being the mother of three when trouble crossed their doorstep again. Patricia, playing with a golf club, accidentally swung it into Allie's head. The resulting injury required surgery. After the unexpectedly high medical bill for Breanna's hospital stay, the financial burden—not to mention the emotional burden—of this new medical crisis was crippling.

Pam Killingsworth got to know the Winkler family on multiple levels. In church, she discovered, Matthew was a dynamic speaker with a forceful style. He put his whole self into giving his lesson. His charisma in the pulpit held everyone's attention.

Outside of church services, he met his ministerial obligations without fail—counseling with members, making hospital visits and always remaining on hand for youth group activities. During his brief tenure, he increased church membership from 140 to 200 souls.

It warmed Pam's heart when she spotted Matthew sitting in the congregation during the announcements and *a capella* singing of old-fashioned hymns, because he always held the baby. And he often spoke in and out of the pulpit about his love for Mary and the girls.

At school, Pam often saw Matthew at the girls' basketball games. But for many other activities, his responsibilities at church kept him away. Pam encountered Mary far more often. She drove Patricia and Allie to and from school every day with Lady, the Great Dane, riding shotgun. One day she arrived in a Toyota Sienna mini-van. When Pam asked about her new wheels, Mary said, "Yes, Matthew is going to take care of me and the girls." Pam thought that was an odd thing to say, but read nothing into it.

More often than not, Mary showed up for school events in a pair of overalls, a shirt and a turned-up baseball cap, pushing a stroller. She was active in the PTO, attended the school festivals—both the Spring Fling and the Fall Carnival—and often dropped in for lunch with the girls. She was there after school for the girls' music lessons with a private instructor—Patricia studied piano, Allie, voice.

Patricia was the family tomboy. She wore dresses to church, but was far happier in a pair of jeans or pants. She read a lot and was a good student, but always had to have something to do. She loved playing video games and competed hard with Pam's 19-year-old son, the youngest of her three boys. They all loved playing with baby Breanna when the Winkler kids were at the house. The young men were at a loss sometimes with Allie. She was a little prissy and loved to play with dolls and girly games. But she was a social butterfly who wrapped them all in her spell.

Pam got a real kick out of the times when Patricia and Allie came to school saying that they spent the night with friends because Mommy and Daddy went out on a date. Trained in children's behavioral problems, and an old hand at noticing the children who were experiencing turmoil in their home life, Pam never noticed any red flags with the two Winkler girls. After Allie's initial trouble adjusting to a new school, both girls seemed happy and well-adjusted. Pam was certain that the Winkler couple had a great relationship. They walked together in the park, as a couple or with their children, often accompanied by a dog or two. They were often seen holding hands, smiling at one another and laughing together. The couple planned a five-day trip on April 20 to celebrate their ten-year wedding anniversary. Their happiness seemed undeniable. The enjoyment they got from their children and from each other was obvious enough to generate positive comment and smiles from observers.

Fourth Street Church of Christ secretary Betty Wilkerson shared Pam's assessment of Matthew and Mary's married relationship. She never saw anything amiss. She never heard yelling or demeaning comments like the ones remembered by the church secretary at Matt's last position. Mary came in often to share lunch with Matthew. They interacted with each other over the meal like a wholesome, "all-American" married couple.

CHAPTER 17

Though they'd since moved to McMinnville and then Selmer, Matthew and Mary maintained friendship with Glenn and Brandy Jones in Pegram. They traveled with the three girls up north to visit over the Memorial Day weekend and had a relaxing, fun-filled time. The Joneses noticed no signs of discord in the Winkler family.

The two couples got together again for the Joneses anniversary celebration in August. Glenn wanted to purchase a gun for home protection. Brandy was hesitant to have a weapon in the house. They discussed this conflict with Matthew and Mary.

Mary said, "Brandy, you'd probably be more comfortable if you went to a firing range and learned how to use the gun. Matthew took me and taught me how to use ours, and I wasn't bothered by it any longer."

On December 1, Mary made a large deposit into the joint account she shared with Matthew at Regions Bank through the ATM. The $6,455 check was drawn on T.C.C. Co-operate Limited, and it was fraudulent. At that time, it was unlikely that Mary knew the check would bounce. It was probable that she believed she'd won one of the many sweepstakes entries she submitted.

Just before Christmas, Selmer Elementary School celebrated an annual tradition, Breakfast with Santa. Mary and

Matthew beamed with pride as Patricia and Allie sang a duet during the program.

In McMinnville, Evon Dennis, the Winklers' former neighbor, opened a Christmas card postmarked in Selmer. The photo greeting inside filled her with delight. It was a picture of her old Christmas tree surrounded by Matthew, Mary and the two little girls she adored, and the new baby she had never seen.

Meanwhile in Huntingdon, Matthew's father Dan didn't want his mother spending Christmas all alone. On October 23 that year—after fifty-six years of marriage—she lost her 74-year-old husband Wendell to cancer. Dan brought her up to his home for the holidays and invited the rest of the family. The new widow spent the day surrounded by children, grandchildren and great-grandchildren. Matthew, Mary and their brood then drove to Knoxville for a two-hour visit with the Freeman clan.

On New Year's Eve, Pam Killingsworth planned a surprise fiftieth wedding anniversary celebration for her parents. Matthew came in early to help her set up the projector and get ready for the event. He was very quiet that night, not his typical talkative self. She wondered what was bothering him. When Mary arrived with the children, Matthew took Breanna and carried her around all night.

That month, Mary enrolled for nine credit hours at Freed-Hardeman University School of Education. She wanted to complete her degree and find a teaching position working with special needs children.

By early February 2006, Mary knew her December 1 deposit did not clear. On February 11, she visited Regions Bank and changed the mailing address on the account from her street address on Mollie Drive to a post office box rented in her name only.

On February 15, a day she had classes at Freed-Hardeman in Henderson, she walked into First State Bank in that town with $100 cash. She opened an account there in her name only, providing her cell phone number and her post office box address as contact information.

Six days later, Mary wrote a check for $7,000 from that account and deposited it in the joint account at Regions Bank to cover the overdraft caused by the bad check from December.

She went to the post office and filled out a change of address form to divert all of the mail addressed to the Mollie Street location to her post office box.

Brandy Jones and Mary finally got together again in person. They had dinner at the Olive Garden and then browsed through a book store. Mary talked about her marriage and her new community. "I am happier than I have ever been. We would never even think of leaving West Tennessee."

Mary also spoke about problems she had with her family in Knoxville. She complained that her father and her adopted siblings had let her down. They didn't come to events, or offer her any emotional support. She said she had, for all intents and purposes, separated from them.

In early March, Matthew went to Freed-Hardeman with Mary. While she went to class, Matt registered for the master's program in Bible. He would start his graduate studies in the fall.

Matt's father Dan, now teaching classes at the University, ran into the couple in the parking lot. Matt told him about his enrollment.

"Is Mary going to continue her schooling, too?" Dan asked.

"Yes," Matt said. "She'll finish up in December." He explained that they'd cleared up their credit card debt when they received a settlement from an accident in Nashville, where an intoxicated woman ran into Matthew's car. "We were very thankful we were able to do that," he added, with a smile to Mary.

"When she finishes up in December, we'll take all of the monies she makes with her new job and first, we'll pay off the mini-van, and then we're gonna pay off the school loans. Then, we'll be debt-free." Matt's pride was obvious, and Dan congratulated the couple on their improved financial situation. Mary did not mention the ongoing mess at the bank, nor did she mention the correspondence and check she just received.

Mary's letter from Saatchi and Saatchi in Canada read:

We are pleased to advice [sic] you that you are one of the winners in the second category of Lottery Draw held on **SEPTEMBER 19th, 2005**.

Your ticket with serial number **38745014AL** drew the lucky winning numbers **22-87-76-44-24**.

You are therefore entitled to the sum of **US $250,000.00** payable to you by bank draft, money order of certified check.

Enclosed is a check of **US $4900** which was deducted from your winnings.

The purpose of this check is for the payment of the *Non Resident Government Service Tax (GST) Payable in Canada*.

The tax amount is **$2,950.00** to be paid either by **WESTERN UNION OR MONEYGRAM.**

You are advised to contact your claims agent

LINDA SMITH Tel 1-778-862-7083,
Monday——Saturday, 7:30 am. . . . To 6:30 pm . . . (Pacific Standard Time)
For further instructions on claiming your big winning.
Congratulations!!!!!!!!!!!!!!!!!!!!!!!!!!

Yours Truly,

John Tyler
(Promotions Manager)

Mary deposited the enclosed check into her First State Bank account in Henderson on March 13. She did not remit the $2,950 as instructed. Three days later, she wrote a check for $4,000 on her personal account and deposited it in the joint account at Regions Bank in Selmer.

On Monday, March 20, Mary deposited a $4,880 check from Trust Financial Services into First State. That same day, she submitted two checks from First State to Regions Bank in the amounts of $2,000 and $4,000. After banking hours, she slipped another check for $1,500 along with $300 in cash into the night drop box.

Both the $4,900 and $4,880 checks she deposited in First State were worthless. Because of that, there were insufficient funds for the checks she wrote to Regions Bank.

Mary was in a state of panic. The next day, it only got worse.

CHAPTER 18

Selmer Elementary School hired Mary as a substitute teacher. Tuesday, March 21, was her first day on duty.

Regions Bank drive-in teller Amy Hollingsworth called Mary's cell phone and said, "Ms. Winkler, I cannot deposit the fifteen-hundred-dollar check you left yesterday, because there are insufficient funds in the First State account. I did deposit the three hundred dollars in cash into your account."

"I appreciate you calling me about this," Mary replied. "I'll check with First State Bank. I'm in a classroom right now and can't talk."

When Mary didn't call back to continue the conversation, Amy phoned her again.

"I can talk now, the children are resting," Mary said.

Amy told her, "There are no funds for the three checks you wrote on First State. It is illegal to make those deposits in our bank. You need to come in and talk to the bank manager."

"Thank you for calling," Mary said.

"Come in and talk to the bank manager about the overdrawn account and it can be handled," Amy insisted.

Mary did not respond.

After a pause, the banker continued. "If you are not able to come in, it will be turned over to the security department."

"Thank you for calling," Mary said again.

The next Regions Bank employee to call was Jana Hawkins. "Ms. Winkler, your account is overdrawn by nearly five thousand dollars."

"I'm aware of that," Mary said. "What are my options? Can I take my husband's name off of that account?"

"No. You can't remove a name from an overdrawn account. But if you come in tomorrow morning at eight-thirty, we can arrange for a five-thousand-dollar loan to take care of the problem with the overdraft."

"I know I've made a bad situation worse, but I can't fit five thousand dollars into my budget. I want to meet with y'all tomorrow, but I'm in class right now. I'll have to call you back later."

The school day ended at 3 P.M. Patricia stayed after school for an extracurricular activity. Mary drove off with Allie to pick up Breanna from the sitter. As she drove past the park, she saw Matthew walking Lady, the Great Dane.

She went home and called Regions Bank at 4:15. Paulette Guest answered the phone and explained to Mary, "We've been calling you because of the check you wanted to deposit. We can't do it."

"Why not?" Mary asked.

"Because there's no money behind those checks. We talked to First State, and they've already returned the first check, so we know there's no need to deposit the latest one. Your bank account here has been frozen. You need to come down and see about this."

"Frozen?" Mary asked.

"Yes. No money can be deposited or withdrawn until you come in and work this out."

"Why is it frozen?"

"Because, Ms. Winkler, you have been kiting checks, and that is a criminal offense."

"I don't understand."

"If the bank doesn't get this worked out—and I'm sure if you come in, we can—but if you don't come in and see about this, there could be criminal charges for doing something like that. We need to see you tomorrow morning."

"Okay."

"And you need to come to the bank with your husband. Both of you have to be here."

Mary made no response to that demand.

After Matthew returned home, Mary headed out again. First, she drove to Selmer Elementary for Patricia. They rented a couple of videos and then picked up dinner at Pizza Hut before returning home.

The family ate pizza, gathering around the television to watch one of the rented movies, *Chicken Little*, together. Between 8 and 9, Matthew and Mary got the girls cleaned up and tucked into bed.

When the girls were asleep, Matt's griping began. Mary had at least two stories about this discussion. One was that he was ranting about his hurt feelings concerning some action taken by the church administration. She said that she listened to him vent until he got it out of his system. The other version was that he was angry about the banking situation and her inability to handle the finances correctly. She said that she told him he had to go to the bank with her in the morning and he refused, saying that she had to keep him out of that mess.

Whatever topic generated Matthew's distress, he eventually calmed down, and he and Mary sat down to watch a movie. In the middle of it, Mary fell asleep. When it was over, Matt woke her up and they went to bed.

Mary didn't understand why, but she knew she felt very uneasy that night. Her sleep was fitful. She awoke over and over, and it was difficult getting back to sleep each time. When the alarm shrilled the next morning, she was exhausted.

THE DOWNFALL

"Unto the woman he said, 'I will greatly multiply thy sorrow and thy conception; in sorrow thou shalt bring forth children; and thy desire shall be to thy husband, and he shall rule over thee.'"

—*Genesis* 3:16

CHAPTER 19

The alarm clock went off at 6:15 and the distant wail of the baby penetrated Matthew's fog of sleep. He hated it when his rest was disturbed by crying and he was annoyed that the baby monitor was turned off. He placed a foot on Mary's rump and shoved. "Shut her up. This is ridiculous," he growled.

Mary tumbled out of bed from the force of the push and headed for the bedroom door, but she wasn't moving fast enough for Matthew. He sprang up and hurried down the hall ahead of her.

By the time Mary reached Breanna's room, Matt was leaning over the crib. His thumb and forefinger pinched the baby's nostrils together; the rest of his hand covered her mouth.

"Stop it, Matthew. You can't do this to her, she has problems. Can I have her?" Mary demanded.

Matthew threw his hands up in the air and said, "I'm tired of it." He slammed his open palm against the door frame as he left the room. He grumbled and muttered as he stomped back down the hall and collapsed on the bed.

Mary cuddled Breanna, stroking her back, murmuring soothing words into her ear and rocking her gently. She changed her diaper and slid a pacifier into her mouth. The crying stopped, the baby's breathing pattern changed and Mary knew she was asleep. She eased her back into the crib, covered her and left the room.

Mary was angry. She went into the kitchen and started preparing coffee, then stopped. She was upset about the method Matthew used to quiet the baby. She called it suffocation, and she'd seen him do it to the other girls. But Breanna had respiratory problems, and Mary knew it was especially dangerous to do it to her. It had to stop. The cruelty had to stop now.

Mary walked through the doorway to the master bedroom, past the closet, up to the door of the bathroom on Matthew's side of the king-size, barley-twist poster bed. "I want to talk."

Matthew snuggled deeper into the covers.

"I want to talk now, Matthew."

He didn't even flutter his eyes in response.

Mary spun around, went to the closet and grabbed the Remington 870 Express shotgun off the shelf. She went to her side of the bed and planted her feet in the pile of decorative pillows lying on the floor. She pointed the shotgun in Matthew's direction. "I want to talk," she repeated.

Matthew did not respond. Not a word or a movement. Not even a grunt in acknowledgment of her presence.

Mary pulled the trigger. The noise of the blast shocked her. The acrid scent of gunpowder tickled her nose. Matthew rolled off the bed and sprawled on the floor. The reality of what just happened stunned Mary. She headed for the door.

Across the hall, the firing of the shotgun awoke Patricia. She did not recognize the sound and in her sleep, it blurred with the memory of the noise her daddy made the time he fell to the floor, knocking over the night stand. She got up and headed for her parents' room.

Mary reached the foot of the bed and saw Patricia in the doorway.

Patricia saw her father on the floor. She heard him gasp, "Call 9-1-1."

Mary closed the distance between herself and her child. "Stay out there, Patricia," she said as she shut the door.

Mary knelt by Matthew's side. Blood oozed from his

mouth. She grabbed the edge of a sheet and wiped the blood away.

"Why?" Matthew asked as the blood continued to pool in his mouth and trickle past his lips.

Mary wiped his mouth again. "I'm sorry. I love you," was all she said. She disconnected the phone from the wall, set it on the floor beyond Matthew's reach and then disconnected the receiver.

She left the bedroom, pulling the door shut behind her, and faced Patricia and Allie, who had since gotten up and joined her sister. "We have to leave and go far away. A bad man hurt Daddy. We need to go before he hurts us, too."

"Daddy said call 9-1-1," Patricia reminded her.

"I did. I did," Mary lied. "We can't wait. We need to go now. Go get in the car while I get the baby." Mary went into the third bedroom, grabbed Breanna and a pair of the baby's socks. She went out the back door to the carport and strapped the three little girls into the mini-van.

She darted back into the house and snatched up the shotgun, stuffed it in its brown carrying bag and zipped it shut. She didn't spare another glance for Matthew. She left the bedroom door open as she raced down the hall. Concealing the gun from the girls, she locked the back door and stowed the murder weapon in the rear of the van.

She backed out of the carport, headed down the driveway and out of town. Inside her home, her husband, the father of her three children, slowly bled to death on the floor of the room where she once shared his bed.

CHAPTER 20

Mary fled her home with no idea of her ultimate destination. Her first thought was to take the girls to Matthew's parents, Dan and Diane Winkler, where she knew her daughters would be safe. Then she remembered that her in-laws were on vacation.

She thought about going to Memphis to await the Winklers' return to Huntingdon, but she'd never been to that city and didn't know her way around. Instead, she crossed the state line into Mississippi and continued heading south. The compulsion to keep moving dominated her decision-making. She kept driving until she was forced to stop for gas near Jackson.

While she filled the tank, Allie spotted the shotgun in the back of the minivan. "Mommy, why did you bring Daddy's gun?" she asked.

"In case the bad guy that hurt your daddy tries to hurt us," Mary said.

The children were restless after four-and-a-half hours in the car, and Mary needed time to think about what to do next. All she wanted to do was spend the last days with her girls having fun. Before "the bad days" arrived, she wanted to fill their minds and hers with happy memories.

At times, she could not believe what had occurred that morning in her bedroom. At others, the roar of the shotgun and sight of her husband's bloody mouth played in a stark, continuous loop. Through this mixed state of denial and acceptance, she looked for a hotel with an indoor swimming pool to entertain her children. She spotted a billboard advertising one, but when she stopped, they had no vacancies. The clerk at the counter gave her directions to the Fairfield Inn.

After checking in, she took the girls to Wal-Mart and bought them swimming suits and a change of clothes. While she played with them in the hotel pool, she thought about where they would all go tomorrow. The first place that came to mind was Baton Rouge. She knew the streets there, but had no idea what she'd find. She knew that Hurricane Katrina left a lot of devastation in Louisiana. Would things still be chaotic in that city? Would there be anything to do with the girls?

Then she remembered the many times that Matthew promised Patricia and Allie a trip to the beach. Patricia had been once when they lived in Baton Rouge, but was too young then to remember it now. Matthew always intended to take them, but each time some work- or family-related problem interfered and the promise was never fulfilled. That was the perfect solution. She'd take the girls to the beach.

When they returned to their hotel room, her daughters were full of questions about Daddy. Mary deflected their inquiries with a litany of comforting words. They went out and picked up dinner, but Mary was too uptight to eat. She grabbed a bag of popcorn on the way back to the Fairfield. She nibbled on it that night to quiet her sour stomach, but even that was difficult to get down. Mary disconnected the phone cord from the wall jack. That made it impossible for Patricia to make a phone call while Mary was busy getting the baby ready for bed.

Meanwhile, back in Selmer, Regions Bank had closed for the day. The bankers there were not pleased with Mary Winkler. Checks came in and were returned marked "insufficient funds." Since the Winklers missed their scheduled meeting that morning, they bankers now began considering their legal options.

The next morning, Mary pulled out her cell phone and checked for messages. There were several from the church looking for her and her children. She knew time was running out. She listened to a voicemail from her father. She wanted to reach through the phone and rip his head off. She didn't want to hear from him. She didn't want to talk to him. She didn't want to see him.

She put her cell away without returning any of the calls. She ignored the pleas from the many anxious callers who were worried about the safety of her little girls.

When she hung up, Patricia asked, "Are we going home to Daddy, now?"

"No," Mary said. "Daddy called and left a message. He said he's resting at the hospital and wants us to stay away another night so we can all come home at the same time."

Mary packed up her girls and the new purchases, and hit the road, heading for the Gulf Coast. She took Highway 49 out of Jackson heading southeast. Just past Hattiesburg, she turned onto Route 98 and crossed the state line into Alabama. When she hit Mobile, they stopped for lunch. Mary still had no appetite, but she made sure the girls were fed. She took Interstate 10 across Mobile Bay, then left the interstate heading south, arriving in Orange Beach about an hour later.

Alabama's small sliver of coastline, with thirty-two miles of beach lapped by the turquoise waters of the Gulf of Mexico, is squeezed in between Mississippi and Florida. The city of Orange Beach gets lots of tourist dollars, but rarely makes headlines.

2006 was not a typical year. Before the end of March, notoriety had struck twice. Mayor Steve Russo became the target of state and federal investigations and indictments into bribery, failure to disclose conflicts of interest and ethics and election law violations. Then he topped that off by getting busted for possession of marijuana. He resigned two months earlier, in January.

For a couple of months, peace reigned in the coastal town until another unsavory event drew the media's attention to Orange Beach. This time, the scope of the coverage was national. Mary Winkler chose to vacation on their shores after shooting her husband in the back.

She selected beachfront accommodations with incredible views of the gulf at Sleep Inn, a six-floor hotel with 117 rooms accessed by interior corridors. She and the girls checked into their fourth-floor room on the afternoon of March 23.

They went shopping, this time at the Dollar General store where she purchased more clothing and swim floaties. They played in the sand on the beach and splashed in the swimming pool. Then Mary loaded up her daughters in the mini-van and headed to the Waffle House for dinner. She never made it.

Mary thought it had been a great day. The next morning, she planned to hit the road and head back to Tennessee. She'd deliver the girls to Matthew's parents. And then? She simply did not know what would happen next. She did know that she'd done something wrong and there'd be a big price to pay for her actions. The most painful part was her awareness that, because of what she did, she might never see her girls again.

Still, she experienced a moment of surprise when she saw flashing red and blue lights in her rear-view mirror. That feeling was quickly replaced by resignation. She knew why she was being stopped. She knew her time had come. She regretted being caught so far from home, but there was nothing she could do about that now.

They might lock her up for life. Keep her girls away from her forever. Turn them against her. But there was one thing no one could ever touch. She would always have the memories of her daughters' happy smiles and exuberant laughter during this odd but comforting trip to the beach.

CHAPTER 21

The next two days for Mary Winkler alternated between hours of intensity, at the focus of law enforcement, judges and her in-laws, and hours of boredom as she sat alone with nothing to do but stare at blank walls. Questioned by authorities, she admitted to her role in the death of her husband. She signed custody of her three girls over to her in-laws. She waived her right to fight extradition to Tennessee and then made the long drive back to Selmer in the company of Sheriff Rick Roten and Officer Byron Maxedon.

When church member Dorothy Weatherford heard about Mary's imminent return, she went to the McNairy County Justice Center and got the list of items that prisoners are allowed to have behind bars. She carried it to Wal-Mart, since, by jail rules, everything had to be new and in its original packaging. She picked up socks, underwear, a toothbrush, toothpaste, deodorant and other assorted toiletries. She returned to the jail hoping to drop them off, but couldn't, as Mary had not yet arrived at the facility. Later that day, Dorothy's daughter called after seeing video of Mary's arrival on the news. Dorothy returned to the jail with her package. Since Mary was allowed to have two books in her possession in her cell, Dorothy included a Bible inscribed with "From the ladies at 4th Street Church," and a book of devotions.

Dorothy was the first to bring supplies to Mary Winkler, but she certainly wasn't the last. Over the course of Mary's incarceration, the church members were so generous, they brought in more than Mary could use, and the excess items were passed out to other prisoners.

Attorney Steve Farese of Corinth, Mississippi, received a phone call from a friend explaining Mary's plight and her inability to afford a good attorney. As soon as he got word of Mary's arrival in Selmer, he made the short drive from his home to the McNairy County Justice Center.

He sat down across from Mary and introduced himself. At rest, with gray hair surrounding unremarkable features, his was the kind of face forgotten the moment he was out of sight. But when he began to talk, his features livened with emotion and Mary could see his concern for her glowing in his eyes. He saw vulnerability in her downturned head and little-girl face, he heard it in her soft, childlike voice. He promised he would do everything he could to defend her against the charges, and she believed every word he said. He vowed to return on Monday and she knew he would.

As soon as he left the jail, Farese called Leslie Ballin, an attorney in Memphis whom he'd worked with on other cases. "Do you want to come to Selmer?"

"All right. How much is the retainer fee?" Ballin asked.

"It's *pro bono.*"

"Steve, hold on, there must be something wrong with my cell phone. I thought I heard you say *pro bono.* Are you crazy?"

"Leslie, it's the right thing to do." Steve outlined all of his reasons and Ballin signed on for the case. Mary Winkler now had a high-powered defense team.

Sunday morning was a somber one at the Fourth Street Church of Christ as members gathered for their first service after Matthew's death. Sharon Pinckley, who taught the first- and second-grade Sunday school class, looked across the hall and realized nobody was there to teach the

2- and 3-year-olds. It was Mary Winkler's group and no one thought to find a substitute.

In adult Bible class, church elder Robert Shackleford warned the group not to speculate about why their popular young minister was killed. "Perhaps over time, we will better understand why this has happened. Be very cautious about what you say or even what you think." Rumors and gossip are destructive forces, he told them. "The simple fact is that no one knows why, except maybe for Mary herself."

He urged the congregation to pray for the children, their grandparents and Mary Winkler. "Mary is a member of this church family, and we may be some of the closest family she has at this point. Forgiveness is a cornerstone of our faith. If we don't have forgiveness, then we don't have anything."

The sanctuary was filled with flowers as well as worshipers for the morning service. The church's youth ministry group presented the most dramatic arrangement—sixty-two yellow roses—one for each of the children in the congregation.

Church elder Drew Eason led the congregation in a prayer for help from their Father to get through this difficult ordeal, and said, "Thank you, Lord, for the time we had with Matthew Winkler." He prayed, too, for Mary: "We ask that she would confess her sins and repent in such a way that she will ultimately have a home with you."

After a tearful rendition of "No Tears in Heaven," church elder and McNairy County Mayor Wilburn Ashe spoke. "We are here this morning with heavy hearts. Our emotions are running high." He reminded the members that little was known about the murder. The only things they knew with certainty were that Matthew Winkler was dead, his wife was in jail and their children were without their parents. "These three little girls we know do not have a daddy right now, and for all practical purposes, they don't have a momma. Those children have got a good home that they're in, but it's not Momma and Daddy." He warned of the dangers of speculation and loose talk. "We've got to do two things. We've got to remain close to God and we've got to remain close to one another."

Jeremy Weekley came down from Freed-Hardeman University in Henderson to deliver that morning's sermon. "God knows exactly what we are going through," he comforted the audience. Echoing the message of a song sung earlier by the congregation, he quoted from Revelation 21:4: "He will wipe every tear from their eyes. There will be no more death or mourning or crying or pain, for the old order of things has passed." He then added, "The present tribulations are no comparison to that which lies ahead for us."

After that harsh warning, he reassured them that their church would survive these tragic events. "This life is not all there is, there is something more."

At the Huntingdon Church of Christ, the elders assumed Dan Winkler would not be available to preach that day, and arranged for a substitute. But Dan rose in the pulpit and delivered a sermon about love, kindness, gratitude and forgiveness. He expressed appreciation for the 400 members who filled the pews. "We love no one more than we love you."

He thanked law enforcement officials and the news media for their assistance in locating his granddaughters and said, "I'm thankful for the Huntingdon Church of Christ and the town of Huntingdon. What wonderful support that Huntingdon will give these three precious babies." He spoke of his gratitude for America itself, saying that calls have come from all over and people have traveled hundreds of miles to embrace them and weep with them for a short time.

Dan talked about the challenges facing him and Diane in raising his grandchildren, but added, "I look forward to being a daddy again." He thanked God for the time he had with his son and cried as he talked about the man he'd raised. "I know the kind of husband and father he was and what a man he truly was."

Sunday afternoon visitation at the jail ran from 1 until

3 in the afternoon. Dorothy Weatherford entered the sparse visiting area, containing only a soft-drink machine, a bench and one table. When Mary was brought from her cell, Dorothy moved into place in front of the window. They each picked up a telephone receiver on opposite sides of the Plexiglas. Dorothy said, "Mary, I wish you could have looked to me and trusted me and told me, 'Hey, there's problems.' I'm old enough to be your mother. I wish you would have come to me to fill that role when you had trouble."

Another church member visiting Mary that day was Pam Killingsworth. She told Mary that everyone was praying for her.

"I loved him so much," Mary whispered. "I'm so sorry for everything. I hope everyone will forgive me."

"Mary, if things were so tough, why didn't you talk to me, or someone from the church?"

Mary hung her head and shook it back and forth. "I don't know."

"Keep praying," Pam urged her.

"I know," Mary said. "God is going to take care of us."

Selmer had not seen this amount of attention from the rest of the world since four tornadoes ravaged western and central Tennessee, killing four people in McNairy County in 1991. The one that touched down in Selmer ripped through town, cutting off all the power for days. One man died, crushed between two vehicles in a used car lot. More than thirty residents received treatment at the local hospital, and dozens more were transported to hospitals outside of the county.

That was on March 22, 1991, fifteen years to the day before Matthew Winkler died. Once again, events on March 22 drew the eyes of the nation to this small town and its people.

In the decade-and-a-half since that disaster, life passed by unnoticed by anyone outside of the county. As Russ Ingle wrote in the *Independent Appeal*:

*McNairy County, with its hot summers and long
winters, has bred for generations a way of life that
had at its center a need to endure. Here we wave at
people we don't know, drink sweet tea and like our
catfish with lemon and onion. Beauty pageants, ben-
efits and church on Sunday are part of the very fab-
ric in this small community. Here a trip to Wal-Mart
is as much a social gathering as a necessity.*

*In the wake of Matthew Winkler's death, all things
small town suddenly vanished. The violence that occurred in one moment's time resulted in the eyes of a
nation peering into our once vaguely known existence.*

On the afternoon of Monday, March 27, Mary wore
shackles and clutched attorney Steve Farese's hand as
deputies escorted her into the small courtroom of General
Sessions Court Judge Bob Gray just down the hall from
the jail. They made an odd couple walking together to the
table. Farese, with his wattled neck and gray sweep of hair
combed over his bald spot, towered over his short, dark-
haired, doe-eyed client.

She sat by Farese's side for her arraignment with her
head down and her back to the audience. She did not once
glance at her father or at the row behind her, filled with
members of the church. The women there sobbed and
dabbed their eyes with tissues throughout the proceedings.
The courtroom was full, with reporters and photographers
occupying most of the other seats.

The judge opened the proceedings by addressing Mary
directly. In a warm Southern drawl, he said, "Ms. Winkler,
the purpose of having you here today is for the court to ad-
vise you of certain rights that you have with the charges
filed against you. And I know that Steve Farese is an experienced attorney and has probably gone over this with you
already, but it's my responsibility to go over them with
you again.

"In addition to advising you of your rights, we're going

to set the matter of a preliminary hearing. Ms. Winkler, the STATE OF TENNESSEE versus *Mary Carol Winkler* . . . you are charged with first-degree murder."

He then read the affidavit of complaint to her and advised her of her right to counsel, to remain silent and to have a preliminary hearing. "Do you have any questions?"

Mary raised her head and delivered the only two words she spoke in court that day in a firm, determined voice. "No, sir."

After a discussion between Gray and the attorneys at the bar, the judge announced that any discussion about bail would be delayed until the preliminary hearing scheduled for Thursday, March 30. In five minutes, the arraignment proceedings were over and Mary was escorted back to jail.

Clark Freeman, Mary's father, left the courtroom with a sheriff's deputy, who took him to a private office. En route, he responded to reporters' shouted questions, saying that his daughter was doing "as well as she can." But he would say no more.

Prosecutor Elizabeth Rice didn't have much to say to the journalists either, telling them only that all the evidence would be presented in court later. When asked about motive, she said, "I just think it's important for us to let this play out in court and not get into specific details of what it is or what her rationale is for it."

To the media's great disappointment, the defense attorneys weren't much more forthcoming. Leslie Ballin declined to answer questions about Mary's state of mind, but said that the defense might order a psychological exam. Steve Farese said that investigators had not told him what motive, if any, Mary had given them. When asked about marital problems, he said, "Have you ever been in a relationship? They all have some problems."

The media engulfed the church members as they emerged from the courthouse. Most of them did not speak, but Anita Whirley said, "It hurts us very much, but we're going to stand behind her one hundred percent. I told a sheriff's deputy, anything she needs, we'll get for her."

Janet Sparks reiterated the church's support for their former preacher's wife, saying, "Mary is a sweet child and we just love her."

CHAPTER 22

Monday evening, Tom Cauley, director of the McNairy County Chamber of Commerce, was preparing to leave his office in the building next to the Shackleford Funeral Home when he heard an unusually high level of traffic noise outside. He investigated and discovered that his car was blocked by satellite trucks and other media vehicles arriving from every direction.

He approached the vehicles hemming him in and said to the drivers, "If you all will just let me move my car, you can have my whole parking lot." It wasn't sleepy old Selmer any longer. With Matthew's funeral scheduled for Tuesday, he wondered if he'd be able to get to work.

At the funeral home, a line of mourners snaked through the building and out the door. One hundred people stood inside. Another hundred and fifty queued up on the sidewalk.

There was no grieving widow to comfort and hug. Mary's absence—and the reason for it—added to the oppressive atmosphere in the room where Matthew lay in a bed of satin.

Patricia and Allie, accompanied by a flock of family members, walked over to the casket. The girls sobbed and reached out to stroke his cheek, pat his head, touch his hands. Patricia cried out, "Daddy, why did you leave us?"

The adults around her fell into painful silence. As her Great Aunt Linda put an arm around her shoulder, a moan, deep and heavy, laden with sorrow, rose from Patricia's throat. All across the viewing room, hearts broke at the terrible sound of the small child's immense pain.

The next morning, with the approval of Dan and Diane Winkler and law enforcement, Mary was escorted from her jail cell to the funeral chapel. The widow stood by her husband's casket alone and cried silent tears before being taken back to lock-up.

Soon after that visit, Mary's attorney Steve Farese appeared on the *Today* show. He said his client was "very detached from the gravity of the overall situation, very reserved, very quiet, very confused and overwhelmed."

Hundreds gathered at the Fourth Street Church of Christ for the 11 A.M. funeral service of Matthew Brian Winkler. The 500-seat sanctuary was filled to capacity. In a room in the church basement, the overflow crowd watched the service on closed-circuit television monitors.

News media were not allowed inside. As a local, *Independent Appeal* reporter Russell Ingle would have been admitted, but he chose not to enter the sanctuary. He didn't know Matthew personally and didn't want to make anyone there uncomfortable because of his job.

Dan and Diane Winkler followed Matthew's flower-covered casket into the church. With them were the three innocent and bewildered young girls, 8-year-old Patricia, 6-year-old Allie and 1-year-old Breanna.

The two oldest went up to the coffin again and touched their father. When she returned to the pew, Patricia asked her grandmother, "Nana, will the police find the person that killed my daddy?"

"Yes," she assured her, "the police will get the person who killed your daddy."

"Nana, that person broke my heart," the little girl said.

Dan Winkler and family friend Eddie Thompson led the service. Dan had conducted many funeral ceremonies in his long years as a preacher, but never thought he'd do so for one of his own sons. Matthew's brothers Daniel and

Jacob each read a passage from scripture. Dan delivered the eulogy, sharing memories of his son from his birth to his death. There were occasional light anecdotes, but most of his talk bore a serious tone as he reflected on Matthew as a devoted husband and father. "Matthew was a fine, loving person, but his life was cut short," he said as intense emotion crackled through his voice.

At 11:55, the mourners exited from the church to confront a mob of media. Most ignored the cameras and microphones pointed in their direction. Eddie Thompson, though, paused to respond to questions about Matthew's daughters. He said, "They're having peaks and valleys, but by and large, they're incredibly happy. We love these girls dearly." He gave details about the special fund, set up under Tennessee's Minor's Trust laws, to pay for the necessary counseling and education for the three fatherless girls. Elders of the Fourth Street Church of Christ paid for the expense of the fund's website so that more money could go to Patricia, Allie and Breanna.

Many of those who attended that morning followed the funeral procession on its sixty-mile route to Carroll Memorial Gardens on Highway 22 in McKenzie, near the elder Winklers' home in Huntingdon. By his son's final resting place, Dan said, "Our family isn't the first to go through something like this. King David lost two sons at the hands of others. God Himself knows what this is like."

In fifteen minutes, Dan closed the graveside ceremony with prayer. He hugged and kissed each of his three granddaughters. Patricia and Allie both picked a flower from the elaborate arrangement on top of the casket, holding them close to their chests as they returned to the car.

CHAPTER 23

The courtroom in Selmer filled again on Thursday, March 30, for the scheduled preliminary hearing. Before the proceedings began, Mary's father Clark stepped up to the defense table, placed his hand on his daughter's shoulder and cradled the left side of her neck. He whispered into her right ear. Mary nodded in response.

When the court was called to order, Steve Farese addressed the judge. "May it please the court, Your Honor, at this time, after conversing with my client and co-counsel, we have decided to waive this opportunity for a preliminary hearing."

Judge Gray turned to Mary. "Ms. Winkler, would you stand for a moment, please? As I mentioned before, you are represented by very experienced and capable attorneys, but I need to make sure that you do understand that you are knowingly and voluntarily waiving your right to a preliminary hearing after having a chance to speak to Mr. Ballin and Mr. Farese. Is it your desire at this point to waive your right to a preliminary hearing?"

In a child-like voice, Mary said, "Yes, sir."

After a brief sidebar, the judge made sure Mary understood that her case would be remanded to a grand jury. "I also understand from your attorney that you will not be seeking bond today."

"That is correct, Your Honor," Farese answered for his client.

The grand jury set to meet in June would decide if there was enough evidence to support the murder charge.

On the sidewalk in front of the courthouse, Farese and Ballin paused to speak with the media. When the reporters asked why they did not want a preliminary or bail hearing for Mary, Farese said, "She still has trouble focusing on important issues."

Ballin added, "Her condition is pretty fragile right now, and we are concerned about it. Also, a case like this, where Mary's state of mind at the time of the event is an issue, we want to have a forensic psychological examination, and it should be done real soon. And we think it's in her best interests to not have bail right now.

"I want to say something else: In this type of case, it's like a marathon. This is not a sprint. We are going to come out of this, as you've seen today, very slowly and methodically, and hopefully we're going to do the right thing for Mary's case."

Farese interrupted. "There is another consideration here, also. And that's the consideration of the Winkler children. We feel it does no one any good to hear bad things about the mother of children. We don't think it does anyone good to hear gruesome things about their late father. We don't think it does Matthew Winkler's parents, kin, people, any good to have to suffer any more than they've already suffered.

"This is not a circus. This is a legal proceeding. It happens all over the free world every day. And all we want is a fair trial for Mary Carol Winkler. We don't want the field tilted in any way. All we want is a fifty–fifty shot at representing her to the best of our ability."

When asked if Mary was on suicide watch, Farese said, "I am concerned about her emotional state. One of those concerns is whether she would harm herself."

Ballin added that he had faith in the professionalism and judgment of the McNairy County Sheriff's Department. The defense team had the utmost faith in the department's ability to protect Mary from herself, he said.

That evening, the two attorneys appeared on the Greta Van Susteren show on the Fox News network. Greta asked Ballin, "Leslie, why didn't you have a preliminary hearing today, which would have required the prosecution to lay out part of its case?"

"Didn't need it," Leslie Ballin said. "We knew what the charges were. We anticipated what the prosecution was going to put on, as far as proof. We talked to the prosecutor about giving us some early discovery, which she graciously agreed to do. Plus, there were some other issues concerning what the proof was going to be.

"Mr. Winkler has recently been buried. The grieving continues and will continue for a long, long time to come. For that family to hear details of what happened just wasn't going to do any good, especially for those three young kids."

She turned then to Farese. "Steve, if I saw your client in the cellblock today and I had a conversation, what would be my impression of her?"

"Your impression would be someone that's, at this point in time, very withdrawn, very reserved, having difficulty understanding your questions contextually, the deer-in-the-headlights sort of look."

"Leslie, do you agree with that?" she asked Ballin.

"Yes. And she is at times lost in space. You talk to her, she doesn't follow a lot of the theme, the subject matter that you're wanting to talk about. And she's kind of bewildered at times."

Farese said it wasn't a circus, but to outside observers, it certainly appeared as if the curtain had risen on the first act in the defense of Mary Winkler.

CHAPTER 24

On March 31, McNairy County deputies transported Mary Winkler to the office of clinical psychologist Dr. Lynne Zager in Jackson. When she received the call from the defense team to evaluate Mary's mental condition and her competency to stand trial, the doctor was excited. She remembered when she listened to the news of Mary's arrest on the radio in her car. Mary, she thought, might be suffering from post-traumatic stress disorder. Dr. Zager would have the opportunity to investigate that possibility firsthand. Even after twenty-four years of forensic evaluation, Zager found this case very interesting. She agreed without hesitation to provide her services *pro bono*.

Zager started the first session with Mary by explaining the limits of confidentiality under these circumstances. She informed Mary that she was granting permission to Zager to reveal anything they discussed to the defense team, and if the case went to trial, everything Mary said could be repeated in open court.

Although cordial, polite and willing to answer questions about her social history, Mary would not look Dr. Zager in the eye when they talked. Zager administered the Multiphasic Personality Inventory, a psychological assessment tool with 567 questions designed to uncover anyone who was either trying to paint a falsely positive picture or appear mentally ill when they are not.

Zager found significant defensiveness in her client, and

determined that Mary was attempting to appear as if she did not have any mental health issues. Beneath that denial, Zager concluded that Mary did have problems in her thinking, trusting and psychological functioning.

On Sunday, April 2, Mary Winkler greeted more than a dozen visitors at the McNairy County jail, including her father and two of her sisters. Friends from the church brought in cards from members who were unable to come. That day, like every day of her incarceration, Mary wrote a letter to her daughters. She never mentioned the events that led to their separation, but she assured the girls that she loved and missed them.

For the few days that followed, it seemed as if Steve Farese and Leslie Ballin were everywhere. One or the other—or both—held court on television, doing their best to sway public opinion in their client's favor.

On April 3, they appeared on *Larry King Live*, where Ballin said, "Everything that she is, is inconsistent with the charges."

To the amusement of the cosmopolitan host Larry King, Farese brought his folksy flair to the interview: "My father always says, 'If *ifs* and *buts* were candy and nuts, what a merry Christmas it would be.' And it truly would be a merry Christmas for the prosecution if all the speculation from them was true, but it's certainly not true."

Ballin expanded on his earlier statement, saying, "This is so inconsistent with what twenty-nine years of the practice of law has taught me. Certainly, you have the off-case where a good person commits a crime, but in this particular case, it's just so unusual. I don't have a two-hundred-and-fifty-pound, six-foot-five, tattooed, one-eyed defendant sitting behind me. This is just unusual. It isn't supposed to happen."

Another guest on the show, Tennessee's Chief Medical Examiner Doctor Bruce Levy, snatched the focus away from Mary and put it back on the victim, saying that Matthew essentially bled to death. "A shotgun is full of many small metallic pellets. When they strike the body, it's like a billiard-ball effect; they go in every direction, and they strike pretty much all the internal organs and cause lots and lots of bleeding, both internally and externally."

Steve Farese appeared on the *Nancy Grace* show on April 6. As a rule, Nancy, a former prosecutor, had little patience with defense attorneys, and Farese was no exception. Her tone was immediately hostile. "When I asked you the other night, 'Did your client get a chance to visit her husband's body before he was buried?' you had not talked to her at that time. Now that you've spent a day in court with her, did she get to say goodbye to her husband one last time?"

"Nancy, I did get to talk to her today, and intentionally did not ask that question."

"Why? Why? Why?"

Mocking her repetition, Farese said, "I thought you might want to know the answer. Know the answer. Know the answer."

"Is it because you don't want people to know that she got out of jail to visit her husband?" she pressed. "I mean, why would you want to keep that a secret?"

Farese responded with a non-answer. "That doesn't interest me whether she did or did not get out of jail."

"Well, you just said you intentionally didn't ask, so obviously you'd been thinking about it a lot."

"No, I intentionally didn't ask, because it didn't enter my mind to ask."

"But you just said you intentionally didn't ask, so obviously you thought about it, so it did enter your mind."

"Nancy . . ."

The host interrupted. "You've been thinking about it, and you've been thinking about me a lot."

"Guess what?"

"Yeah?"

"You're right on both accounts."

Nancy then moved on to badger McNairy County Sheriff Rick Roten. He wouldn't comment on the funeral home visit, either, insisting that it was a private matter.

Farese and Ballin did scores of other interviews including *Dateline NBC* and *People* magazine. But of all the inquisitors they faced, the only one they refused to consider for a repeat performance was Nancy Grace. They said that they didn't think she was "very nice."

In another show about the Winkler case, she asked a Baptist minister what he knew about the churches of Christ.

"It's, unfortunately, a very legalistic sect, and they tend to use methods of intimidation and pressure," he said. He added that the churches of Christ believe that they and they alone have the key to heaven's gate.

Nancy responded, "You make it sound like a cult."

"It's kind of a borderline cult, unfortunately."

Church of Christ adherents across the country were up in arms. Even those who hadn't seen the show heard about it from friends or read about it in a churches of Christ publication, *The Christian Chronicle*.

The editorial board of that periodical expressed their shock at the comments on Nancy's show, writing:

The worst of these characterizations and insinuations ranges from charges of being a cult to dismissing us as mindless "fundamentalists" and conservatives. This is not the same church we know and love. It's painful and frustrating to find our congregations so seriously misunderstood, especially since we recognize the untold labors of love and ministry, teaching, worship and community involvement that go on continually, to say nothing of millions of dollars we donate to the poor and needy around the world. We know these charges to be false, inaccurate stereotypes not based on fact.

They ended their long opinion piece with an admonition to the flock:

We must neither be addicted to the approval of the wider culture, nor stubbornly picking fights over doctrinal details. If we love, our difference will be noted. While the church we love is countercultural and always will be, we should show the heart of Christ to our culture in our actions and attitudes.

As for the media's recent treatment . . . Jesus reminds us that such experiences should be cause for joy: "Blessed are you when people insult you, persecute you and falsely say all kinds of evil against you because of me. Rejoice and be glad, because great is your reward in heaven."

Fair or not, it was clear that the church would be on trial as well as Mary Winkler when the court convened in McNairy County.

Back at the jail, a different kind of media excitement was underway. Nearby Hardeman County resident Robert King, an employee of New York–based Polaris Images, had an assignment to shoot pictures for *People* magazine.

According to the sheriff's department, King came into the jail with Mary's attorneys. He signed in as an investigator. Once inside, he took photographs of Mary. No one is certain if the lawyers knew about this ruse or not.

There had to have been a lot of legal wrangling in the prosecutor's office, because an indictment charging him with impersonation of a private investigator was not handed down for ten months. Once it was, an arrest warrant was issued by the sheriff's department, and Robert King faced a potential prison sentence of one to two years.

CHAPTER 25

In the midst of all the media frenzy, Bio-Recovery Solutions went unnoticed as they slipped a team into the house on Mollie Drive. The business of the Murfreesboro, Tennessee, company involved traveling to locations where dead or injured victims left behind blood, body fluids and other contaminants. Following the guidelines set by the Centers for Disease Control and OSHA, they cleaned up the stains and bacteria, saving the family members of the victim the horrible anguish of doing it on their own.

On May 8, Patricia met with her new counselor, Diana Crawford, for the first time. After that visit, Crawford sent the Winklers a note telling them to start giving the girls the letters from their mother a few at a time right before their next appointment. She also urged them to explore all the details of their first visit with their mother in advance to prepare the girls and reduce the possible trauma.

Behind bars, Cynthia Gibbs, supervisor of the women's section of the jail, signed a letter of disciplinary action against Mary Winkler. Gibbs spotted another inmate passing a prescription drug to Mary, who accepted it. She confiscated the pill before Mary could ingest it. Mary lost her rights to visitation on Sunday, May 7.

Unaware of this restriction, some of Mary's family traveled from Knoxville to Selmer to see her. They were turned away.

The next Sunday, Mother's Day, her visitation privileges resumed. Inmate and mother Mary Winkler did not greet the day showered with hugs, kisses and happy greetings from her three little daughters. She didn't even want them to come and visit her—not while she was in jail wearing the orange prison uniform, trapped on the other side of a sturdy piece of Plexiglas.

It was just an ordinary day for Mary. The lights came on, as usual, at 5:30 in the morning, the cell door opened about half an hour later. She made her way to a breakfast of sausage, toast and scrambled eggs. Then, she went to church service.

Mary's life had settled into a dull routine with the twenty or so other women in the jail. By May, the volume of mail had dropped since its peak of fifty to sixty letters a day right after her arrest. But she still got a plentiful supply—a daily delivery of fifteen to twenty. Mary often passed out correspondence to female inmates at mail call, a privilege that made her the target of jealousy from some of the others.

Prisoners—burglars and drug offenders for the most part—often harassed her for being a murderer. Whenever one of them asked Mary about killing her husband, she turned away and walked back to her cell.

Television reception in the recreation room was limited to one local channel. Mary sometimes joined the others to watch soap operas, Oprah and Doctor Phil. When the latest on her case aired, some inmates pounded on windows and walls, hollering, "Mary Winkler, you're on TV!" Mary ignored them; she never watched the news coverage.

She spent most of her time writing letters, playing cards and talking on the telephone when she could. Although silent when she initially arrived, she now talked and laughed frequently with the less judgmental inmates.

She spoke of her children constantly, but Matthew's name rarely crossed her lips.

In Huntingdon, three little girls struggled to cope with the loss of both their mother and father. Only 8-year-old Patricia was mature enough to grasp the gravity of the situation. Questions about the pivotal events of March 22, 2006, tormented her days and haunted her dreams. She did not understand how her mother could not have realized the consequences of her actions before she pulled the trigger.

Dan and Diane Winkler tried to focus on relearning their parenting skills and changing their lifestyle to accommodate three young children—it had been decades since their sons were small boys. And their children never faced the extreme trauma that now lay heavy on their granddaughters.

The couple tried to ignore the innuendo and hints of spousal abuse, the excuse of self-defense and the smearing of their son's reputation that seeped out from the defense team, but it was impossible. They dreaded the upcoming days in the courtroom.

In legal circles, McNairy County had earned a dubious reputation, dating back to the days of Sheriff Buford Pusser. Of all the counties in southwestern Tennessee, the jurors there were more likely than others to side with the defense if the attorneys could paint a portrait of the deceased as being someone who "needed killin'."

This proclivity was not lost on Mary's defense team, who would certainly want to take advantage of that mindset if they could.

Beneath the pleasant, backwoods demeanor of Steve Farese was a keen legal mind and a man capable of being a shrewd courtroom performer. He demonstrated for years that he had inherited the skills of his father, Big John Farese, a legendary court performer in Mississippi.

Steve Farese defended a white law enforcement officer charged with the execution-style murder of a black teenager. Not only did the jury find him guilty of only the lesser charge of criminally negligent homicide, but the judge sentenced the policeman to a mere one year of supervised probation. After it was served, the court expunged the record of the crime, as if it had never happened. Fellow attorneys named Steve Farese one of the top ten defense attorneys in the nation.

Leslie Ballin worked with Farese in the defense of Howard Michael Mullins, the Memphis Federal Express pilot charged with beating his wife to death and burning up her body. Mullins was acquitted.

Ballin's track record on his own was equally impressive. He'd successfully defended Jeremy Hunt, a former star of the University of Memphis basketball team against charges of assault, and actor Anthony Anderson on rape. Outside of the courtroom, his laid-back, jovial demeanor and easy smile were in sharp contrast to the outraged anger that erupted in the courtroom on behalf of his clients.

Against these formidable adversaries, the state's team was an unknown factor. Elizabeth Rice led the prosecution now, but voting day was coming up in August, and Rice was not running for re-election. Nothing could be more unsettling for a victim's family than the unknown. Dan and Diane were adrift in an ocean of it.

They braced themselves for the worst. They turned to prayer, fellowship in the church, friends and family members for spiritual and emotional support. But nothing could prepare them for the onslaught that was to come.

CHAPTER 26

After hearing testimony from just one witness—Special Agent Chris Carpenter of the Tennessee Bureau of Investigation—the Grand Jury of McNairy County issued a true bill of indictment on June 12, 2006. They found that Mary Carol Winkler

> *did unlawfully, feloniously, intentionally and with premeditation kill Matthew Brian Winkler . . . against the peace and dignity of the State of Tennessee.*

The next day, for the first time since her arrest, Mary received a letter from her daughters.

> *We miss you. We love you. We want to see you.*

Mary clutched the paper close to her heart as the comforting words echoed in her mind.

On Wednesday, June 14, Mary appeared in court in her orange-and-white uniform, an ankle chain binding her legs, and handcuffs around her wrists. She dabbed her nose with a tissue throughout the proceedings.

Judge Weber McCraw asked if she understood the charges against her and she softly said, "Yes, sir." Then she told the judge her attorneys were in the room to act on her behalf.

Steve Farese said, "We have seen the indictment and

gone over it with [Mary]. We enter a plea of not guilty at this time for her." The defense submitted twenty-five motions to the judge. The first one was a request for bond. McCraw set a hearing on that matter for June 30.

They filed another motion with the intent of suppressing the statements Mary gave police on the grounds that she wasn't properly advised of her constitutional rights, and, since the statements weren't voluntary, they were in violation of her right against self-incrimination.

They also filed to suppress evidence from the mini-van on the grounds that it was seized illegally and in violation of Mary's Fourth and Fourteenth Amendment rights. Additionally, the motion alleged that she was illegally arrested because there was no probable cause to detain her.

Other motions included a plea that the court require the prosecutors to announce whether they intended to seek the death penalty, and a request that a special questionnaire be given potential jurors other than the one that the court usually gave.

Although defense attorneys described all their motions as routine, Deputy Clerk Nancy McClain disagreed with them on the questionnaire issue. She said it was the first time she'd heard that one in the thirteen years she'd been with the McNairy County court system. Typically, potential jurors provided their home address, age and marital status. The defense wanted to add some additional questions: whether or not the potential members of the panel knew the Winklers, had heard of the case or had formed an opinion about it, along with other questions relating to the planned defense strategy that they were not willing to reveal at that time.

They also wanted the jurors interviewed outside of the presence of other potential jurors during jury selection. They requested this individual questioning because they planned to ask those in the jury pool about "their familiarity with the crime, the victim or the probability of innocence or guilt." They believed that the "sensitive and potentially embarrassing questions exploring the prospective jurors' bias or prejudice" might cause some not to speak openly or honestly if they were in the presence of people they knew in the jury pool.

The judge did not rule on any of the motions, but set an October 30 date to go to trial. After the hearing, deputies escorted Mary to her jail cell, a short walk down an adjoining hallway to the courtroom.

Outside of the courtroom, Farese told reporters that he intended to call two or three people to testify about Mary's character. "We'll put on proof of whether she's a threat or danger to herself or the community as a whole, where she will be living, what she will be doing, show a history of her non-violent background." He complained that Mary wanted to be in contact with her children, who were in the custody of Matthew Winkler's parents, but he could not get a response from them. "All I've asked for is, 'Could you send a picture of the girls? Could you tell us how they are doing in school?' We aren't asking for much."

When asked about the police statement that Mary confessed to the murder, he said, "Just because they interpret a statement as being one thing, we don't necessarily see it as being the same thing."

Ballin added, "We've seen a copy of the statement. Not a confession to me." Asked about Mary and Matthew's ten-year marriage, Ballin said, "Each of those years, each of those months, each of those days of marriage has a history to it. Things that led up to March twenty-second need to be told to this jury."

CHAPTER 27

On Sunday, June 25, just fifteen minutes before the end of visitation, Mary noticed the arrival of a group not on her visitors' list. For the first time in three months, she looked into the faces of her three little girls. They arrived with Dan and Diane Winkler and family friend Eddie Thompson.

Patricia and Allie's lower lips quivered. Mary said, "It's okay to cry." And they did. The most forceful sobs came from Patricia.

Mary, shocked by the unexpected visit, and embarrassed to be seen by her children with her status as a prisoner so obvious, told them over and over how much she loved them and missed them. It was awkward, unnatural, speaking through handsets behind a barrier to the children she carried in her womb, rocked to sleep, kissed and hugged more times than she could count.

Dan held up the littlest one to give Mary a good view of the baby. Breanna stared at her for a while, then gave her a big smile. Mary urged them to set her down on the floor and let her see Breanna walk—she missed her daughter's first steps while in jail.

Mary commented on Allie's longer hair. Allie said that she was letting it grow out because she thought long hair was pretty. Patricia told her mother all about her new school. The jailers allowed the visit to run over the scheduled time by thirty minutes. Then, the bittersweet interlude was over and Mary went back to her cell.

The counselor and grandparents had worked with Patricia and Allie for weeks to prepare them for this day. Nothing, though, could ease the sorrow in their hearts as they walked out, leaving their mother behind. They fell asleep that night on tear-dampened pillows.

Mary's first visit to Dr. Zager's office was plagued with difficulties caused by the complexity of transporting a prisoner. Zager decided it was far less of a hassle for her to go to Mary in Selmer than to have the deputies bring her to Jackson. They had three additional sessions in the McNairy County Justice Center that spring, with Mary opening up more and more each time. During one session, she pulled a photograph of Matthew out of her pocket and showed it to Zager. Mary said that she always carried it with her.

After the fifth session, on June 27, Zager reached a diagnostic conclusion. Mary, she believed, suffered from post-traumatic stress disorder. Its origin dated back to the death of Mary's sister, Patricia, when Mary was 13.

Since then, Mary had experienced numerous dissociative episodes where she lost track of herself and had trouble with impulse control. Mary also had dysthymic disorder, a mild form of depression. Zager believed that Mary was in a dissociative state when she shot Matthew, which explained why she had no memory of the shooting.

With Assistant District Attorney Walter Freeland by her side, District Attorney General Elizabeth Rice strode into a crowded courtroom on June 30 toting a shotgun. It wasn't the actual murder weapon—that was still in the lab for analysis—but it was good theater. She wanted to display a clear reminder of the crime committed by Mary Winkler. She wanted the judge to deny bail.

Leslie Ballin argued first on Mary's behalf. He pointed out that Mary had the opportunity to post a $25,000 bond when she was arrested on March 24 in Alabama. Since she did not bail out, but waived extradition instead, she'd shown a good faith effort to comply with the law. He surprised Matthew's parents when he said that the state had not produced any evidence to indicate that Mary—the woman who pulled the trigger and killed their son—was the aggressor in this case.

Ballin proposed that Mary be released on her own recognizance because of her standing in the community. He reminded the judge that Tennessee law required that suspects be released on the least possible amount of bail. He then cited reports from psychologist Lynne Zager indicating that Mary did not pose a significant risk.

Rice argued that Mary should not be issued bond because she faced a capital murder charge with the possibility of the death penalty. She chastised the defense attorneys for grandstanding and engaging in theatrics, rather than focusing on facts. To demonstrate the state's belief that Matthew's murder was premeditated, she produced the autopsy report. There was no doubt that he was shot in the back when he was lying down. The pellets perforated his ribs, shattered his spine, tore through his stomach and caused numerous internal injuries to other organs and tissues. As the cold hard facts of the autopsy report echoed in the courtroom, Mary bent her head and sobbed.

The state's first witness in their battle to keep Mary behind bars prior to trial was Sergeant Roger Rickman, an investigator with the Selmer Police Department. As photos from the crime scene were displayed, he related his observations of the victim's body, pointed out the telephone lying in the middle of the floor with its cord unplugged, and drew attention to the blood spots on the bed in the master bedroom. Rickman verified that the photos correctly demonstrated how Matthew's body was positioned and the location where he was found. Pointing to a close-up of Matthew's face, Rickman said that the bloody saliva coming from Matthew Winkler's mouth was proof that he had kept breathing for a while after he was shot.

Prosecutors called Special Agent Brent Booth of the Tennessee Bureau of Investigation to the stand. He read the written statement Mary signed the night of her arrest in Alabama, in which she admitted to holding the gun when it blasted Matthew in the back, and then fleeing from the scene without seeking help for her dying husband. Women from Fourth Street Church of Christ, hearing the details for the first time, were visibly shaken. Tissues flew from purses and passed up and down the row to dab wet eyes and runny noses.

Rice whipped out the shotgun she'd brought into court. Booth testified that a similar shotgun was held two-and-a-half to seven-and-a-half feet from Matthew's body when it was fired.

The questioning then moved to Mary and Matthew Winkler's finances. Booth testified about the $17,500 worth of fraudulent checks that Mary deposited in banks in Selmer and Henderson. He alleged that the irregularities in Mary's banking practices bore all the earmarks of check-kiting, a term used for the illegal transfers from one bank to another to disguise the absence of a shortfall in the account balances. He also noted that Mary made several withdrawals totaling $500 from two different Selmer banks on the day before Matthew's body was found. On cross-examination, the defense so persistently badgered Booth about the possible differences between the shotgun in the courtroom and the actual murder weapon that Judge McCraw stopped the inquiry, insisting that they move on.

The first witness called by the defense was Alicia Jones, a professional nanny in Nashville who had known Mary Winkler for seven years. Matthew was the youth minister at Bellevue Church of Christ where Alicia's family went to church and she took care of the Winkler children for four years. Alicia visited Mary nine to ten times in the jail. Alicia said that although she had not talked to Mary about what happened with Matthew, she did not believe Mary would be a danger to herself or anyone else, and would follow the rules and come to court when ordered.

Pam Killingsworth, the assistant principal at the local elementary school, took the stand next. She described Mary as very quiet, very patient and a good mother, who was an even-tempered person and slow to get angry. She, too, supported Mary's request to be out on bail.

Jimmie Smith, a retired psychiatric nurse and Fourth Street Church member, followed Pam to the stand, saying that Mary was not violent. The attorney showed her a letter written by a staff member at the jail stating that Mary was a good inmate. Jimmie said, "That sounds like the Mary I know."

Mary's sister Shannon Roberts explained that her father would get the money together for bail, but he was not very wealthy. She said Mary would follow all the court's guidelines, "Even rules that are minor and not that important."

Kathy Thomsen from McMinnville said that Mary could live in her home, and two employers—including a dry cleaning business—had already offered Mary Winkler a job in her town. Walt Freeland stepped up to cross-examine the witness. His prematurely white hair made him appear older than his years. He sported a gray moustache and a white beard so closely cropped it looked more like overgrown bristle. His rosy lips provided the only hint of color in his face. He asked Kathy if she knew what Mary had done. "I know she murdered her husband," Kathy said, "but I do not think Mary would murder anyone in my house." She admitted to having a gun in her house, but said she would remove it if ordered by the court. "I've been thinking about doing that already."

In rebuttal of the arguments presented by the defense, the prosecution called Cynthia Gibbs, the jailer who wrote the letter in support of Mary, to the stand. She testified about Mary's drug infraction while in jail.

In closing arguments, defense urged the judge to set bail. They argued against flight risk, pointing to Mary's good character, her obvious lack of planning for the trip to Orange Beach and her unwillingness to jeopardize her father's home. Additionally, he said, Mary had employment offers and a place to live in McMinnville. She would comply with telephone report schedules, in-person visits to the probation or police offices, an electronic bracelet—whatever the judge deemed necessary. He concluded by requesting that bail be set at the lowest amount possible.

The state countered that Mary's freedom should be denied, because this was a capital case. Mary fired a shotgun into the back of Matthew Winkler while children were in that house, and how he later died proved that the killing qualified as capital murder, Freeland contended. She disabled the phone, preventing any possibility of Matthew seeking and receiving help, then left on a beach vacation. Freeland said that she premeditated all of this when she went to the closet, got a gun and fired the shot into the back of Matthew Winkler.

Judge McCraw stated he'd review all the exhibits and testimony presented, and make his ruling at a later date.

CHAPTER 28

On July 7, Judge Weber McCraw issued a written ruling setting bail for Mary at $750,000. He imposed several conditions on her release. He required that Mary live with Kathy Thomsen at her McMinnville residence in Warren County, with all weapons being removed from that home; that the defendant be supervised by the state probation department, complying with all their rules; and that she would not leave the county except for meetings with her lawyers or visits with her children. Upon receipt of the ruling, Steve Farese said, "I'm just surprised at the amount. For her, that's tantamount to no bond at all."

On July 14, the defense filed a motion requesting that the judge reduce bond to $315,000, allowing Clark Freeman to use his home as collateral. Judge McCraw denied that request on July 31.

On Wednesday, August 9, when the parties gathered before the bench again, the dynamics of the prosecution shifted. District Attorney General Elizabeth Rice stepped into the background, leaving Walter Freeland in the forefront. Election Day had come and gone, Rice's days were numbered. Michael Dunavant defeated Ed Neal McDaniel. He'd take over her position in early September.

In a hearing that lasted four-and-a-half hours, the defense presented motions to suppress Mary's statements because they were not voluntary as required under the Fifth Amendment, since police should never have treated her as a suspect in the first place.

In addition, they argued that Mary's Fourth Amendment rights had been violated as well, when law enforcement searched her home and vehicle. "We are alleging that the search and seizure of the defendant herself was without probable cause, [without] articulate facts, without good reason. She was simply the subject of an AMBER Alert," attorney Steve Farese told the court. "If the safety of the family was the only objective of Tennessee, then Alabama overstepped its authority. Alabama had no right to arrest and seize the person of Mary Winkler. They did so illegally." He added that there was no arrest warrant and no probable cause for one.

Assistant District Attorney Freeland disputed the defense's allegations. "Officers at every level acted appropriately and went beyond the bounds of what they were required to do." He insisted that they read Mary her rights, and Mary's statements were voluntary.

"To say there wasn't an arrest warrant for her at that time, really doesn't make that much sense," he continued. "Mr. Farese well knows you don't have to have a warrant for a felony arrest. There just has to be a reasonable and articulable suspicion."

And the reason was there, he said. "Almost immediately upon the stop, not Mrs. Winkler, but one of her children, volunteers the information that 'Mama's got a shotgun in the van.' If Orange Beach police officers hadn't acted exactly as they did act, this would be the grossest case of negligence on the part of police that I can imagine."

Defense Attorney Leslie Ballin argued, "What we understand happened is that the Alabama authorities—acting on the request of the Tennessee authorities—immediately put her under arrest. That is a violation of her rights."

In argument, prosecutors presented testimony from Orange Beach police officers Jason Whitlock and Travis

Long, Jr., Alabama Bureau of Investigation Agent Corporal Stan Stabler and a special agent from the Tennessee Bureau of Investigation.

Ballin concluded the defense's arguments by reiterating the allegation that the state lacked probable cause.

Judge McCraw deferred his decision to another day. Immediately following the proceedings, the defense thought that all was in order for Mary's release that afternoon. But that day, the court clerk's office was closed—as it was every Wednesday—and the judge wanted the bond agreement reviewed by that office before he signed off on it.

Mary's family stood patiently outside of the courthouse hoping to see Mary walk through the doors. At 6 P.M., Farese delivered the bad news—Mary would not be released that day.

The next morning at 9:45 A.M, Tyrone Byrd of Alpha Bail Bonds in Somerville delivered documentation to Circuit Court Clerk Ronnie Brooks. Brooks checked to make sure that that company as well as the other business involved, Williams Bonding Company, had certification to write bonds in McNairy County.

With the paperwork complete, Brooks approved the agreement and faxed it to the judge and the district attorney general for their signatures. Things looked good for Mary's release. She changed out of her prison uniform and into the street clothes her father provided. Then, McCraw talked to a judge in another county and learned that Williams Bail Bonds was suspended from issuing bonds there in 1999. Thursday and Friday passed while Mary remained behind bars and the courts untangled a bureaucratic jumble of outdated records on Williams Bonding Company, and Williams was cleared to issue the bond the following week.

On Sunday, August 13, murder struck McNairy County once again. The community was stunned. One homicide a year was unusual—and now they had two in less than six months. Law enforcement found 22-year-old Ruth Sigrist dead from a shot to the head in a friend's home in the nearby town of Bethel Springs—the ugly result of a love triangle gone bad. On Monday, they arrested Bonda Cummings and charged her with negligent homicide. Exactly one year later—on August 14, 2007—Bonda was found guilty and sentenced to three years.

That same day, Mary's attorneys continued their dance with authorities to gain their client's release from jail. Finally, on Tuesday, all the hurdles were cleared. Family and friends gathered in the lobby of the McNairy County Justice Center. The moment Mary stepped through the door, she was folded in her father's embrace—the first time he hugged his daughter since Christmas. When Dorothy Weatherford, among the crowd of well-wishers, saw her friend in real clothes—a black skirt, striped top and black flats—for the first time in months, she smiled. The two women hugged. "Keep in touch with me, Mary," Dorothy said. Mary nodded and reached out to grasp the hands of her lawyers.

They took her first into the court clerk's office. The staff there was a bit baffled. *Why did they want her to see us and us to see her?* They plastered awkward smiles on their faces and said, "Hello." When Mary and her attorneys just stood there, the confusion of the county employees increased. *What do they want? Do they expect us to go up and hug her?*

At 11:55 A.M., Mary walked out the front doors of the Justice Center flanked by her attorneys Steve Farese and Leslie Ballin. They stopped to speak to reporters. Mary's head remained bowed as the two men spoke for her, explaining the conditions of her release. "We would specifically request of all the press—not just the ones here today, but the magazines, the newspapers, the national press—please respect her privacy as they have respected the privacy of the Winkler family," Farese asked.

They walked Mary to her father's car and faced the reporters again, answering questions about their client. "Her emotional state is fragile, but it's a new world and a new day for her today. Certainly, she's apprehensive. But I think as the days go, just as she became acclimated to jail, she'll become acclimated to the free world. She will have to get used to carrying a purse again. She mentioned that today," Farese said with a rueful smile.

When asked about Mary's visitation with her children, he said, "There has been some disagreement there, which you would understand in any custody arrangements, but we'll try to work through those issues as far as weekly telephone calls and, hopefully, visits as often as possible."

A reporter asked about Mary's monitoring by Warren County probation officials. "Mary will report to a state probation officer in McMinnville immediately," Farese answered. "She will make that call tonight. If she gets there after hours, she will leave a message. She will call back tomorrow."

Another journalist asked, "Will she start work at the dry cleaners immediately or will she have some down time?"

Leslie Ballin fielded that question. "We'll play that by ear. That's not a decision that either Steve or I would be involved in. Whatever she feels is best for her. She's going to have some adjusting to do."

Follow-up inquiries dealt with Mary's ability to weather negative reactions from folks in McMinnville. Ballin said, "We told her to go forward, keep her head high, although she didn't today.

"She did not come out here and jump for joy that she's out on bond, as you might expect from someone being locked up for almost five months now. But she came out and displayed the calm, meek person that I know her to be. Preparing her for the unknown, we talked about living her life as normally as possible."

CHAPTER 29

Clark Freeman drove off with his daughter in his '94 Cadillac, taking her straight to her former home on Mollie Drive to pick up clothing and other personal items. It was a strange experience for Mary to enter that empty house.

The sound of children, playing and laughing, squabbling and crying, once filled the four walls. Now, all that remained was a dusty silence. The two dogs who once welcomed her with yips of joy were now living with her sister in Knoxville. In their absence, nothing greeted her but the dark memories of a distant day.

The last time she'd passed over the threshold, her husband of ten years lay dying on the bedroom floor. Now his body was gone and all signs of his blood were washed away by the ardent ministrations of Bio-recovery Solutions. Here and there were pockets of dishevelment, and empty spaces where computers or portraits once stood, all evidence of the law enforcement search.

Mary went straight to the laundry hamper and lifted the lid. She dug through the dirty clothes and pulled out a shirt belonging to Matthew. She held it to her face. She inhaled deeply. She remembered his presence, his touch, the love they once shared. Now it was gone. But even the pull of the trigger could not take those memories away.

As if she were rewinding the hands of time, Mary followed the same roads, in reverse, that she'd journeyed with

Matthew a year-and-a-half before, when they moved to Selmer for a new and better life. Now she returned to McMinnville to begin again—but this time, she was alone.

Mary did, however, have someone keeping an eye on her—her new probation officer Donna Dunlap. She would meet with Donna every week until the commencement of the trial.

She moved in with Kathy and Rudy Thomsen and their son in a home on Fairview Road perched atop a hill on the outskirts of a congested downtown. At first, she kept to herself, coming out of her room for meals, but little more. In a short while, though, she integrated into their family life. She developed a playful relationship with the Thomsens' teenaged son. She called him her "big little brother." He called her his "shorter older sister."

Mary entered Cleaners Express, where she once was a customer. She now was an employee of owners Paul Pillow and Matt Hash. She had a great manner with customers, and even many who didn't know her loved catching a glimpse of her timid smile. She still had many friends in town, and they came in to greet her, often bringing their dry-cleaning business there. Some friends brought gifts to Mary. Others gave her cash. Occasionally, Mary encountered hostility from a customer, but Paul watched over her and was always ready to jump in and shield her from harsh words and ugly glares.

She didn't talk at work about what happened to Matthew. But every now and then, she'd mention his name in conversation. If they were talking about a particular food, she might say, "Matthew really likes that." Or if a television show was mentioned, she might say, "That was one of Matthew's favorites."

Mary resumed attendance at Central Church of Christ. On the first Sunday, people lined up outside to hug Mary when she arrived. Tears glistened on her cheeks as she made her way into the sanctuary.

It was a large congregation, though, with nearly 600 members. With the addition of Mary, it became a divided

one. Not everyone was pleased to have her in their midst—
even people in the same family were on opposite sides
when it came to the question of Mary. Some welcomed her
with open arms. Others struggled with Christ's admonition
to forgive and to judge not. The latter were looking for a
demonstration of remorse or an act of contrition from
Mary, and found none.

The problem was magnified because so many church
members had known Matthew, had great respect for his
work as youth minister and remembered him fondly. Mary
quietly left the dissension there behind, attending services
at the smaller Arlington Church of Christ.

She socialized a bit, going to lunch with friends and having dinner at the home of former neighbor Evon Dennis,
across from where Mary and Matthew lived on Franklin
Street. She returned to the chair of her beautician, Stephanie
Fann, who regularly cut the hair of Mary and the girls—and
occasionally Matthew—when they used to live in McMinnville.

Mary's sister drove to the Thomsen home to reunite
Mary with Lady and Lucy Lou. The dogs filled a tiny
piece of the emptiness in Mary's heart. But a family visit
raised a new dilemma. There was no extra room in the
Thomsen home—where could her family stay when they
visited?

JoAn and Dewey Cantrell came to the rescue. When
JoAn's mother passed on, she'd inherited her house, complete with furniture. Occasionally, they had one of their
grown children in the home for a short period of time, or
visitors from out of town stayed there for a weekend, but
for the most part, it sat vacant and neglected. Nothing had
been done to it in years. They offered it to Mary.

The court mandate required that Mary live with Kathy
Thomsen, so she couldn't move into the Cantrell house,
but it would be the perfect place for visiting family to stay.
Mary spent her free time there, keeping busy, fixing it up
for company. She cleaned every room, scrubbing the wood-
work, scouring the sinks, chasing away dust bunnies and

cobwebs. She picked out colors, painted every room and added personal decorating touches.

When she was finished, the transformation surprised and delighted JoAn. There was one thing, though, that made JoAn uneasy. Scattered about the home were Mary's family pictures, including many photographs of Matthew. She averted her eyes from his image. After all that had happened, the presence of Matthew's face in Mary's home "just seemed too weird."

CHAPTER 30

On September 22, the defense requested a postponement of the October 30 trial date because they needed more time to discuss the case with the newly elected district attorney general. Four days later, Judge McCraw granted that request, putting the trial on the calendar for the February 2007 term without setting a specific date.

The other decision the judge announced that day did not please the defense. He denied their motion to suppress the statements Mary made in Alabama after her arrest.

Farese told the media that he planned to continue the fight to suppress evidence seized from the parsonage. He said that the police did not have the necessary search warrant when they began their investigative exploration of the Winkler home.

With a pounding heart, Mary drove with her sister Tabatha from the Thomsen home in McMinnville to Huntingdon on the other side of Nashville. She had not seen her daughters' faces for three months. For the first time in half a year, she'd be able to touch them, kiss them, hug them.

She pulled into the parking lot of the Huntingdon Church of Christ. She went straight to the gymnasium and flung open the door, her eyes scanning the vast room, seeking sight of her little girls.

Before her arrival, Dan Winkler brought over Cokes, ice and popcorn, as well as a supply of disposable diapers for

Breanna. He introduced Mary to the two family friends, Betty Pritchard and her daughter, Beth Guess, who'd be supervising the visitation. Then, he left to go next door to his home in the parsonage and pick up the children.

Dan escorted the girls to the gym and left as they ran toward their mother. Patricia and Allie immediately threw themselves into their mother's arms, giving and receiving kisses and hugs. Breanna hung back a bit—half a year's absence was a formidable length of time for an 18-month-old. After a little coaxing, she, too, joined in the affectionate exchange.

Patricia spotted her "Aunt Baba" on the sideline, rushed over to her for a hug. Allie knew Tabatha was her mom's sister, but didn't really remember her. Breanna had never met her.

They spent their time together playing and talking about everything but the event that caused their separation. The two hours passed far too quickly for Mary Winkler. After a flurry of exchanged I-love-you's, the girls were gone. Mary made the long drive back to McMinnville with her sister, alternating between sparkling moments of recollection to somber periods of dead silence that lasted for miles.

Back in Huntingdon, Dan and Diane talked to their granddaughters about the visit with their mother. They were shocked to learn that Mary told the girls that the police were wrong—she'd had nothing to do with the death of their father. Hearing this lie, the elder Winklers' attitude toward Mary took a dramatic negative turn. One month later, the accusations of Mary's family would harden their hearts forever.

Mary asked for permission to travel to the Ladies Christian Retreat at Thompson's Station in Williamson County, Tennessee, on the weekend of October 13. Her attorneys argued that she would benefit from the spiritual guidance, fellowship and support she would find there. Judge McCraw denied the request.

Mary was disappointed, but it was not her most important concern. She hungered for her next visit with her daughters. She had every reason to believe it would happen soon. Then, in mid-October, the November issue of *Glamour* hit mailboxes and newsstands across the country.

In the article about Mary, Clark Freeman came to his daughter's defense. "Mary Carol could not bring pain to anyone . . . You know the saying, 'She couldn't hurt a fly'? If a fly buzzed over the table at dinnertime, Mary Carol would open the door and help it find its way out. That's who Mary is.

"I know her finger was on that shotgun. And I know a lot of what has been described about the shooting is true. But Mary Carol didn't do it. Not the Mary Carol I know."

Steve Farese lashed out at Matthew Winkler. "Only Mary can talk about Matt and his temper and how controlling he was." He claimed Matt "ruled every aspect of his wife's life." He told her which dresses to buy, and he told her what to eat. "Mary didn't do anything without first checking with Matthew," he said in the interview.

The defense attorney asserted that "a too-obedient wife and a too-controlling husband" were "a recipe for disaster." He insisted that by the time she pulled the trigger, "Mary did not know up from down, and was literally trapped."

Clark Freeman told the interviewer for *Glamour* that he knew something was wrong in the marriage but if he had believed things had gone "very wrong," he would have talked to Mary and encouraged her to confide in him and accept his help.

But a month after the publication of *Glamour*, where he claimed to be pretty much clueless, Clark appeared on *Good Morning America* talking about the extremity of the abuse. "Physical, mental, verbal was strong. I don't know how she took it. She's a stronger individual than I am."

At one point, Mary's family claimed that they had seen Mary only twice in the last five years, but on the morning news show, Clark claimed that the abuse became obvious in the last three years of Matt and Mary's marriage. "I saw terrible bruises, the heaviest of makeup covering facial bruises. So one day, I confronted her. I said, 'Mary, you are coming off as a very abused wife. Very battered.' And Mary, she would hang her head and say, 'No, Daddy, everything is all right.' "

After this attack on the victim, clear lines of demarcation were drawn. The dispute over the custody of Patricia, Allie and Breanna Winkler escalated into all-out war.

CHAPTER 31

On New Year's Eve, Mary and her sister Tabatha went out with Mary's employers, Matt Hash and his life partner Paul Pillow, to the New York Grill, a popular hang-out in downtown McMinnville. Paul said that he tried to get Mary to join in a champagne toast in honor of the occasion, but all that Mary wanted was Mr. Pibb.

Luis Correa and his wife, Libby St. John, were there with friends that night. They recognized Mary Winkler sitting at a table and were shocked to see her giggling and drinking.

One of his friends went up to Mary's table and asked her, "Are you the preacher killer?"

Mary said, "Yeah. You want to be next?"

According to Luis, her companions at the table roared with laughter at her retort. When Mary sidled up to the bar to engage in her secret vice, Luis used his cell phone to snap photographs of her with cigarette in hand. Sitting beside her was an open bottle of beer.

Luis sold the images to WMC-TV. His wife Libby told Action News 5 that she wasn't bothered by Mary's drinking and smoking, but she was disturbed by her unwavering cheerfulness. "This doesn't look like a woman worried about anything. If I thought there was a chance I wouldn't see my children again, I wouldn't be celebrating in such fashion."

Paul Pillow rushed to Mary's defense, telling anyone who would listen that "She's not the preacher's wife any longer. He's dead now. She's not married to anyone. She's nobody's wife. She's her own person now." And he continued to insist that she was not drinking.

However, the owner of the New York Grill told WAFF 48 News that Mary had drinks at his establishment three or four times over the past few months.

The parties to the criminal case gathered in Selmer in advance of the trial on February 22 for a hearing on the defense's motion to suppress the evidence seized from the parsonage. Drew Eason testified about why he and other members went into the Winkler home and how they called the police and admitted them into the residence.

Three members of law enforcement presented the sequence of events that led to each of their actions, and explained that the initial primary motivation was the location of the three missing children. Judge McCraw took all the arguments and testimony under advisement for a later ruling and set the trial date for April 9, 2007.

The prosecution made an offer to avoid a trial, offering Mary Winkler a plea bargain that would guarantee a life sentence—usually meaning 50 years—instead of execution or life without parole. Then, they offered a deal of a 35-year sentence. The defense turned both down.

On March 14, the state lowered the possible consequences for Mary. They withdrew the pursuit of capital punishment. With that off the table, the maximum sentence she faced was 51 to 60 years of incarceration, but no one thought she'd actually spend that much time behind bars. Before trial, prosecutors offered a 20-year sentence, then a 15-year sentence in exchange for a guilty plea. The defense refused those offers, too.

The last half of March was a flurry of legal activity for Mary, but not in the criminal courts. Dan and Diane Winkler filed a $2,000,000 wrongful death suit against Mary, half for compensatory damages and half for punitive damages, in civil court.

In the papers filed, the Winklers alleged that when Mary shot Matthew, she "caused the children much mental pain and suffering at the loss of their father and has taken from them the person who economically provided for them and would have economically provided for them for many years to come." The document also contended that the children were deprived of "parental consortium, attention, guidance, care, protection, training, companionship, affection and love."

On March 29, the attention shifted to the Juvenile Court for McNairy County with presiding Judge Christy R. Little. There were many bones of contention between the parties in the custody case, and attorneys argued for both sides.

Dan and Diane's lawyer, James Adams, said, "My clients didn't ask to be put in this situation. They didn't ask the respondent to kill their son, but it happened. They are in this situation. They have done the best job they can to take care of these three little girls." He urged the judge not to change the agreed custody order, since there was neither a material change of circumstance nor a written agreement between the parties.

Kay Farese Turner, Mary's attorney for the custody case and sister of Mary's criminal lawyer, insisted that the Winklers were doing harm to the children by keeping them separate from their mother and maternal grandfather, and by sending them to an inappropriate counselor.

She also made a request for the children to have an overnight visit with their mother. "Her family is having a large family reunion this weekend in McMinnville. We had hoped against hope that this court would see fit to let these children go and be with these people. They grew up in McMinnville. They lived there a part of their schooling, or the older child did, and they have friends there, they would be comfortable there, and we would abide by anyone this court said should be present to safeguard this in the court's mind."

Adams objected to a trip to Mary's home. He felt the judge should not order a visit until the facts of what really occurred while the children were in the custody of his clients could be shown. He asserted that they never acted out of vengeance or vindictiveness. He insisted that they did not discourage the girls from speaking to their mother. "The children are going through some things right now, as can be expected when their father has been killed by their mother. They're going through some stuff. My clients have not seen fit to force them to speak to her."

Turner presented her client's vastly different point of view. "It is my opinion—and I told the court I practiced law thirty-two years, twenty-five in this area alone. I have never seen such an absolute alienation of children's affections against their parent; and all you have to do, Your Honor, is read from the beginning to the end of those counseling records."

Judge Little admitted that the reports from Diana Crawford were "quite eye-opening," but did not rule on any visitation request. Before that moved forward, she wanted to speak with the two victims of the criminal case, Patricia and Allie Winkler.

The parsonage on Mollie Drive in Selmer, Tennessee, where Mary shot and killed Matthew Winkler.

Courtesy of Diane Fanning

The bedroom on Mollie Drive. Matthew's body lay on the floor between the bed and the bathroom.

Courtesy of McNairy County General District Court

The spot in the bedroom of the parsonage where Matthew Winkler bled to death.

Courtesy of McNairy County General District Court

The unplugged telephone on the floor at the foot of the bed.

Courtesy of McNairy County General District Court

The two fraudulent checks deposited in the bank by Mary Winkler.

Courtesy of Diane Fanning

Fourth Street Church of Christ, Selmer, Tennessee, where Matthew Winkler ministered before his death.

Courtesy of Diane Fanning

Clark Freeman hugs his daughter, Mary, after learning she would be released from jail on bail. Attorney Steve Farese stands behind them, smiling.

Courtesy of Russell Ingle

Mary Winkler flanked by attorneys Leslie Ballin and Steve Farese immediately after her release from jail on bail.

Courtesy of Russell Ingle

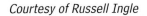

The Shackelford Funeral Home the night of Matthew Winkler's viewing, showing the long lines of people who came to pay their last respects.

Courtesy of Russell Ingle

Mary working at Cleaner's Express in McMinnville while out on bail.

Courtesy of Russell Ingle

Defense attorneys Leslie Ballin and Steve Farese confer during a break in the trial.

Courtesy of Russell Ingle

Corporal Stan Stabler of the Alabama Bureau of Investigation and defense attorney Steve Farese with the murder weapon.

Courtesy of Russell Ingle

Mary hides her face when talking about sexual activity between her and Matthew.

Courtesy of Russell Ingle

Dan Winkler, Matthew's father, being cross-examined by defense attorney Steve Farese.

Courtesy of Russell Ingle

Prosecutor Walt Freeland delivering his closing statement.

Courtesy of Russell Ingle

Defense attorney Steve Farese displays the shoe and wig during his closing statement.

Courtesy of Russell Ingle

Mary Winkler, flanked by attorneys Leslie Ballin and Steve Farese, faces reporters after the verdict.

Courtesy of Russell Ingle

Sheriff Rick Roten hands the notebook containing the verdict to Judge Weber McCraw.

Courtesy of Russell Ingle

Daniel Winkler, Matthew's older brother, in the courthouse. Although he didn't testify at the trial, he made an emotional plea at the sentencing hearing.

Courtesy of Russell Ingle

Diane Winkler, Matthew's mother, at the sentencing hearing, reading from the impassioned letter written by her sister.

Courtesy of Russell Ingle

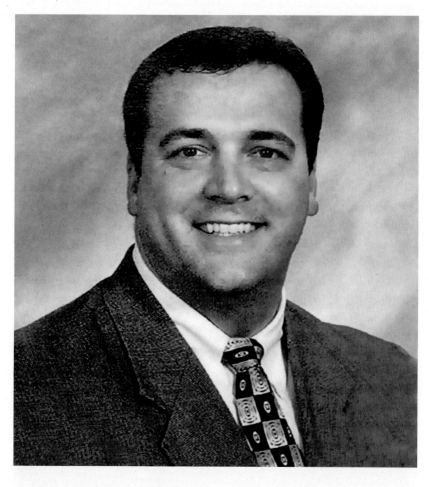

Matthew Winkler at age 30—taken less than one year before his death.

CHAPTER 32

On April 4, 2007—just four days before jury selection commenced in Mary's murder trial—Judge Christy Little gaveled her courtroom to order, brushing a stray strand of her collar-length blonde hair out of her eyes. Representatives of Dan and Diane Winkler were joined by the attorneys hired by Mary Winkler and those on behalf of the three girls, all standing before her. Patricia and Allie waited in another room with Amy Jones from CASA—Court Appointed Special Advocates—an organization using trained community volunteers to speak on behalf of the best interests of children.

Before bringing them in, Little heard arguments from the attorneys. Kay Farese Turner expressed outrage that family counselor Diana Crawford's main expertise was in the arena of termination of parental rights and adoption. She expressed her shock about the lack of care Allie Winkler had received for her head injury in 2005. "This child is hearing voices, this child hears things that other people don't hear . . . Do we see Ms. Crawford refer this child to a psychiatric neurologist? Do we see this addressed anywhere with a qualified psychiatrist?"

After an interruption from attorney James Adams about the admissibility of the girls' records outside of the presence of the counselor who created them, Turner continued. "We also have the older child, who was bonded to the mother, being told—Patricia is being told that her mother is bad, the Winklers telling them what the mother's motives were, discussing the criminal proceedings, and then allowing the D.A. to orchestrate whether or not these children see their mother."

She added that the collusion between the state's attorney and the counselor was "bordering on prosecutorial misconduct. It is bordering on unethical misconduct as it relates to dealing with three children who have, as this court so succinctly said, lost their father, and now they're going to see to it they lose their mother."

The judge stopped this characterization of her remarks and moved on to ask questions of the lawyers present. Wrapping up this portion of the hearing, she elicited their opinions on what needed to happen in the future.

Turner said, "What these children need is reunification counseling. They need counseling that wipes out of their mind the brainwashing and planting of memory."

Adams argued that the temporary custody order was temporary in name only. "This is a valid custody order and . . . the law clearly says . . . that if the court were to just give in to the superior rights doctrine every time the actual parents stood up, then there would never be any finality to any custody orders ever, ever drafted." He reminded the judge that his clients alleged in the petition that a change of custody would cause ". . . substantial harm to the children in our petition, and the guardian *ad litem* [the advocate appointed by the court to represent the interests of another—in this case, the Winkler children] is alleging substantial harm now . . ."

Judge Little requested that Patricia and Allie be brought before her. She focused her blue eyes and round, motherly face on the two girls and tried to put them at ease with simple questions about their daily life. She asked them about their schools and report cards, then inquired:

"And what is your favorite subject?"

Patricia said, "Science."

Allie said, "Social Studies."

Judge Little spoke of her own 7-year-old daughter. "Her

favorite right now, which in the past has been 'recess,' is now Math, which is a very good thing; and she likes the Doodlebops and SpongeBob and *Suite Life of Zack and Cody*."

Patricia nodded in agreement.

"That's cool, isn't it?" the judge asked.

"We like SpongeBob, *Suite Life of Zack and Cody*, *Drake and Josh*, *Zoey one-oh-one*," Allie said.

"*Zoey one-oh-one* is cool. You watch *Hannah Montana* and *The Amanda Show*?"

Both of the girls said, "Yes."

"Oh, so cool. All right, now . . ."

Allie interrupted, "And The Naked Brothers Band."

"Yes; and I bet that doesn't go over real well, because I know I don't like the name."

"I don't either," said Patricia. "They need to change their name, but they're still cool."

"Even though they are naked brothers, they are still cool?"

"Yes," Patricia said.

"I haven't been really happy about that," Judge Little said. "And you have your ears pierced."

"Uh-huh," Patricia answered.

"Wow."

Allie jumped in. "I get mine when I'm nine."

"I did mine in September for my birthday," Patricia said.

"I'm going to get mine when I'm turning nine," Allie repeated.

When the judge determined they were relaxed and comfortable speaking with her, she steered them to more serious matters. "I wish we didn't have to meet like this, you know that? And I'm so sorry that you lost your daddy. It's been tough, hasn't it? It's been a bad year."

"Uh-huh," Allie agreed.

"I guess you could classify it— How do you classify it?"

"Well . . ." Patricia began.

"What does that mean?" Allie interjected.

Patricia continued, "It's been bad, but I made new friends, too. So there's good and bad."

"You know, a lot of people were concerned about you, and are still concerned about you. You've got a whole court-room of people in there concerned about you, and then all the lawyers that are in here and everybody else; and then you've got your little sister, too, that you—although she's younger—she's a part of the package, too."

"Yes," Patricia said.

"And you take care of her, make sure she's okay? And I'm sorry that you haven't been able to see your mom."

"I don't want to," Patricia said.

"Well, let's don't jump to that, okay? Let's just take it kind of one step at a time here." The judge then walked them gently through the events from their mother's arrest to the funeral. When asked what their grandfather told them about what happened, Patricia and Allie were walk-ing over each other's answers so much, it prompted the judge to say, "We'll just let Patricia talk, and then we'll let Allie talk, all right? Go ahead."

"He told us that Mama called one time," Patricia said.

"One time?"

Allie interrupted. "I want to say that part."

Patricia continued. "She's been calling, and then I talked to her, and I told her I didn't want to talk to her, or I didn't want her to write anymore to me. And then— I can't re-member what he's told us—a lot, too. And then Allie's go-ing to tell you about what happened."

"Okay, Allie," the judge said.

"One time when she called, it was Breanna's birthday."

"Yes?"

"And we had to go over to Gigi's to celebrate it, be-cause our mother said she was coming over."

"And who is Gigi?"

Patricia answered, "Our grandmother, Eloise Boyd. She's our great grandmother."

Allie interjected, "And he was telling that he was disap-pointed at her and stuff, and then he called the judges."

"He didn't call the judge," Patricia contradicted.

"His lawyers," Allie said.

"No, yes, no, he called . . ." Patricia began.

"I'm speaking now," Allie interrupted.

The judge intervened. "It's Allie's turn. Y'all sound like lawyers in a courtroom. Allie, it's your turn, dear."

"And he called his lawyers. And if she would have come here, she would have been put to jail until the court," Allie said.

"Because what? What did she do?"

"Because she wasn't allowed to come here, but she said she was coming here. But just in case, we went over to Gigi's," Allie said.

Patricia added, "March ninth was Breanna's birthday, and she had called up a few days earlier and said that she was going to come over. And Poppa called her back and said she wasn't allowed because she would be trespassing. She didn't even ask to come over, and she said if . . ."

The judge interrupted. "Don't you think that's kind of neat that she wanted to come to the birthday?"

"Yes, well, he said if she . . . was going to trespass, then he would have to call the police."

Allie spoke up. "Why, why we went over to Gigi's is because one time our—her father, he came . . ."

The judge tried to turn the conversation to their mother's sisters, but Allie persisted in staying on the subject of her mom's father. "And then our granddaddy came over, and he said he was going to take pictures. But our Poppa said no, said they had to go talk on the porch, he could visit with us for five minutes. So he, then he called our mom so he could talk to her, but they said no."

Patricia said, "Because that was before she— before I told her not to— before I talked to her."

"Yes, and so," Allie continued, "and then he got the phone, so he had to leave and he was not allowed to come back to our house . . . because they would take pictures and make our daddy look bad, bad man and stuff."

"Who said that?" the judge asked.

"Our Poppa," Allie said.

"He had to tell us, because they were already doing that, Mama and Granddaddy," Patricia said in her Poppa's defense.

The judge cut off the conversation. "Now, you know that may not necessarily be absolutely true, right?"

Both Patricia and Allie said, "I don't know."

Patricia added, "Because, I mean, like, my friends have been saying, like, they saw us on magazines and . . ."

"Stuff," said Allie, completing her sister's sentence. "Well, that's not exactly. He said that—because our aunts would take pictures of us a lot, and they would be taking pictures and make our daddy look bad, like he was being mad, a bad man, so she could get away with it."

"Okay," the judge said with a sigh. "Let me just tell you one thing. Us old people . . . sometimes, we do things we shouldn't do, and one of those things is— You guys need to enjoy being a nine-year-old and a seven-year-old and really not have to worry about all this stuff now."

"Well, I mean, like, I want my Poppa to tell me all this, because I want him to tell me the truth and what's going on," Patricia objected.

"Right, but . . ." the judge began.

"So . . ." Patricia tried to continue.

"But," Judge Little said, "you know that story about 'There is two sides to every story and sometimes three'?"

Allie said, "Uh-huh."

"Maybe you should keep a more open mind about it, because your mom has gone through a lot, and she has attorneys that are fighting really, really hard just to get a chance for her to see you and talk to you."

Both girls shake their heads.

"And you know, there may be another side to this story that we don't know about, and it may come to a time where, you know, you— Wouldn't you like to just see her and ask her some questions?"

"We have already saw her once," Allie said.

"Yes, but just once. Wouldn't you like to have a chance to just talk to her about it?"

They both shook their heads and Allie said, "No. And then . . ."

"Why?" the judge said, cutting her off. "I guess that's the big question."

"Because she did a mean thing, and it really hurt us really bad," Allie answered.

"But we all do bad things, though," the judge said.

Patricia burst into tears.

"I'm so sorry," the judge apologized.

"She's emotional," Allie said.

"She's emotional. She's emotional," the judge said as she struggled not to get emotional herself. "Can we have some Kleenex, Bailiff, the good kind?" Turning to Patricia, she said, "We're going to get you some good kind. We have this old nasty hard County kind, and then I have my own private stash."

"This is what happened," Allie began.

"I don't want to see my mama after what she did," Patricia insisted.

"And see, like, this is how it began," Allie explained. "Our mama, she had been robbing banks."

"Well, not robbing banks, but going . . ." Patricia said.

Allie continued, "She had a plan to get some money from a bank, so then, early in the morning, they would call her. So she told our daddy and he was mad at her."

"He wasn't mad at her," Patricia said, "he was disappointed in her."

"Disappointed in her, so she just shot him," Allie said.

"For no reason," Patricia added.

"Who told you all that stuff about the bank and all that?" Judge Little asked.

Ignoring the question, Allie said, "And then she . . ."

The judge repeated, "Who told you about the bank and the bank calling and the 'disappointed' and all that?"

"I can't remember," Allie said.

The judge turned to Patricia. "Do you remember?"

Patricia shook her head no.

"Was it your Poppa or . . . ?"

"I don't know," Patricia insisted.

"I can't remember," Allie said again.

"Would it have been . . . ?"

Allie cut off the judge. "And he—I remember this part—our Nana, she said our mother lied to us. She said that she called nine-nine-one [sic]."

"But she didn't," Patricia said.

The tissues arrived for Patricia and then the judge said, "Let's talk about prior to that. You love your mom."

"No," Patricia said.

At the judge's urging, the two girls admitted that they did have a good relationship with their mother and she was never mean to them. Then, she asked, "From the time this incident occurred, prior—back, back—when you were younger or when you were in kindergarten and all that, did you get along with your mom?"

"Uh-huh," Patricia said.

"You loved your mom."

"Yes," Allie said.

"She took you to ball games and movies and ballets or whatever, and you had a good relationship, right?"

Both girls nodded.

"And that night, you went with her, you were with your mom. And you missed your mom when you didn't get to see her for a period of time, right?"

"Well, before I knew she killed my daddy, I did," Patricia said.

"Okay. Okay. And now that you know what you think that you've been told, who all has told you that?"

"That my mom killed my daddy?" Patricia asked.

Then in unison, the sisters said, "Nana and Poppa."

Allie explained her daddy's absence at church, then said, "So they knocked down the door and found him dead. And Patricia said she heard a loud knock when— that night, she said she heard it."

"I heard . . ." Patricia began.

Allie interrupted. "Then when we were in the hall, Trisha said she saw a gun."

"No, I didn't," Patricia contradicted her.

"Yes, you did."

"What happened was, I was— We were sleeping, and I don't know how early it was, and . . ."

"Because you had to go to bed early? On a Tuesday night you go to bed by eight-thirty, right?"

"Yes," Patricia answered. "And, well, what happened was, we saw— Well, I heard— I don't know if Daddy fell on the floor, or somebody— or if Mom— or if I heard the gunshot. I don't know what happened. What it was, I heard a big kerplunk. And I woke up, because I was scared. And I— And I was going to go to Mama and Dad's room to see if it was like a thunderstorm or something, and Daddy was on the floor, face down. And he was like— He sounded like he was hurt."

"Right," the judge encouraged her to continue.

"So, I didn't see any blood, though."

"Okay."

"And then—and the youth ministers called— The elders called a person that knew Uncle Jacob, one of Uncle Jacob's friends . . .

"And then, Uncle Jacob called Nana and Poppa."

"No, no," Allie said.

"Uh huh," Patricia retorted.

"Some police came to Nana and Poppa's house and they told them," Allie said.

"No, they didn't," Patricia argued.

"I remember," Allie insisted. "I have a better memory than you."

"But, Allie, they were in their holiday. And Uncle Jacob called Nana and Poppa and told them that they found Daddy dead, and then they— and then the police called

them and told them that they found us and we were—
Well, before the police called them, before anybody found
us, there was, like, an AMBER Alert, and they were—for
missing children, and they told— And they . . ."

"Where did you think you were going?" the judge asked.

"Mama said when we were going to Alabama, she said
Daddy wanted us to go here."

"For like a vacation?"

Both girls nodded and then Allie said, "No, just in case
that man would come again."

"Yes," Patricia agreed.

"So that's what we thought," Allie added.

Patricia clarified, " 'Just in case,' she said. 'Just in case
the man came again, we would be gone, he couldn't hurt
us.' And then we were going to Alabama, I was like, 'Where
are we going, why can't we go back to see Daddy?' and she
was like, 'Well, Daddy would want us to go here.' And I was
like, 'Can't we go pick up Daddy?' And she said, 'No.'
She's like, 'No.' "

"No, Trisha," Allie interrupted. "She couldn't say that,
because she told— because we— because she told us at
the house that she was calling nine-nine-one [sic]."

"I know."

"I remember," Allie said.

"She said that he was at the hospital, and then I asked,
'Can't we go pick him up,' and, see, 'get him over here?'
And she's like, 'No, no.' And I'm like, well, 'Yes.' And
she's like, 'Because Breanna might be, like, crying and
stuff.' "

The judge told the girls that there would be a trial next
week and said, "The only issue that I have to decide is, do
you see your mom, do you not see your mom, the what-if's
of the future."

Both girls said, "We don't see her."

"Why?"

"Because I don't want to," Patricia said.

"We don't want to," Allie corrected.

"And Poppa said if I ever wanted to call my mom, he

would call her, because he wants what's best for me. And he said . . ."

"Us," Allie corrected again.

"Us. And he said, 'If you ever want to talk to your mom, just tell me and I'll call her.' But I've never wanted to."

The judge allowed Kay Farese Turner to ask a few questions. Turner asked the younger girl, "Allie, do you have headaches?"

"Well, I kind of do, because I've got an ear problem, but my ear is healing better."

"Do you ever hear voices telling you to do things?"

Allie nodded her head. "Yes, like sometimes I hear a voice. Like sometimes Nana and Poppa are calling my name, but then I get up and then I get out and go, 'Yes, ma'am?' and, like, 'Ma'am?' And they said, 'I didn't call you.' And I'm, 'Didn't you call my name?' They said they didn't call my name."

Turner turned to the oldest girl. "Patricia, when did you first learn that your daddy had died? You said that you learned that after you got back?"

"No. We were in the hotel. And I went first. And they— because they were going to tell both of us."

"They said that our daddy had gone to see Jesus," Allie said.

"Yes," Patricia agreed.

As the questioning continued, both girls insisted they knew nothing about the district attorney or lawyers, they just knew that they didn't want to see their mother. Then Turner asked, "Do either of you ever write your mom and send her any of your pictures or anything?"

They both said, "No."

"You never wrote her?"

"I wrote her once," Patricia said.

"We just wrote her once," Allie said.

"Did she ever respond to that letter?"

"No," Patricia answered.

"Did you send her your report cards or pictures or anything like that?"

"No."

"Why not?"

"Because I didn't want to," Patricia insisted.

Turner tried to get Patricia to admit that her Poppa told her that her mother or granddaddy would sell the pictures to media outlets, but Patricia refused. Turner then asked, "And you didn't want to send her a picture of you, like your school pictures or anything?"

"I mean, we sent her one picture," Patricia said.

"She asked for them, didn't she? She wanted you to send her some."

"Yes, we sent her a picture last year of when we went to Disney World, and we had a— we took the castle in the background," Patricia explained.

"How did you send it?"

Patricia furrowed her brow.

"I saw a letter that said 'Mary Winkler,' and so— and then— and then I— They let me put it in the mail with my other letters to go to someone else."

"So you know it got mailed then."

"Yes, we know," Allie replied.

The attorneys argued back and forth with the judge over making additional inquiries. Patricia interrupted the discussion. "I don't want to be asked any more questions."

"That answers that," Judge Little said. "I get tired of it, too, sometimes." She asked the deputies to escort Patricia and Allie out of the room. Before they exited, Turner asked, "Can I ask the girls one thing?"

"Sure," the judge said.

"Girls, can I tell your mom that you love her?"

Patricia nodded and Allie said, "Yes."

The judge commented on the obvious coaching of the two girls. Then she dismissed the court without setting a new date, deciding instead to await the outcome of the up-coming trial.

THE JUDGMENT

"He that is without sin among you, let him first cast a stone at her."

—*John* 8:7

CHAPTER 33

That evening, members of the Fourth Street Church of
Christ met in the sanctuary for their regular Wednesday
night service. Jeremy Weekley, who assumed Matt's position as pulpit minister the summer after his death, prayed
for the church body to find strength to persevere in the
weeks ahead. He made a special appeal for God's blessing
on those among them who would testify at Mary Winkler's
trial.

At the McNairy County Justice Center, they prepared
for the media onslaught, setting up a designated room for
their use. Inside the building, they replaced burned-out
light bulbs, cleaned and made repairs. Outside, they spruced
up the grounds, mowing the grass and trimming the shrubs.
The sheriff reviewed security concerns and assigned tasks
for the trial. A lot of people in Selmer were looking forward
to when it would all be over—no one more than Sheriff
Roten.

Anxiety ruled the day for the 160 county residents selected for the jury pool—some were eager to serve, others
filled with dread. One willing man went out to the farmers'
supply store and purchased an automatic goat feeder. He
was certain he'd be chosen, and he didn't want his live-
stock going hungry. He didn't make the cut.

An unwilling candidate, who worked out of an office in
her home, fretted over her wardrobe. "I don't have enough

nice clothes to last three weeks." She didn't have to worry, she was not selected.

At least one person who received a summons was not anxious at all. Sharyn Everitt, who lived across the street from the Winklers on Mollie Drive, and once had a run-in with Matt over her dog, was certain she would not make the final panel. She was right.

The questioning began on the morning of Monday, April 9. They came in to face the attorneys seven at a time. They were asked about their knowledge of the case, their willingness to set aside pre-formed opinions and their ability to give Mary a fair trial. Other topics covered included domestic abuse, brainwashing, the appropriateness of lying to children and familiarity with firearms and gun safety. By the end of this first day, only fourteen prospective jurors had crossed that hurdle.

By the end of Tuesday, the count was up to forty-two, but that was not sufficient for Judge Weber McCraw—things had to move faster. He ordered that the groups be doubled in size for Wednesday's session to fourteen jurors at a time. His plan worked. By the end of court on Wednesday, a panel of sixteen was selected. Although four of the chosen were alternates, no one—not even the jurors themselves—would know who they were until it was time for deliberations to begin.

The group consisted of twelve women and four men. The state had eliminated prospective panelists of both genders. The defense reserved all of their strikes for males in the pool. The jurors ranged in age from 20 to 62, and were predominately white—only two were black, no surprise in a county where the population was 92 percent Caucasian. Among the group was a truck driver, a drafter, a machinist, two factory workers, a retired Baptist minister, a secretary, a teacher's aide and a handful of housewives.

The judge passed out an information sheet reminding them that they needed to be prepared when they returned to court in the morning. They should bring enough clothing and prescription medications for two weeks, make sure their bills were all paid and arrange for mail pick-up in their absence. First thing in the morning, their real lives were put on hold.

Their temporary quarters were a mile from the courthouse at Southwood Inn. Televisions, telephones and radios were removed from their rooms. Even the newspaper box outside was shrouded with a black plastic garbage bag by order of Judge Weber McCraw.

They could not bring their cell phones or laptops. They were not allowed to visit the motel's breakfast room or leave the facility for any reason unless accompanied by authorities.

The expense of the trial for this county of less than 25,000 residents, with its low tax base, was staggering. The state government would pick up some of the bills, but they did not cover the overtime accrued by deputies having to guard the courtroom by day and the jurors by night. Nor did they cover the cost of the jurors' lodging. At $69 per night, the county's outlay there alone could easily exceed the ten-thousand-dollar mark before trial's end.

On Thursday, April 12, Mary Winkler entered the courtroom, with a cross around her neck, a wedding band on her finger and a prayer in her heart, to face the judgment of her peers.

CHAPTER 34

Judge Weber McCraw stepped up behind the bench and brought Mary Winkler's trial to order. He had a thoughtful face framed by thinning, graying hair. Bushy eyebrows rested over brown eyes on a long oval face with full lips. By the end of every day, a heavy 5 o'clock shadow darkened his chin line.

Prosecutor Walt Freeland stepped before the podium in a gray suit and a gray, black and white striped tie to present the opening argument for the state. With his white hair, rounded shoulders and sagging face, he looked tired before he started.

"Why?" he asked the jury. "That was the last word spoken on this earth by Matthew Winkler, and his last word was addressed to the person he thought he could trust—his wife, the defendant Mary Winkler. And he said it as he lay dying on the floor of the bedroom of his own house in his own home in Selmer, McNairy County, Tennessee. He had been shot in the middle of the back as he lay sleeping in his bed by his own twelve-gauge shotgun."

The lawyer introduced himself and his co-counsel, Michael Dunavant, the regional district attorney general, and then continued. "The state will not produce any evidence of any good reason why Matthew Winkler was murdered by Mary Winkler, because there is no good reason why Matthew Winkler was murdered by Mary Winkler.

"The 'Why?' question is a question that is used to develop suspects. There's more than a suspect in this case—the state's proof will be, there is a perpetrator, which we will show committed an unlawful act, a deliberate act and a premeditated act. What the state will prove is that Matthew Winkler was, in the words of Mary Winkler, 'a mighty fine person.'

". . . He finally had his own church—the Fourth Street Church of Christ in Selmer. Finally had his pulpit. He was only thirty-one years of age. He had met his wife Mary about ten years or so before at Freed-Hardeman, which is a Church of Christ school in Henderson. And in his career, he'd been in various places as a youth minister. He'd been in Baton Rouge in Louisiana, he had been near Nashville. He'd been in McMinnville—all as a youth minister.

"Finally, he had gotten his pulpit job here in Selmer, I believe, in about February 2005. He was a son, his parents were alive. He was a brother, he had two brothers. And he was the father of three precious little girls. He was a man, the proof will be, that did not deserve to be murdered."

He talked about the discovery of the body, and locating Mary and the three girls. He then moved on to Mary's recorded conversation with law enforcement, which he planned to play in court. "And you will hear that Mary Winkler is very calm. She's not excited. She's not sad. She is—as the patrol officers described her upon the stop—she is stoic, which means she didn't show emotion.

"And you won't just have to rely on the testimony of the officers who stopped her, because you will hear her voice on this tape, and you will hear the general sort of questions asked about her rights, and did she understand those? And her comfort is mentioned, and she is supplied drinks.

"You will hear her several times say to Corporal Stan

Stabler, words to the effect, when she was asked questions, 'No comment' or 'I don't want to talk about that yet.' But the conversation progresses and she concedes—and this is the Thursday evening after the Wednesday morning shooting—she concedes that she had a good marriage. That there were no major, major problems. And she uses words that indicate that she was in control of this situation. She says words basically, 'There's no *Poor me*. I'm in control.'"

". . . You will hear her say that she has her nerves now, she's has her self-esteem and she guesses her 'ugly' just came out. You will hear those words almost verbatim. And when asked her plans about what she planned to have done after this, she says, 'I didn't have the money to go to Mexico, of course. I was coming back to west Tennessee. I was going to bring the children back to stay with the family.'

"And when she was asked, 'Your parents?'

" 'No, the family. They're good people.' And she was talking about Matthew Winkler's family. She was talking about Poppa and Nana, and she was talking about, not her family, but Matthew's family.

". . . She told Stan Stabler—you'll get to hear it on the audio—he was asking about how this happened, and if there was any thinking about it. You will hear her say, 'I've been battling not to do that forever.' You will hear her on the tape when asked, she states it was not planned, but when asked if she had thought about doing it, she indicated to Stan Stabler that it 'had crossed minds.'

". . . Now, the state, I have told you, will not produce evidence of any good reason why Matthew Winkler was killed, because there is no good reason. However, the state will give you evidence to show that this was no accident. That this was a premeditated act, because of things that had been happening over which Mary Winkler was in control. Mary Winkler was in control of the family finances. Mary Winkler signed, if not every check, the overwhelming number of checks in this matter."

Freeland described the financial problems, which included counterfeit checks and check-kiting by Mary, immediately before Matthew's death. "Many gullible people take the phony check and think they have won the lottery they never entered, and wire the money off to this nonexistent company and thereby lose money.

"The proof will be that Mary Winkler was not such a victim. She took the checks all right. She took several of them. And she deposited them in banks. And it was the bank's fault, obviously, but some of these were credited to her account. But she was not a victim, the state's proof will be, because unlike a real victim, she didn't fall for it, she didn't wire the money, she just took the phony checks and put them in the bank.

". . . She set up an account in her name—her name only—in Henderson. She had as the contact, not as her home number on Mollie Drive, but her own cell phone number. She was the only one who ever had contact with that bank. The account was set up on February seventeenth of 2006. The state will give you evidence that six days before this . . . she had gotten a change of address at the Selmer post office directing that all mail come, not to Mollie Drive, but exclusively to her post office box. Again, the house of cards that she set up was falling down.

"There were telephone calls after telephone calls to Mary on March twenty-first from Regions Bank. 'Mary, you have to come in.' 'Mary, this is illegal, what you're doing.' 'Mary, we can work it out, but you have to get Matthew to come in so that we can straighten it out. You are five thousand dollars overdrawn. You have got to have to get this straightened out.'

". . . There was telephone call after telephone call saying, 'Mary, you've got to come in tomorrow. You've got to bring in Matthew. We've got to get this straightened out.' Well, *tomorrow* was March twenty-second. *Tomorrow* was the day that Matthew got shot.

". . . There will be evidence that she asked people at

Regions Bank before March twenty-second, perhaps the day before: 'Can I take my husband off the account?'

" 'You can't take your husband off the account, because there is a negative balance.' This was not a good reason to kill Matthew Winkler, but the state's proof will be that it informed her mind and formed the intent that she had after her sleepless night on March twenty-first, knowing that that next day Matthew and she had to go to the bank and get her problems straightened out."

Freeland summarized the ballistics and medical examiner's evidence and then said, "[Y]ou will hear evidence that there were seventy-seven number six steel birdshot recovered from Matthew's body. That shotgun blast blew apart his ribs. That it perforated his ribs, his lung, his diaphragm, his stomach, his spleen, his pancreas and his adrenal glands. That his ribs were fragmented and thrown throughout the inside of his body, causing him to bleed to death. And you will hear testimony from her that despite these massive injuries, that Matthew Winkler could have lived for several minutes after this. That the shot was from one to three feet from the end of the muzzle to his back."

He informed the jury that they would hear testimony from Matthew's oldest daughter and what she saw on the morning of her father's death. "You will also hear testimony that some months later, months after this event, months after the charge, Mary is at an establishment in McMinnville. A man walks in and says, 'We got a preacher killer here? Are you the lady who killed the preacher?' And you will hear testimony that she laughed and said, 'You wanna be next?' "

At the defense table, Mary's mouth formed the word "Wow!"

"You will not be given a good reason why, but the state will show you ample evidence that Mary Winkler willfully, unlawfully and intentionally killed Matthew Winkler. A man that did not deserve to die."

Freeland delivered even the most emotion-laden words in a matter-of-fact fashion. He addressed the predominately female jury without passion or outrage. He seemed incapable of summoning the energy required to express animated concern for the 31-year-old man who was dead, or for the three little girls who no longer had a father.

CHAPTER 35

In a black suit and a red tie, Steve Farese stalked to the podium with the pent-up energy of a Thoroughbred delayed at the starting gate. As he began to speak, his face distorted as if he were pained by what he had to say. "Good morning. Matthew and Mary Winkler had what appeared to everyone who observed them—those on the outside—to have had a marriage made in heaven. But behind closed doors, it was a living hell.

"As I listen to the prosecution submit to you that they were going to have a child eight years old at the time on that stand to testify, it breaks my heart," Farese said looking as if he would cry.

Walt Freeland jumped to his feet. "Objection. May we approach, Your Honor?"

After a brief sidebar, Farese continued. "If that does occur, it should break your heart. Because this child has been kept away from her mother since September of 2006. Her own mother, who was out on bond, could not see her." His voice raised an octave, his emotions obvious.

"A child who reportedly saw nothing when first interviewed, now has seen everything. A child who loved her mother, who wanted to touch her mother, who wanted to be with her mother, who wanted her mother to be found innocent, who hoped that this was an accident, now hates her mother. That should break your heart.

"The proof will show that these three girls were Mary's only reason for living. They were her flowers. They were her ray of sunshine each day. Because a huge cloud loomed over that household. Mary Carol and Matthew were married after dating from July of 1995 to October of 1995. August, September, October, Matthew asked her to marry him after three months of dating. That's a whirlwind romance. But he was handsome. He was charismatic. He was the perfect husband—until they married.

"And then, like many marriages, people find out there are differences. That would not be unusual, but these differences were unusual. And I submit to you that we will show you proof that he would destroy objects that she loved. He would isolate her from her family. And he would abuse her. Not just verbally. Not just emotionally. Not just physically. In other ways, too. And that this was constant.

"And she lived a life where she walked on eggshells. Because Matthew was wrestling with his demons, too. He had a father that he couldn't satisfy. A father who was well-known, respected, legendary in the Church. But didn't give Matthew what he needed—positive reinforcement. He gave him negative reinforcement. And Mary knew that was hard on Matthew. And Mary took it."

Farese backtracked, offering, with tenderness, a portrait of Mary growing up in a strict household, experiencing the death of a sister and welcoming her adopted siblings into her home. He then returned to her marriage.

"The proof will show that Matthew Winkler, whenever things did not suit him—his shirts weren't ironed correctly, if the car wouldn't start, if something didn't work—Mary was his whipping boy. He didn't like the way she talked. He didn't like the way she walked. He didn't like it because she was too fat. He would tell her she couldn't eat lunch because she was too fat. She wasn't perfect and she had to be perfect, because she was a preacher's wife. And not only did she have to be perfect, her children had to be perfect."

Farese complained about the time the state spent talking about Mary's financial motivation for shooting Matthew, then said, "I submit to you, the proof will show, yes, Mary wrote almost every check, because Mary did everything Matthew said to do. The proof will show that Mary was not the academic. That Mary's not the smart one in the family. Matthew was the smart person, and we'll submit to you the proof to show you that. No, Matthew did not sign those checks, because Matthew always set up Mary to fail.

"Their finances were in shambles—and who do you think got blamed for that? Mary did try to get Matthew's name off that so it wouldn't affect Matthew's credit. That was his thinking. We'll submit to you proof that he told Mary to set up her own account so if bad checks, insufficient funds, came back, it would not be on his account, and to get his name off that account. We will submit proof to you from that stand, from people that say Mary did nothing without Matthew's approval. That Matthew was in control. She would not lift a finger unless Matthew said to. That she couldn't get her hair cut unless Matthew said she could get her hair cut. She could not buy Christmas presents for the children unless Matthew said so."

He criticized the Tennessee Bureau of Investigation's policy to not perform audio or video recording of statements. He spoke of his gratitude to Alabama's investigative bureau, which did tape-record the first interview, because it showed Mary's state of mind more clearly. "She wasn't thinking about herself. She was thinking about her children—and one other thing, something that had been more important to her before March twenty-second, 2006, than anything else: protect Matthew's name.

"She will say it more than once. 'I don't want his name smeared.' 'There's no sense in his name being smeared.' Every time they asked her what happened, I submit to you the proof will show, she said, 'I can't talk about that right now.' 'I don't want this to go public.' She was still protecting her children from knowing about their father. And was protecting her husband in his death. She said, 'Let me take all the blame.' 'Put it on me.' She was still in that mode, 'Put it on me.' As long as the children are okay, 'Put it on me.'

"Because, ladies and gentlemen, she could take what had been dished out to her. She could take it. She thought that was the way it was going to be. Nobody knew about it, because she hid it—except for a couple things. Whenever you have a secret, there's always a few clues that slip out. I don't care how careful you are. There's always a few clues that slip out.

"Taken one by one, I would submit, those clues don't mean anything. But when you put them together, they do. Trips to the doctor for a swollen jaw. A black eye not covered up adequately with makeup. Little things. Not being able to buy your own clothes. Little things that can be found on computers. Little things that add up to her existence— but she took it.

". . . Mary can take it for herself, but she could not let her children take it for her. You will hear from the stand what happened on the morning of March twenty-second of 2006. Mary had always tried to talk to Matthew about his problems. She loved him. I don't know why. She loved him. She wanted him to change. To be a better person. She thought he had it in him. They had three children. All she wanted to do was talk to him.

"Mary'd been threatened before. She'd had that shotgun pointed at her before. He threatened to cut her brake lines. He threatened to cut her into a million pieces if she talked back to Matthew the way that one of Matthew's brother's wives talked back to him."

That morning, Farese said, ". . . she was going to get his attention. And there was only one way to get his attention—with the very thing that he'd always threatened her with—the only thing that he appeared at six-foot-one and two hundred and forty pounds to fear. The shotgun."

Farese described the events of that morning, bringing Mary to tears. He pointed to his client and said, "Mary was invisible. She lived in a shadow. Mary was a second-class citizen. Matthew Winkler was the face of that family. He was the preacher. He was the important one. He was the handsome one. He was the charismatic one. And he was the mean one.

"Nobody was going to believe Mary—in her mind, at that time—about what happened. Nobody was going to believe Mary. So Mary thought about one thing, and that was her children. She grabbed them up. She didn't grab clothes. She didn't grab anything of any importance that would indicate planning. And she left."

He discussed Mary's frenzied trip south, the upcoming mental health testimony and Mary's inability to see the children. Then he wrapped up his statement. "You will be the judges of, number one, whether a crime was committed. And number two, if so, what crime was committed. There was no premeditation, and there'll be no proof of it. There was no planning, and there'll be no proof of it. They had to come up with something. And I submit to you they're trying to use these finances in the record that had nothing to do with it.

"Proof will show that now they have some guy who comes up and said, 'Are you the preacher killer?' They're trying to use that for proof, because they didn't have any. They're trying to use her own daughter against her, because they've turned that love into hate.

"Mary may not be a perfect person. But Mary Winkler was a good wife and a good mother. Unfortunately, she wasn't perfect."

Throughout, Farese's voice was lyrical, alternating between poignancy and outrage. When he spoke of his client, he often almost whispered, caressing each word. At other times, when he talked about the deceased victim, he shouted and pounded his fist on the podium. With the power of his emotions, Farese planted the first seeds of sympathy for Mary in the hearts of the jurors. He would tend that garden well throughout the trial.

CHAPTER 36

The prosecution called its first witness to the stand, Matthew Winkler's father, Dan. Dan sat with an erect posture in a black suit and black-and-silver tie, with his hands folded in his lap. He nodded frequently. His spoke in a confident, calm tone of voice with little or no apparent emotion. But his face gave his heart away. A bright red flush highlighted his cheekbones, and intensity burned deep in his eyes.

Freeland guided him as he related his background and the family biography. He then helped Dan recount the night of his birthday in 2006, when he learned of the death of his son. Dan spoke about being informed that his daughter-in-law was responsible for Matthew's death, his first meeting with her at the jail, his reunion with his granddaughters and how he learned about his son's adverse reactions to drugs on two occasions. Freeland then questioned him about how he was caring for Matt's children. "At some point after you and your wife got custody of your grandchildren and started to raise them, I guess, as your own, did you attempt to get them any therapy?"

Dan nodded and said, "Immediately."

"And who paid for the therapy?"

"We did until TennCare [Tennessee's Medicaid program] kicked in."

"Did you tell the therapist to plant anything in the little girls' minds?" Freeland asked.

"Absolutely not."

". . . When you were with the children, at home, when you weren't working, did you attempt to influence them or poison their minds against their mother in any way?"

"We have not," Dan declared without hesitation.

"Are you aware of whether or not your wife did?"

"Not in my presence, and if I know her, no."

"How do they, at least, appear to be doing now?" Freeland asked about the children.

"Incredibly well."

"Now, Mr. Winkler, I'm going to ask you: Are you a party to a lawsuit in which you are suing Mary?"

"Yes, sir, on behalf of the children."

"Is your testimony today in any way affected by the money you hope to get out of that lawsuit?"

"Absolutely not."

Freeland switched gears. "Do you have any knowledge from what you observed as to who ran the finances in your son's household?"

"Yes sir. Mary."

"Mary?" Freeland asked with a slight overtone of incredulousness.

"Mary."

"Do you know that was just a default on Matthew's part, or how do you know, if you know, how that came about?"

"Several years ago, Matthew was involved in an automobile accident in Nashville, Tennessee. A lady was under the influence of either alcohol or drugs and rear-ended his car, and they received a financial settlement for that. And he was sharing this with me and was thankful for what he was able to do. From that financial settlement, he said, he was able to call all his creditors . . ."

Farese interrupted. "Objection, Your Honor. Can we approach?"

"That's okay," Freeland said. "I'll withdraw that question. But do you know from anything other than what Matthew told you that Mary was in charge of finances? Did Mary ever indicate anything to you, or did you ever make any observations independent of Matthew about her being in control?"

"I suggested to my son on one occasion, that it would be . . ."

Farese spoke up again, "Objection, Your Honor. Non-responsive."

"That's all right. I withdraw the question," Freeland said again, and then turned back to his witness. "Are you aware of anything you personally observed of any physical abuse by Matthew of Mary?"

"Not at all."

"Are you aware from what you personally observed of anything that could, in any way, be described as emotional abuse of Mary by Matthew?"

"Not at all."

"And by emotional abuse, I'm including even something like nagging, carping or complaining, or anything of that nature by Matthew to Mary?"

"Not in our presence."

"What was your observation of Matthew growing up in that regard, did you observe any physical abuse by Matthew to anybody?"

"No, sir."

"Did you observe any emotional sort of abuse by Matthew to anybody?"

"No, sir."

"Now, children of ministers and preachers often have the reputation, perhaps, of being hellions growing up, when they spread their wings. Did you ever observe anything of that in Matthew?"

"No, sir," Dan said with a soft smile.

One member of the press was tossed from the courtroom that day. Ted Parks, a correspondent with *The Christian Chronicle*, a publication of the churches of Christ, refused to follow instructions from the judge.

He had a noisy still camera and kept jumping up in the back, snapping pictures and being disruptive. Judge

McCraw spoke to media liaison Sue Allison about this annoyance. Sue brought Ted out into the hall to tell him it had to stop.

Sue barely had time to sit down in the courtroom before Ted was at it again. The judge gestured with his thumb to Sue to "Get him out of here." Sue got up to deal with the problem. Ted saw her coming and snapped shots off as fast as he could. McCraw later said that it reminded him ". . . of a child stuffing candy into his mouth as fast as possible to get as much as he could before his mom stopped him."

Out in the hall, Ted taunted Sue. "I got everything I wanted already anyway." He went into the media room, where he snapped shots of the Court TV monitors before deputies escorted him out of the building. He was the only reporter Sue had to rebuke throughout the trial.

CHAPTER 37

The tone in the courtroom changed dramatically when cross-examination began. Dan faced the man who just be-smirched his son's character in front of the jury and video cameras during opening arguments.

Farese began with a polite, solicitous and considerate demeanor. He obviously wanted to position himself as the nice guy in the coming confrontation—a brief prelude to the verbal attack awaiting the witness. The ominous ap-proach of severe questioning hung in the air.

With the niceties aside, Farese asked Dan a series of questions to get him to admit that his oldest son, Daniel, had marital problems at one time. The relevance of that badgering was not apparent. Then Farese moved to the events immediately after Matthew's death. "You were in-terviewed by the police concerning what you knew about the disappearance, and about what you knew were going on at the time?"

"Yes, sir."

"Okay. And you gave them a statement? Or they took information from you—that would probably be a fair statement, wouldn't it?"

"Yes."

"Yes. Did you say anything to them—in all fairness to you, Mr. Winkler, you may not have had any reason to—did you say anything to them about Matthew having episodes while taking medications . . ."

"No, sir."

". . . that you recall?" said Farese, finishing his incomplete sentence.

"No, sir."

"So it wouldn't be in your report?"

"No, sir."

"But evidently, since then, you have given statements to someone concerning Matthew having episodes while on medication, bizarre actions, or whatever, I think hallucinations—and I apologize, sir. You had to tell someone that in order for Mr. Freeland to ask you that question, correct?"

"Correct," Dan said with a nod.

"So who did you tell first? Who was the first person you told about Matthew's hallucinations?"

"The former district attorney, Elizabeth Rice."

"Okay, and when did you tell her?"

"I cannot recall the exact date," Dan said.

"Well, was it a time while she was still in office?"

"Yes."

"Okay. Who else was present?"

"It was a phone conversation."

"Why did that issue come up? Why did the issue about Matthew's bizarre behavior come up in that telephone conversation?" Farese asked.

"Because of quotes from either you or your comrade in the newspapers."

"Okay. And my comrade? Meaning, Mr. Ballin?"

"Correct."

"The other defense attorney?"

"Yes."

"So you read in the newspaper, what? What were the comments?"

"That there was some life-threatening . . ." Dan began.

Prosecutor Freeland stood and interrupted. "I'm going to object to getting into prejudiced statements that he made . . ."

"Would you approach, please?" Judge McCraw asked.

After two minutes at the bar, Farese resumed the cross-examination. "Mr. Winkler, if you could listen to my question carefully—without saying what you read—did you call Ms. Rice as a result of reading some article in the newspaper?"

"No, sir," Dan answered, looking confused. "I don't recall. Would you state your question again?"

"And I may be misstating it. I think I know where you're going," Farese said. "You had an opportunity to talk to Ms. Rice concerning the reaction that Matthew had with some medications, correct?"

"Yes, sir."

"Okay. Did you call her, or did she call you?"

"I can't remember that."

"You all had a telephone conversation, though?"

"Yes, sir."

"And whoever called whom, it was concerning some things you read in the newspaper concerning Matthew. Without going into details, what exactly was said?"

"The phone call was not for that specific purpose."

"Did it come up in that conversation?"

"Yes, it did."

"And, as a result of that, did Ms. Rice ask you, 'Did Matthew ever exhibit any violent tendencies?'"

"I can't recall the details of the conversation," Dan said, shaking his head.

"Okay, but you felt it necessary to explain some of his bizarre actions during that conversation?"

"I felt it necessary to respond to what had been said in the newspaper."

"Okay, what were you trying to explain to Ms. Rice? You talked about an incident in Pegram. What happened in Pegram?"

"What I said happened earlier," Dan replied with a defiant thrust of his chin.

"And I'm asking you again, what happened?" Farese followed with testiness in his voice.

"That he had taken medication for a tooth problem. And had an adverse reaction, and had hallucinated thinking someone was trying to kill him."

"As a result of that, he did what toward Mary?"

"Locked her out of the house."

"So that's it?" Farese said, disbelief etching the edges of his words. "That's all that happened? He locked her out of the house?"

"To my knowledge."

"There may have been some things that happened that's beyond your knowledge?"

"Certainly."

"Certainly. Now, there was a second occasion that this happened. Where did this happen?"

"In McMinnville, Tennessee."

"And what happened, what was your understanding of what happened, in McMinnville?"

"That again, a strong drug was given to him for a stomach problem that caused an adverse reaction of hallucinating."

"Okay. How did these hallucinations manifest themselves?"

"The same way."

"So he locked her out of the house again?"

"No, sir, where he thought that someone was going to kill him."

"So how did he act out toward Mary?"

"I do not know," Dan said with a tight shake of his head.

"Okay. Now, you would agree with me that these revelations are not written down anywhere, correct? The revelations about the remembering about Matthew's reaction?"

"I have no knowledge of whether they are written down or not."

"Well, did you think they were important to help explain his actions?"

"I thought they were important enough to express to the former D.A."

"To the former D.A., but not to any agent or policeman or investigator or anything else?"

"No, because my conversations with them were prior to the statement in the newspaper."

"I understand that. But what I'm saying is, you didn't reach out to any TBI agent, to any FBI agent, any Selmer police officer to talk about this?"

"I went directly to the district attorney."

"Directly to the district attorney. When she was the district attorney?"

"That is correct."

"Mr. Winkler, you said when you went to see Mary at the jail, you said, 'I'm so sorry for all of this,' correct?"

"Yes, sir, 'I'm so sorry for this' or 'for all of this' or 'I'm so sorry.'"

"That sounds like something that Mary would have said to you, doesn't it?" Puzzlement furrowed his brow.

"Should have."

"But you're saying that Mary said nothing to you."

"No, sir. Not to my recollection."

"Okay. Are you saying that Mary," swinging his arm to his client, "didn't tell you that she was so sorry for all of this?"

"I'm saying that she did not say that to me."

Farese moved on to the trust fund that had been set up for the benefit of the Winkler children. He insinuated that the fund was not legitimate or above board because a family friend, Eddie Thompson of Thompson and Associates managed the fund. He also questioned the use of the funds. "Have you never asked your dear friend, Mr. Thompson, how much money is in that fund?"

"On purpose, I have not."

"But you're saying, therefore, that no money has been expended from the fund?"

"There has been a recent trip to Disney World that the trustees asked if we would like to take. And outside of that, to my knowledge, there has been no expense taken out of the fund."

"When you say the trustees suggested for you all to take a trip to Disney World, is that correct?"

"Yes, sir."

In an incredulous tone, Farese said, "They just came up and said, 'You know, we've got a lot of money in this fund, it may be just a good idea for you to go to Disneyland' [sic]?"

"They asked us if we wanted to do so, on spring break."

"The reason I'm saying that was—was that also a time when Mary was trying to see her children?"

After a long pause, Dan said, "Be more specific, please."

"What I'm saying is: It's difficult for Mary to see her children because they are in school, correct?"

"Correct."

"You all didn't want to disrupt their school, their regular school schedule, correct?"

"Correct."

"So, if the children were going to be out of school, spring break would be a good time for Mary to get to see her children, correct?"

"Would be a possibility," Dan said, nodding his head.

At the prosecution's objection, the testimony was again interrupted. After the sidebar, Farese continued to belabor the same point, implying that the only purpose of the trip to Disney World was to prevent Mary from visiting the children. Farese insisted and Dan denied that Mary's attempts to see her children were constant.

The court recessed for lunch. After the break, Farese delved into questions about the temporary custody agreement. He accused Dan and his attorney of misleading Mary about the permanence of the situation. He then turned to the two-million-dollar civil lawsuit. "You know Mary doesn't have any money, don't you?"

"Yes, sir."

"So you're suing her because—why?" Farese asked.

"Punitive and compensatory damages."

"I understand. But you know she doesn't have any money?"

"Not currently."

"Okay. So, what you want to do is make sure she never has any money."

"That she doesn't benefit from these proceedings," Dan insisted.

In a testy tone of voice, Farese snapped back, "What I'm saying is, you want to make sure that she never has any money, yes or no?"

"No, sir."

"Yes or no?"

"No."

"Well, if she has any money, and you all are suing her for it, and if you all were to get a judgment, you would take that money. Is that correct?"

"If anything came from these proceedings, yes, on behalf of the children."

"But that's not what the lawsuit says; the lawsuit says nothing about coming from this proceeding, does it?"

"No, sir. It says 'compensatory and punitive damages.' "

"For the death of Matthew Winkler?"

"Correct."

Farese battered Dan again, his voice becoming more strident with each phrase. "You don't want her to have any future, you don't want her to have any dreams, you don't want her to have any money, you don't want her to have her children, do you?"

"I don't know that you can say that," Dan objected.

"I just did, sir," Farese retorted. "I'm asking you a question."

"Okay, repeat the question, please."

"Do you want her to have her children?"

"When?"

"Today."

"No, sir."

Farese approached the witness with a document in his

hand. "Again, Mr. Winkler, this is a legal document that appears to be the complaint we've been talking about, isn't it?"

Dan glanced down at it and said, "Yes."

"It is about punitive and compensatory damages."

"It is."

"Is that correct?"

"Yes, it is."

Farese moved to have the wrongful death civil suit document entered into evidence. Prosecutor Freeland objected on grounds of relevance. Once again, the attorneys gathered at the bench. Judge McCraw ruled in favor of the defense and the document was admitted.

Farese switched his questioning to another topic. "Now, in the Church of Christ, who is the head of the household?"

"The Bible says that the husband is."

"Now, my question is, in the Church of Christ, who is the head of the household?"

"If you go by what the Bible says, the husband is."

Farese refused to concede that the question was asked and answered until he got an answer without any caveats. "My question is, in the Church of Christ, who is the head of the household?"

"The husband is," Dan finally obliged.

"Thank you," Farese said with a nod. "If the husband is the head of the household, what does that entail? What is contemplated by the meaning of 'the head of the household'?"

"That he sets directions for the family dynamic . . ."

"And," Farese began, and then stopped. "Excuse me, sir."

Dan continued, "While at the same time, according to what the Bible teaches, he cherishes his wife and honors her."

"But he is the boss of the house?"

"He sets the dynamic for the direction of the family. What do you mean by 'boss'?"

"Who decides what goes on in that household?"

"The husband takes into consideration and then if there is a disagreement, I don't know that there is any policy says that he has to have his way, but the husband is the one that has to set the direction."

"He would be the one who would be making the decision as to whether he would be consenting to his wife," Farese testified, and then asked, "Do you have woman preachers in the Church of Christ?"

"No, sir."

"And why is that?"

Freeland objected to the line of questioning about theology or religion.

Farese snapped back like a tattle-tale kid, "Sounds like a talking objection, Your Honor. Just what you told him not to do a couple of minutes ago."

The judge didn't comment on that, but told the attorneys to approach for a sidebar. After that conference, Farese switched to a line of questioning about a piece of evidence found in Mary's mini-van that the state did not plan to enter as an exhibit because of its dubious chain of custody. "You understand that vehicle was the subject—before it was given to you—of a homicide investigation?"

"I did not understand that."

"You did not understand that?"

"No, sir."

"Well, I mean, the vehicle was searched and inventoried by the Alabama Bureau of Investigation and the Tennessee Bureau of Investigation."

Shaking his head, Dan said, "I never gave it a single thought."

"Well, today, do you know that happened?"

"I never gave it a single thought."

"Well, today, do you know that happened or not?" Farese persisted.

"Yes, sir."

"Well, so you know that the Alabama Bureau of Investigation and the Tennessee Bureau of Investigation had both searched that vehicle. Correct? You know that today?"

"Yes, sir."

"Did you call anyone with the TBI on or about April the sixth, 2006, and tell them that you found something in that vehicle?"

"No, sir. I did not call TBI."

With his impatience etching every word, Farese rephrased the question. "Did you call any of the authorities on or about April sixth 2006, and say you found anything in the van?"

"Yes, I called former District Attorney Elizabeth Rice."

"Ms. Rice is the same one you talked to about Matthew's problems with medicine that's not listed anywhere? Is that correct?"

"Yes sir. That is correct."

"Did you tell them that you had recovered an orange tackle box with shotgun shells in that vehicle?"

"I did."

"Shotgun shells?"

"In the back of the van when we were . . ."

Farese interrupted. "The tailgate on that van lifts up, is that correct?"

"Yes, sir."

"And then there's a space between the seats—the seats you sit in. To the best of your recollection . . . was it under anything?"

"Yes, it was under a lot of things."

"Clothing?"

"I don't recall clothing. There was a stroller and beach toys . . . Those were the items that I recall right offhand."

Just so I'm straight on this—after the TBI and the ABI had conducted their search and investigation in this case, you found an orange box with shotgun shells?"

"Yes, sir, that is correct."

Farese next asked Dan about Diana Crawford, the counselor in Nashville who'd been seeing the children since May of 2006. "Do you remember speaking to Ms. Crawford on or about October sixteenth, 2006, and telling Ms. Crawford that you had spoken to the D.A.

about Mary's visitation with her children? Do you recall that?"

"I did not call to speak to the D.A. about Mary's visitation."

"That's not my question. Did you speak to the counselor and tell her that the district attorney wanted visitation with Mary ratcheted down? Because the district attorney was concerned with the tampering of witnesses and Mary's persona. Did you say anything of the like to the children's counselor?"

"I received a phone call in reference to an article in a magazine."

"Keep going," Farese urged.

" 'Keep going'?"

"I want you to tell the jury what you told the counselor about Mary being able to visit her children and why you were cutting off visitation with them."

"I didn't say I was going to do that," Dan said in the same calm voice he'd maintained throughout the cross-examination.

"What does 'ratchet down' mean?" Farese asked.

"Those were not my words."

"Yes or no, were those the words you gave to the counselor?"

"Yes, sir, and the reason for that was the danger of trying this case in the media."

"I thought the reason was the danger, if Mary was seen with her children, she would be considered as a loving mother, am I wrong?" Farese countered.

The state objected again and the attorneys whispered arguments to the judge. Upon returning, Farese asked, "My question, Mr. Winkler, is, What does 'persona of Mary' mean to you?"

After a long pause, Dan said, "The way she's perceived, I guess."

"The way she's perceived. Would you agree with me that if she's seen with her children, she may be perceived as a loving mother?"

"Depending on how she acts, yes."

"Yes, sir. Did you also tell the counselor that the D.A. wanted visitation ratcheted down? Did you tell the counselor that?"

"He did not say 'visitation ratcheted down,'" Dan said stubbornly, sticking to a strict compliance with exact words.

"Whose words are those?"

"He did not say those words."

"Whose words are those?"

"He said 'contact ratcheted down.'"

"Contact?" Farese parroted with an incredulous look on his face.

"Yes, sir."

"Do you agree that that would have been on or about October sixteenth, 2006?"

"I would say it would be whenever that article came out in the magazine."

"Did you tell Ms. Crawford that an article came out in *Glamour* magazine depicting your son as domineering, overbearing and abusive by Mary's sisters and father? Did you tell her that?"

"I told her that there was an article in there, and I faxed her that article."

"Listen to my question," Farese commanded.

"Okay."

"'Cause I'll ask you a hundred and fifty times until you do answer."

"Yes, sir, I will listen carefully."

"Did you tell Ms. Crawford that there was a major article in *Glamour* magazine depicting your son as domineering, overbearing and abusive by Mary's sisters and father? Yes or no?"

"I'd have to say yes, I guess. I don't recall the exact words, I'm sorry."

"If that occurred on October sixteenth, 2006, would you agree with me that Mary has not seen her children since that day?"

"That's correct—or before."

Farese shot him a wide-eyed look of disbelief. "You sure you want to say that? You want to say 'or before'? I'm going to give you another shot here."

"Okay."

"You want to take that back?"

"Okay, ask your question again, please."

"Okay. When was the last time Mary saw her children?"

With a thrust of his jaw, Dan said, "That was not your question. I asked you to repeat your question."

"This is the way it goes, I get to ask what questions I want to."

"I thought . . ."

Farese cut him off. "Nobody controls me."

"Can I ask you to repeat a question?"

"Yes, you can ask me to repeat a question. Has Mary seen her children since October sixteenth, 2006?"

"No, sir."

"And then you added 'or before that.' "

"And you asked me . . ."

"Do you want to reconsider that?"

"I'll retract that," Dan conceded.

"Thank you. 'Cause that was not the true answer, was it?" Farese continued badgering Dan about visitation for several more minutes.

After this exchange in a cross that by now had lasted three times the length of the direct examination, Farese consulted with attorneys at his table, and Dan whispered a request for a drink of water to the deputy. Farese, whose previous attempt to bring in religion as a point for the defense was stopped, now crept up to the topic again. In reference to counselor Diana Crawford, he asked, "Does her group have a name?"

"Agape," Dan said with a nod.

"What's 'agape'?"

"You mean its location?"

Farese shook his head. "What does 'agape' mean?"

"It's the Greek word for 'love.' "

"Is it a church organization?"

"It's affiliated with the churches of Christ, but I don't know that you'd call it a church organization. I say it's affiliated with the churches of Christ, because monies from the church help support its existence, I guess."

"They rely upon donations that are collected through the Church of Christ."

"Well, they're helped by them."

Farese and Dan exchanged dueling versions of the reactions of the children to seeing Mary in September and the scheduling of an additional visit. After an objection from the prosecution led to another sidebar, Farese continued. "On the day that Mary saw her children, how long did she get to see them?"

"Two hours."

"Who was dictating how long she got to see her children?"

"This was a visit that *we* made available."

"Who was dictating how long she got to see her children?" Farese repeated.

"My wife and I, I guess."

Farese conferred again with co-counsel and then continued. "Mary sent letters to her children, did she not?"

"Could I qualify my last answer?" Dan asked.

"If you need to explain your last answer, I have no objection, sir."

"The two hours was something, I believe, the therapist recommended in the best interest of the children."

After that, Farese accused and Dan denied that Mary's letters were always withheld from the children and her phone calls were never answered. "Our agreement," Dan explained, "was a letter one week and a phone call the next, on Tuesday, and if we weren't present on Tuesday, a phone call on Thursday."

"Whose agreement was that? When you say 'agreement,' that sounds like two people agree to something."

"That's something we set up with Mary while she was in jail."

"But Mary wasn't in jail. Mary was out of jail."

"That's something we set up with Mary while she was in jail here in Selmer," Dan repeated.

"But when Mary got out of jail, she wanted to see her children? Correct?"

"I would say that would be the case."

"What do you mean, you 'would say that would be the case'?" Farese said in a voice dripping with disgust. "That *was* the case, wasn't it?"

"All right, yes."

Farese jerked his papers off the podium and said, "Nothing further," and turned his back on the witness.

CHAPTER 38

The state next called Kacey Broadway to the stand. She worked at Selmer Elementary as a teachers' assistant at the time of Matthew's death. She testified that the day before, Mary spent a lot of time on her cell phone, pacing back and forth, crying and looking distressed.

The witness following her was Doctor Drew Eason, family physician, church elder and Matthew's friend. On direct examination, he recounted the evening when he discovered his preacher's body in the parsonage.

On cross, Farese was more interested in eliciting testimony about Mary's medical condition. "You remember that I asked you last time [at the suppression hearing] a question about her swollen jaw? You remember that question?"

"Yes, sir."

"And of course, you didn't have your records, and you were going to go back and check them. Did you in fact treat her for a severely swollen jaw?"

"I would not describe it as 'severely.' I'm sure it was severe to Mary. It was swollen. She had some swelling of the jaw."

"And what caused the swelling of the jaw?"

"I felt at that time, it was likely due to an infected tooth."

"Is that what caused that swollen jaw?"

"I believe it was."

"Do you know what caused that swollen jaw?"

"I believe it was an infected tooth," Drew reiterated.

When the witness stated that he did not recall the time of the day or night he saw her, Farese asked if his records would reflect that information. Drew said that they should.

Farese then asked, "So on the day that I'm going to show you— Do you have your records with you?"

"I brought some of them."

"Did you say you brought some of your records?"

"In the D.A.'s office. Because my office staff copied them for me, for me to bring."

Farese approached the witness with a document in hand. It was clearly labeled "Mary Alice Winkler" rather than "Mary Carol Winkler." The attorney hammered at the doctor because the record of the visit was filed in Allie's medical folder rather than Mary's. When Drew acknowledged the mistake, Farese asked, "Down toward the bottom, you have 'assessment' and 'new problems.' Would you tell the jury what your assessment is?"

"Abscess with cellulitis," the doctor read, and then explained, " 'Cellulitis,' which means an infection of the skin. 'Abscess' would mean an infection, which could be a pocket of pus, is what could relate to an abscessed tooth— this is kind of non-specific—it could also relate to an abscess, a pocket of pus within the skin. But uh, at the time, I did feel that it was due to a tooth."

"The reason I'm asking you, is that before, you didn't remember treating her at all, do you remember that?"

"I vaguely remembered that at the time."

"What I'm saying is, now why do you remember today why you thought it was an abscess of the tooth?" Farese asked.

"I hadn't thought about it much at the time. I did recall and had a conversation with my wife about that when we got home. And we were talking about that. Mary was going to go see her dentist in McMinnville."

"Here's what I want to know, Doctor. Did you have independent recollection of whether you thought it was an abscessed tooth, or is this something your wife told you?"

"Both."

"Okay. Fair enough. But one thing that we would know, there would be certain things that would jump out at us that would tell us that this is not a child's report, would you agree with me?"

"Yes," Drew concurred.

"Especially on the prescription that was given."

"Correct."

"And what was the prescription that was given?"

"Z-Pak, which is an antibiotic, and a pain pill, hydrocodone and prednisone."

"Which is . . . ?"

"A steroid."

"So the prednisone and the hydrocodone would stand out to me as something that wouldn't be prescribed for a minor, is that correct?"

"That's correct. In some cases, we do prescribe steroids for minors, but not in the tablet form, and not to Allie."

"Now, this was signed by you on seven-fifty A.M. on June the first, 2005, correct?"

"That's correct."

"My copy's not really signed, but that is what's stated on the document, correct?"

"That's correct."

"Okay, and that may be the way you signed it. Which means that would have been around Memorial Day, 2005? Is that correct?"

"If that's when that was."

"Sounds correct, doesn't it?" Farese said, continuing to push for confirmation.

"Yes, sir."

"If someone had come in your office and wanted to find Mary Carol Winkler's records, how would they have found them?"

"She does have a record; this particular note was not in there."

"All the other records were complete and there was nothing of any significance, regular visits, cold, flu, things like that, correct?"

"That's correct."

Drew knew that Farese was attempting to make it appear as if he deliberately concealed that note. He knew he hadn't, but he didn't know how to get that across without sounding defensive.

Once again, Farese pursued the point of the Winklers' religion. "Now, if I belonged to the Church of Christ—you were asked a question by Mr. Freeland about brothers in Christ and counseling—and I wanted to get a divorce, what would be the acceptable problem that I could get a divorce from?"

"Adultery."

"And . . . ?" After a pause, Farese added, "That's pretty much it, isn't it?"

"That's pretty much it," Drew said with a nod.

"If you don't have adultery, you can't get a divorce that's accepted by the Church. Is that correct?"

"We don't expect people to live under certain situations, but in order to, the Church of Christ does believe to have an acceptable divorce so that it would be acceptable for someone to get remarried, would be adultery."

"In other words, you could get divorced, but you just couldn't get remarried for other reasons?"

"Yes. We believe that the only way divorce would be right is adultery."

"I understand, sir. If a minister for a Church of Christ was accused of domestic violence, would that affect his employment with the Church?"

"Yes."

"Did you know Mary Winkler?"

"As well as most men in the congregation would know Mary Winkler."

"What kind of person was Mary Winkler?"

"She seemed to be a nice, friendly lady."

"Compared to Matthew Winkler's personality, how

would Matthew's personality compare to Mary's personality?"

"I think Matthew was much more outgoing," Drew said.

Next to the stand was Investigator Roger Rickman with the Selmer Police Department. Through his testimony, the prosecution entered photographs from the crime scene as exhibits—including a close-up of Matthew's face with the bloody foam coming from his mouth. As the shots were displayed on a large screen in the front of the room, Mary bent her head and sobbed. Lawyer Leslie Ballin patted her on the shoulder.

"Were the wife and three children there in the house?" Freeland asked.

"No," Rickman answered.

"Did this cause you some concern?"

"Yes, sir." Rickman related calling in the Tennessee Bureau of Investigation to process what was obviously a suspicious death.

Ballin conducted the cross-examination. He swaggered to the podium with a feisty air, as if ready to pick a fight with anyone willing. His shaggy brown hair brushed his collar and hung down to his basset eyes. A prominent nose jutted out over a thick moustache, and his chin seemed to have a permanent dark bristle even in the morning.

He immediately attacked the reliability of Rickman's report. The officer disputed Ballin's contention that it was inaccurate because of the presence of a typographical error. Ballin then asked him if he knew how the family photo got into magazines, but Rickman denied any knowledge of that.

On re-direct, Rickman testified that there were no police calls to the Winklers' address in regards to domestic violence. On re-cross, he had to admit that just because the police were not called, does not mean that nothing happened.

Officer Jason Whitlock of the Orange Beach Police Department stepped into the stand to describe Mary's arrest and the recovery of the girls. On cross, Farese asked, "You would agree with me that before Ms. Winkler said anything to anyone about herself or her predicament, she asked y'all to make sure the children could get something to eat?"

"Correct."

"First thing?"

"First thing."

"After a gun's pulled on her?" Farese said with incredulity.

"Yes, sir."

Another Orange Beach officer, Travis Long, stepped in the box. He confirmed the statements of his fellow officer and testified that although there was an audio recording of the arrest, there was no video because of the angle of the camera on the police car.

And with the end of Long's testimony, the first day of court recessed just before 6:30 that evening.

CHAPTER 39

At 8:15 Friday morning, day two of the trial began. The first witness was Investigator Stan Stabler, who worked for the Alabama Bureau of Investigation at the time of Mary's arrest in Orange Beach. His presence on the stand paved the way to introduce the audio recording of his interview with Mary Winkler. The judge admonished the jurors to listen carefully to the tape and promised them that a transcript would be provided.

After playing the complete tape, the judge called a brief recess. When court resumed, Freeland produced the murder weapon and handed it to his witness. Stabler verified that it was the shotgun that he personally retrieved from Mary's van.

Steve Farese approached the witness for cross-examination. "Did you say to Mary Winkler that she was a cold-blooded killer?"

"I said that."

"Was that the truth?"

"At that point, I did not know."

Farese accused Stabler of lying to Mary, and Stabler denied the allegation. Then Farese asked, "Did you tell Ms. Winkler that you were going to turn the recorder off when you left the room?"

"Yes, sir, I did."

"Did you turn the recorder off?"

"I think I did. I thought I did."

"Did you turn the recorder off, yes or no?"

"I thought that I had turned the recorder off."

"Well, you know now, you didn't, don't you?"

"That's correct."

With sarcasm apparent, Farese said, "But you didn't lie to her, that was just a mistake?"

"Yes, sir."

Farese insisted that it was an intentional act—a technique of interrogation—rather than a mistake. Then he said, "One of the techniques that you used in this case was to identify the weak points, the Achilles' heel of Mary Winkler. Is that correct, yes or no?"

"Yes, sir."

". . . The children were the main thing, correct?"

"Yes, sir."

"Because every time Mary Winkler did not answer, did not respond, there was a pause, 'No comment,' you brought up the children, didn't you?"

"Yes, sir," Stabler admitted.

". . . You told Mary Winkler that you knew what had happened, but you didn't know why it happened. Is that correct?"

"Yes, sir."

". . . Was that true?"

"Yes, sir."

". . . Did Mary Carol cry at any time during this interview?"

"Yes, sir."

"Did Mary Carol appear tired to you at any time during this interview?"

"She yawned a couple of times, yes, sir."

"Well, she also told you she had fallen asleep right before the interview, correct?"

"Yes, sir. I did ask her about sleep."

"Did you ask her how much sleep she had in the last few days?"

"Yes, sir."

". . . What did she say?"

"If I recall, she slept on and off, not good sound, solid sleep."

"Did she say how much she had had to eat?"

Freeland objected and the attorneys approached the bench. When Farese resumed, he asked, "Did Mary Winkler ever tell you that she shot her husband? Yes or no?"

"She did not speak those words, no, sir."

"Did you ask her the question, 'Did you shoot your husband?' Did you ask her that question?"

"I think the way I asked her was, 'Why did you shoot your husband?'"

"Listen to my question. Did you ever ask her, 'Did you shoot your husband?'"

"I'd have to refer back to the transcript. I'm not sure."

". . . Did you ever ask her if she intentionally pulled the trigger?"

"No, sir."

"Did you ever ask her if she accidentally shot her husband?"

"No, sir."

"When you tell her that making a statement would only help her, was that the truth?"

"Yes, sir."

"How did it help her?"

"By resolving the matter, we moved on, we got the kids taken care of."

"Oh, by making a statement, you inferred it would help the children?"

"By resolving this, putting it to closure, the kids were going to go through all this . . ."

Farese interrupted. "Listen to my question. You inferred to her if she made a statement, it would help her children, yes or no?"

"Yes, sir."

". . . You've been an investigator twenty-one years, correct?"

"Yes, sir."

"You've seen all sorts of crimes, correct?"

"Yes, sir."

"You've seen crimes that have involved elaborate planning, correct?"

"Yes, sir."

"You've seen crimes that involve very little planning, correct?"

"Yes, sir."

"What evidence do you have that Mary Winkler intentionally shot her husband?"

Freeland objected to the line of questioning again. After a conference at the bar, Farese carried the shotgun in its case up to the witness. He held it straight up in the air, the stock-end resting in his hand, the barrel-end pointing to the ceiling. "Would you please remove the gun from its case, sir?" Stabler pulled it out and Farese continued. "Agent Stabler, would you stand and safely demonstrate to the jury—if you need to have more space to make yourself comfortable, I'm sure the judge will accommodate you. Would you please demonstrate to the jury how that gun is loaded?"

"How it's actually loaded?"

"Yes, sir."

He handled the weapon as he spoke, pointing to different parts of it. "My training is with two types of loads, we call it combat load and tactical load. Basically you can drop a shell in the open chamber and close the action and you've got a round chambered."

"Yes, sir."

"And underneath you can put in multiple shells in the bottom portion of the shotgun."

Farese asked a few questions about the loading of the firearm and then said, "I'd ask you to remain standing and get it ready to rack again."

Stabler pulled back on the slide, positioning the shell, as the unmistakable noise echoed in the courtroom. Farese took back the weapon and said, "Now you and I are about how far apart?"

"About six feet."

"About six feet. And when I rack this gun, it makes a distinctive sound, does it not?"

"Yes, sir."

"It's fairly loud, would you agree?"

"Yes, sir."

"You had no trouble hearing that, correct?"

"Correct."

"And if a man is familiar with a pump shotgun, that's a very distinctive sound to him, is it not?"

"Yes, sir, it is."

"It could be dark, lights could be off, and you hear that, you know what it is."

"Yes, sir, I do."

Farese then questioned him about the trigger pull on this gun—how many pounds of pressure were required to pull it. Stabler made a guess. Farese contradicted him and hassled him about his incorrect answer. Freeland objected that Stabler was not qualified to answer the questions.

Farese snapped back, "Who's qualified? He's answering, Your Honor."

When they returned from the bench, Farese asked more questions about the firearm, this time regarding the weight of it. Stabler resisted all of the attorney's attempts to get him to make an estimate. Farese changed his tack: "If you were carrying this firearm for a fairly long time, how would you hold it?"

"Generally when I hunt, I'll carry it across the chest, carry it over my shoulder for a little bit."

"Because of the weight?"

"The weight and just the discomfort of holding your body in one position for a long time."

"But you don't carry it like this?" Farese said, pointing the gun straight ahead.

"I don't, no, sir."

"Why's that?"

"Safety reasons."

"Safety reasons. Because if you agree with me, if I held this gun in this position and I have my finger inside the trigger housing, that, number one, with my arm extended, as time passes, the weight becomes heavier and drops," he said as he lowered the barrel of the gun. "Would you agree with that?"

"Yes, I do."

"If I am not careful, it will sympathetically put pressure on your right hand and may cause you to pull the trigger? Would you agree with that?"

"No, sir."

"You don't agree with that? Why don't you? Tell me why."

"I don't agree with you, because I don't know that."

". . . Let me ask you this: Could a meteorite hit you in the head right now?"

"I guess it's possible, yes, sir."

"But this is not?"

"I didn't say it wasn't possible, I said I didn't know."

"Could that be correct?"

". . . I said I don't know," Stabler repeated.

"It's possible for a meteorite in the head right now, but it's . . ."

"Objection, Your Honor," said Freeland in an exasperated tone. "It's argumentative."

The judge sustained the objection.

Agent Chris Carpenter from the Tennessee Bureau of Investigation took the stand and told the jury about the time he spent in the Winkler home at the crime scene, and the statement he'd took from Mary in Alabama. He explained the TBI policy not to make audio or video recordings of interviews. He testified that the written statement was in his handwriting, and it was initialed and signed by Mary.

On cross-examination, Leslie Ballin questioned him first about the search of the parsonage, and then said, "But in Orange Beach, you did go into the van?"

"Yes, sir, I did."

"Why did you go into the van? Were you going to drive it?" Ballin asked with a smirk.

"No, sir, I was not."

"Why did you go into the van?"

"Looking in the van for any evidence related to the investigation."

"Would ammunition be something that you would consider relevant to the investigation?"

"Yes, sir."

"Was there any ammunition?"

"None that I found."

"Well, if you expect the people that work under you to be complete," Ballin said in reference to a comment Carpenter made during direct examination, "don't you expect that of yourself?"

"Yes, sir."

"You looked in the van, didn't you?"

"I didn't look in the entire van. I kept my observation and searching through the passenger area."

"Who looked through the entire van?"

"No one looked in the entire van. Special Agent Booth searched through the trunk area and I searched the passenger area."

In an angry voice, Ballin shouted, "You didn't want to look any further, is that your testimony?"

"No, sir."

"Why didn't you look in the van, sir?"

"I did look in the van."

Ballin spewed, "Why wouldn't you look thoroughly in the van, sir?"

"I did look in the van, in the area I was responsible for."

Ballin pounded on the podium and continued shouting. "Who was responsible for the areas that you weren't?"

"As I testified, Special Agent Brent Booth."

"And you were convinced that the van had been looked at, searched thoroughly, before the authorities released it?"

"As you have been reminding me regularly about accuracy and dependency and honesty with the people I work with, Special Agent Booth told me that he had searched the rear of the van."

Waving his arms wildly in the air, Ballin shouted, "Thoroughly?"

"Yes, sir, he . . ."

"Completely?"

"Yes, sir, he said he searched it."

"And you relied on him?"

"Yes, sir."

"And you believed that he searched it?"

"Yes I did."

"And you believed that he searched it thoroughly?"

"Yes, sir, I believed he searched it . . ."

"Otherwise, you wouldn't have released it from police custody, correct?"

"No, sir."

"You would agree with that?" Ballin said in a calmer tone of voice.

"I would agree: Until we had searched it, until we were satisfied, we would not have released it."

"April the sixth of oh-six is the day that you saw Dan Winkler, correct?"

"I would have to see something to refresh my memory."

Ballin retrieved the document from the court clerk and gave it to Carpenter, asking him what it was.

"This is a Tennessee Bureau of Investigation property receipt form dated April sixth, 2006. It is where I received from Mr. Dan Winkler an orange tackle box," Carpenter said.

Ballin asked several questions about the item's physical dimensions and then asked, "Did you send that tackle box or its contents for fingerprint testing?"

"No, sir."

"Would that be because you don't want to waste the TBI's time or money?"

"Is that a question?"

"It sure is," Ballin said with his hands on his hips.

"Repeat it."

"Would you agree with me that, because you were

convinced that the van had been thoroughly searched in Orange Beach, it would have been a waste of your agency's time and money to fingerprint it?"

"No."

"Did you fingerprint it?"

"No."

At 6:15, Carpenter stepped down from the witness stand, prompting Judge McCraw to say, "I think this is a good place to stop for the day."

The long day of testimony etched weariness across the faces of the jury members. They packed up their belongings and headed for the bus. Dinner and bed awaited, and another day filled with more witnesses would come all too soon.

CHAPTER 40

Even though it was a Saturday morning, court was in session at 8:15. Judge Weber McCraw saw no sense in making a sequestered jury sit around the motel with little to do for two days straight. It was more than the day of the week that was different about this session. The sheriff's department had ramped up security that morning. Prior to then, everyone walked in and out of the courtroom at will. There were plenty of deputies around, but they didn't stop anyone. A disturbing phone call changed all that. A very angry man called the courthouse and voiced his displeasure that Mary was not being prosecuted "with enough gusto."

Starting that morning, deputies checked most bags and purses, and made each person stand still and be wanded before entering. The attendees at the day's trial wondered if it was worth all this trouble for what was the most dreaded and boring day in any criminal trial—the financial testimony.

First in the stand was Jana Hawkins of Regions Bank, who told the jury about the Winklers' $5,000 overdraft and Mary's request to remove Matthew's name from the account.

Next was drive-in teller Amy Hollingsworth. She appeared very nervous during the direct examination about deposits in Mary's accounts and the phone calls she had with her over the counterfeit checks.

When Farese approached the podium, it was obvious that the prospect of cross-examination terrified Amy. The defense attorney gave her a hard time for referring to the bank accounts as Mary's when she couldn't say if they were individual or joint accounts. He then got on her for accepting the deposit of the fraudulent Canadian Trust check. By the time Farese released her, she appeared on the verge of tears.

She was followed on the stand by Paulette Guest, another bank teller at Regions Bank and a member of Fourth Street Church of Christ. She related her telephone conversations with Mary about the insufficient funds for the deposited checks she had written on the First State Bank account in Henderson. She testified that she explained to Mary that what she was doing was a criminal offense called "check-kiting." She told the jury that she reminded Mary to come in to the bank with Matthew the next morning at 8:30—the morning of March 22.

Ballin cross-examined her. "You did not, according to your answer to Mr. Freeland, ever talk to Matthew about the account, but you tried?"

"I don't know when I tried."

"But you know you tried."

"I don't know that I tried."

"But you do remember trying to call Matthew, leaving a message, 'This is Paulette at the bank, you need to come in and talk to me about your account'?"

"I don't remember."

"Do you deny doing that?"

"No, sir, I don't deny doing it."

"In addition to calling Matthew and leaving messages, which you may or may not have done, did you ever talk to him at church about it?"

"No, sir, I did not."

Ballin then elicited from her that she'd explained to Mary that the overdraft situation was not dire—there were ways to work the problem out—but the conversation seemed to be going over Mary's head.

After Paulette, April Brown, a corporate fraud investigator for Regions Bank, testified about deposited checks
and telephone transfers Mary made between the different
accounts at her bank. She explained that when the bal-
ances of all the Winkler accounts were combined, the
Winklers were still overdrawn by $3,000.

Freeland next called First State Bank employee Judi
Mills to the stand, who testified about the activity on Mary's
account there. The prosecution wanted her to testify as an
expert on check-kiting, but the defense objected and Freeland dropped the request.

With the minds of observers in the courtroom sufficiently numbed by the banking testimony, Freeland
livened things up a bit by bringing in a firearms expert,
Special Agent Steve Scott. On direct, he testified about the
murder weapon and about his examination of the green
sweatshirt and red T-shirt worn by Matthew Winkler when
he was shot. He said, "I found no dysfunction in the
firearm that would cause it to fire unless the trigger was
pulled with three and three-quarters pounds of pressure."

Steve Farese seemed to relax a lot with this witness.
Some tension drained away from his features and posture.
In fact, at times, the exchange seemed more like friendly
banter between old buddies than a cross-examination.
"Could I summarize your testimony in twenty words or
less, saying that the shotgun did fire the shell that was in
the gun, the pellets and the wadding probably came from
that shell and the pellet that came from that shell made the
holes in the shirts and penetrated the body?" he began.

"That's probably accurate."

"A lot shorter that way," Farese said with a grin.

Scott returned the smile. "It is a lot shorter, yes."

"A couple of things I'd like to ask. You were asked a
question about what would cause the gun to discharge; do
you recall Mr. Freeland asking you that?"

"Yes I do."

"Probably not in those exact words, but first I need to

ask you this: Is there such a thing as an accidental discharge of a firearm?"

"There are times when a firearm can dysfunction me-
chanically in such a way that it can discharge accidentally."

"That's not my question. My question is, is there such a
thing as an accidental discharge by a person with a
weapon that is working perfectly well?"

"Well, let me answer your question by establishing
some definitions first. When in firearms identification,
when we talk about an accidental discharge of a firearm,
we mean that something has dysfunctioned within the gun
to cause it to discharge by accident."

"Can I ask one question here?"

"Yes."

"What do you mean by 'we'?"

"Well, I mean, those in the firearms identification field."

"Okay. Go ahead, sir."

"Then also, we, I, define someone unintentionally shooting a firearm as an unintentional discharge."

"I understand. Okay, then is it possible for someone, in
your parlance, to unintentionally discharge a firearm?"

"I suppose it would be, yes, sir."

" 'Suppose'?"

"Um-hmm," Scott said with a nod.

" 'Suppose'? That's all? You just 'suppose'? You don't
know that that's possible?"

"It is possible, yes, sir."

"Okay, now, not only is it possible, but it's been documented, would you agree?"

"I have actually unintentionally discharged a firearm
before."

"That's my question. And you're the expert, right?"
Farese said with glee.

"I have been qualified so by the court."

"Yes, sir. Now, I've got one other question, and I'm
sorry to even waste everybody's time, but this was a figure-
eight hole on the outer garment, am I correct?"

"Correct."

"Could it have been because the shirt was wrinkled?"

"Yes, sir, that's possible."

"Okay, I was just wondering. Now, just a lucky guess. Now, let me ask you this, Mr. Scott: When you talked about— Have you got the firearm?"

"Yes, I have," Scott said, lifting it up and swinging it around.

Grinning, Farese said, "Will you please display it in a safe manner? I know I don't have to tell you, but I'm trying to limit my liability."

"I do have the safety on, sir."

"Thank you. You stated to the jury that it had two safety mechanisms, am I correct?"

"Yes, sir."

"One on the—and if I use the wrong term, please correct me—it's on the trigger guard."

"It's on the rear of the trigger guard, yes, sir."

"Okay, on the trigger guard and another where it can't be pumped, primed, right?"

"That's not exactly—that is what I said—but when the bolt is locked and the breach is closed, the firearm can't be pumped without using the button to open the firearm, and that's part of the safety design of the firearm."

"I understand. But I don't want you to allude to the jury that that safety device is in effect when one is in the barrel. The safety device is not in effect when you have one in the chamber."

"That's correct, because the firearm will discharge when there is a cartridge in the barrel and the breach is closed and locked."

"Let's take care of that first. Let's put the firearm in the position of being primed."

Scott worked the action on the shotgun.

"Okay, let's assume one's in the chamber."

"All right."

"And you've already demonstrated the two ways that

a shell can be loaded. One, you rack it manually and put it in the chamber, and two, in the feeder and rack it, correct?"

"That's accurate, yes."

"Now, let's now push the safety from SAFE to FIRE, that is, go from black to red."

Scott followed directions and said, "It is in that position now."

"Now, how many safety devices are in effect?"

"There are none, because the trigger can be pulled and the firearm can be discharged."

"Zero. Let's talk about that, too. Because you stated when Mr. Freeland asked you how this weapon can be discharged—you kind of got cut off on your answer, but I heard it—your answer was that by someone pulling the trigger or—and I'm not sure the jury heard the other way—someone pulling the trigger, or— What's the other way for the gun to be discharged?"

"I'm not sure exactly what I said, but by applying three-and-three-quarters pounds of pressure to the trigger itself."

"That's exactly what you said. And there's a difference, would you agree, between those two ways to fire a gun?"

Scott gave Farese a quizzical glance and said, "Set the two ways up for me again."

"Okay, for example, I could be walking through the woods and a stray limb could put three-and-three-quarters pounds of pressure on the trigger, and it could discharge if it was primed and racked."

"Yes, sir, it could."

"It could. Okay, let's say I'm walking with the gun, say I'm hunting quail, the safety's off and the dogs pointed and I tripped."

They talked about the possibility of a sympathetic reflex causing the trigger to be squeezed on the shotgun and then Farese switched the conversation to a 40-caliber Glock. He asked Scott about accidental discharges on that weapon, but Scott pled ignorance. Then, Farese accused him of being evasive for his unwillingness to state whether or not that shotgun was a good weapon for a woman to use. Hefting it, he asked, "Is this gun heavy or light for a woman?" When he didn't get an immediate response, he added, "Let me guess, you don't know 'cause you're not a woman?"

After a pause for the laughter to die down, Scott nodded his head and said in his deep, definitely masculine voice, "I'm not a woman."

Farese posed with the firearm, trying to ask a question, but Scott wouldn't let him finish. Scott kept interrupting the lawyer with questions like "What exactly do you mean by 'elbow bent or arm extended'?"

Exasperated but amused in spite of that, Farese said, "If I ask you what time it is, you're not going to tell me how to build a clock, are you?"

Over the laughter, Scott said, "No, sir."

"If this barrel lowers, will it apply pressure to my finger on the trigger?" Steve asked as he lowered the gun.

"I don't believe so, sir."

"Then why is it applying pressure on it now?"

Scott was perplexed. Farese got him to stand and take the firearm and then told him he'd have to hold it for ten minutes. Freeland objected. The attorneys met with the judge in a sidebar. All the while, Scott held the gun in his right hand. Without any resolution to the question, the judge released Scott without any further testimony.

CHAPTER 41

Judge McCraw didn't like leaving jurors idle all day, but in rural areas of the Bible Belt, court on Sunday was not an option. He reconvened the courtroom on Monday morning, but the trial itself got off to a late start. One of the male jurors was dismissed for a minor, unexplained reason. Sue Allison, court spokesperson, assured the media that it was simply business as usual, there was no mysterious subplot and nothing malicious was going on behind the scenes.

When testimony began, Doctor Staci Turner, forensic pathologist and assistant medical examiner, took the stand to tell the jury about the autopsy she'd performed on Matthew Winkler's body. As the doctor detailed the victim's injuries, Mary Winkler looked down sniffling and wiping her eyes with a tissue. Turner corroborated the earlier testimony of Sergeant Rickman, saying that the aspirated blood on his mouth indicated that he'd breathed for some period of time after he was shot. She added, "I would expect him to die within minutes."

The next witness was Matthew's mother, Diane Winkler. She appeared determined to maintain her control throughout the ordeal. Thick, chin-length brown hair framed a stern face. Her eyes were deep hollows, her lips a ribbon of disapproval. Across the courtroom, her husband Dan sat forward in his seat, his hands folded on his crossed knee. His dark hair had a startling swath of white in the front, a slight splashing of gray at the temples. His

firm jaw and straight nose gave him the look of a patri-
arch. Typically, compassion and understanding resided in
his eyes. But as he gazed on his wife in the witness stand,
those emotions were replaced with a determined intensity
and focus, as if he could, with a look, instill in her the
strength and fortitude she needed.

Diane started out seeming unflappable, but when she
was asked about the night she learned of her son's demise,
her voice wavered and she came close to tears. She pulled
herself back together and donned an emotionless mask to
suppress her inner turmoil.

Freeland led her through a re-telling of her experiences
in the immediate aftermath of Matthew's death. Then he
asked her, "Now, the girls have been back with you since
late March of 2006?"

"Yes, sir."

"Now, during that period of time, have you ever attempted to turn the little girls against their mother?"

"No, sir."

"Have you attempted to poison their minds in any way?"

"No, sir."

"Are you aware of, did you observe or did you hear,
their grandfather or their great-grandmother do the same?"

"No, sir."

On cross, Farese questioned Diane about keeping Mary's
letters away from the children. She testified that the children opened them when they arrived, for a while. But when
the correspondence grew repetitious, the children lost interest and tossed them aside after only the briefest glance.
On the advice of the counselor, they held on to the daily
letters and gave them to the children once a week.

"When did they start throwing the letters aside? What
month?"

"I don't remember that, sir."

"Well, was it May? Did they throw them aside in May?"

"I don't know, sir."

"Did they throw them aside in June?"

"The answer's the same. I don't know, sir."

"Well, you know when you talked to the counselor and told her that they didn't care about their letters anymore. You know that, don't you?"

"I don't remember the exact time, sir."

"Was this at a time when you decided to cut off visitation with Mary after she had only one visit with her children after she'd gotten out of jail?"

"It could have been shortly after that, I don't remember."

"Because the children enjoyed their visit with Mary, did they not?"

"They enjoyed playing with her."

"And they enjoyed hugging and kissing her, too?"

"I don't know, sir, I wasn't there."

"Well, you were told."

"I don't know, sir."

"They told you how much they enjoyed being with their mother, didn't they?"

"No, sir, they really didn't."

"You didn't say that to the counselor, Ms. Crawford?"

"Not that I remember."

"Are you denying that you said that to Ms. Crawford, yes or no?"

"I don't remember."

"Do you deny that you said it?"

"I don't remember."

Freeland objected that she'd already answered the question, bringing the defense's badgering of the victim's mother to a halt for the moment. Farese continued on to another topic. "When the children were brought to the jail to visit with Mary, were you with them?"

"I was."

"Was that an expected visit to the jail?"

"No, sir."

"Y'all didn't tell Mary that you were coming, did you?"

"No, sir, we didn't."

"Mary didn't ask for the children to come see her in jail, did she?"

Nodding her head, Diane said, "Yes, she did want the girls to come see her."

"In jail?"

"Y'all were the ones trying to work up the visit," Diane insisted.

"In jail, is that correct?"

"That was where she was at the time, sir."

"Right. Talking about wanting to work up the visit, we were the ones trying to get her to see her children when she was out of jail, correct?"

"Only one time that I remembered."

"One time?"

"That *you* worked up the arrangement."

"That I worked up the arrangement?"

"Yes, sir."

"What arrangement did I work up?"

"Y'all were trying to work up the arrangement for Mary to see the girls one time—one time."

"So we just wanted— Mary wanted to see her children, one time. Is that what you're saying?" Farese grew more agitated with each passing question. He paced in tiny circles behind the podium, waving his arms in the air.

"Yes, sir."

"Where were you getting your information?"

"From you."

"I've never spoken to you in my life."

"From our lawyers."

"You got your information from your lawyers?"

"Yes, sir, because that was the way it was supposed to be."

"Yes, ma'am. I understand. We didn't talk to y'all, correct?"

"Correct."

"We obeyed the rules. We didn't try to talk to you. Or to Mr. Thompson, correct?"

"Right."

"We went through your lawyer, correct?"

"Correct."

"And Mary got to see her children one time?"

"Yes, sir."

"Are you saying that's what we agreed to? For Mary to see her children one time in eight months?"

"That's what was worked out."

After a pause, Farese said, "I want you to look at that jury, Ms. Winkler."

"Okay," she said turning in their direction.

"Look at 'em. I want you to tell that jury that 'Our agreement was for Mary to see her children one time in eight months.'"

"That was the only agreement that was worked out between our lawyers."

"There was no agreement, Ms. Winkler, and you are well aware of that."

"No, sir, I am not."

"Y'all cut off visitation," he said, poking his finger in Diane's direction and then making a wide swing of his arm to point at his client, "between Mary and her children."

"We cut off visitation between Mary and her girls when Mary lied to her children in the gym. But we were willing to work something else out if it was a supervised visit."

"Did Mary lie to those children in the gym?"

"Yes, sir."

"Were you there?"

"No, sir, I was not."

"Did you hear her?"

"I did not."

"You're the person that told the counselor that Mary lied to her children in the gym. Is that correct or incorrect?"

"That is correct, sir."

"Are you aware that the children told the judge that no such conversation ever took place? Are you aware of that?"

"I am, sir."

Farese's voice shrieked up an octave. "How are you aware of that? Who told you that?"

"That was told in the juvenile court."

"Who told you that?"

"Our counselor—not our counselor, but our lawyer."

"Mr. Adams told you that?"

"Um hm," she agreed.

"The children have in fact, denied . . ."

Freeland stood and said to the judge, "I object, Your Honor, as to hearsay and relevance to a murder trial, this is family court."

Farese snapped back, "Nothing family about this, Your Honor."

"The court finds it relevant," Judge McCraw said. "But beyond that, I ask that you rephrase your questions."

"Yes. Yes, Your Honor," Farese said, then turned back to Diane. "Just so I'm straight on this, you know the girls have told the judge that their mother never told them any lies?"

Freeland spoke up again, "Objection as to hearsay."

"I'll move on. I'll move on," Farese conceded. He questioned her about Mary's housekeeping and other remarks she'd made to the counselor. Then, he asked her, "Did you ever tell the children that their mother murdered their father?"

"We told the children that their mother had shot their father."

"You didn't say 'murdered'?"

"I'm sure we didn't. She shot him, he died."

"You never said 'murdered'?"

"I don't remember that we ever probably used that term."

"What did you tell the children about why their mother shot their father?"

"We didn't know why at that time."

"So they just made it up on their own that Mother stole money from the bank?"

Freeland objected. The judge sustained and Farese

asked, "Did Patricia ever tell you that she hoped what happened to her father was an accident?"

"Yes, sir."

"Did you then in turn tell her that it wasn't an accident? That her mother shot her father intentionally?"

"We didn't know that at the time, sir."

"Did you say that?"

"The girls loved their mother, and that has not changed."

"And the girls still want to see their mother, do they not?"

"No, sir, they don't."

"Well, what has changed from September of 2006 when the girls wanted to live with their mother and now?"

"Well, it's called publicity, and what's been in newspapers, what's been in magazines and what they heard in school. We do not watch the news at home. We do not take newspapers. We do not take magazines. So what they found out, is what they have learned from friends in school."

"What they have found out is what they have learned from friends in school," he said with a shake of his head. "Let me ask you something. Have you reported that to the counselor?"

"Yes, sir."

"That the children are learning from kids at school what's going on in the case?"

"Yes, sir."

"So that'll be on the counselor's records about the children, correct?"

"Yes, sir."

"The truth is that anything that would be on the TV about Mary, you would tell the children about it and use the excuse that you didn't want them to hear about it in school. Is that correct or incorrect?"

"That is incorrect."

"So if those records indicate that, Ms. Crawford is wrong again."

"Sir, the only time we ever talked to the girls about anything is when they came home saying what someone at school had seen or what they heard their parents say. And the only thing that we ever told those girls was when they would come home and ask. We always told them that we would always tell them the truth. We never went beyond that and we never dug in deep on anything."

"What was the truth that you told them?"

"It depended on what they were asking at the time."

"Well, if they asked, 'Why did this happen to Daddy?' what is the truth that you told them?"

"Well, that we really don't know."

"You didn't tell them that Mary stole money from the bank?"

"If that was one of the things made public, and that was one of the things they were asking, we would tell them that. We would not deny it, but we were not authorized to bring things up with them."

"You weren't?"

"No, sir."

"Who were the ones to bring things up? Go ahead, tell the jury who were the ones . . ."

Diane cut him off. "I just told you that—what they would hear from friends in school."

"Okay. So, in September of 2006, this financial stuff had been brought up, is that what you're saying?"

"All I can tell you is just, when we would discuss things with them, we would not go into detail with them. They're children."

"They're young, correct?"

"That is correct."

"And they don't understand what's going on, correct?"

"Neither do we at times," Diane said.

"But they don't especially, because they're children."

"But they're very smart children."

"They're like little sponges, they can absorb material, correct?"

"They are smart enough that they can figure things out."

"And did Patricia figure it out that her mother was going to move to Georgia, remarry and have another child? That Patricia would live with Mary and the other two children would live with you? Did she figure that all out on her own?"

Diane sighed. "That was something that she made up and told a friend at school, whose mother contacted me because she was concerned about that. And I told her, 'I didn't know anything about that.' And we approached Patricia and asked her, 'Where are you going with that?' And she cried and she said, 'All I want to do is be normal and be like other children here at school.' For which, we told her that it's not the truth. 'Your mother is not moving to Georgia . . . ' "

"Did she also tell you that all she wants to do is to be normal and live with her mother?"

"No, she did not say that part. She said that she wanted to be normal and she wanted to have her daddy and her mother and be a normal family."

"Sure, and she loved both her mother and her father, correct?"

"She does."

"Did she say she wanted to come to court and testify to make sure her mother goes to prison? Did she say that?"

"No, sir."

"So if anybody told that to the counselor, that would be a lie, wouldn't it?"

"No one's told that to the counselor."

Farese then harassed her about not telling Mary about the time Patricia broke her arm, or that the girls were in a minor car wreck. Then he asked, "Did you try to prevent Patricia from testifying in this court?"

"It was not our decision that she testify."

At the defense table, Mary, dressed in pink, rolled her eyes and dropped her forehead in her hand.

"Did you do anything to discourage the district attorney?"

At an objection for the prosecution, the lawyers went into another sidebar with the judge. After skimming over

some other topics, Farese turned his questioning to the
September visit between Mary and the girls.

Diane testified that after returning home, the girls
showed her the presents they got from their mother, and Patricia said, "Nana, mother said she did not kill Daddy, isn't
that wonderful? She said that the police in Alabama did not
tell the truth."

"You said you don't want the children to have scars,"
Farese said.

"Of course not. We want them to heal and learn how to
deal with what they've been through."

"Do you realize that Patricia will have a big scar when
she gets home?"

"I don't know what you're talking about."

"I'm sure you don't," Farese said with disdain.

CHAPTER 42

Prosecutor Freeland stood up and announced, "The state calls Patricia Winkler."

Minutes passed in anticipation. Everyone in the courtroom knew the emotional intensity of the daughter's testimony would be in sharp contrast to the stoicism presented by Matthew's mother.

The video cameras were turned off and no audio recording allowed, by order of Judge McCraw. The journalists, who'd been watching the trial feed in the adjacent media room, now saw only a still shot of the state seal of Tennessee. They packed up and moved into the courtroom, squeezing into already crowded rows of reporters.

Previous witnesses filled the space in the witness box—the larger men actually made it look cramped. Now, Patricia looked lost in its vastness, appearing even tinier than she was.

Mary's attention zeroed in on Patricia—she didn't move her eyes from her daughter's face for one moment throughout her testimony. A soft smile stole across Mary's lips, her eyes softened and glowed with warmth at the first glimpse of the girl. That expression remained fixed in place as long as Patricia was in the courtroom.

Freeland established that the little girl knew the difference between the truth and a lie, and the importance of telling the truth. When he asked her about her age and her school, Patricia fell apart, sobbing uncontrollably. Judge McCraw whispered to her.

When she regained her composure, Freeland continued, eliciting basic biographical information. Then he said, "I'm going to ask you about the morning you left the house with your mama. Do you remember waking up that morning?"

Patricia talked about the "big boom" she heard, and about seeing her daddy on the floor crying.

Freeland asked, "Did you hear Mommy say anything after you left, about what happened to your dad?"

"When we were going to Alabama, she said he was in the hospital."

"And how was your mother—how did she look?"

"Mom just looked like her normal self."

"Did you ever see your daddy be ugly to your mother?"

"No, sir," Patricia said shaking her head.

He talked to her about her time at the police station and then asked, "Did you ever ask your mother where you were going?"

"I asked her where we were going and she said we were going someplace special. I asked her if we could go pick up Daddy. She said, 'Daddy couldn't take it with all of Breanna's crying.'"

Farese handled the cross-examination of the child with exquisite tenderness. He talked to her about her trips to Gatlinburg and Disney World, then asked about her visit with her mother in Huntingdon last fall. "Were you happy to see her?"

"Yes, sir."

"Did you hug her?"

"Yes, sir."

"Did you kiss her?"

"Yes, sir."

"Did you tell her you love her?"

"Yes, sir."

"You just talked about happy stuff?"

"Yes, sir."

"Not about any of the stuff we're talking about here?"

Patricia shook her head. Farese talked with her about her counselor and then asked, "Why didn't you see your mom again?"

" 'Cause I didn't want to see her."

"You had a good time and liked seeing her in September. Suddenly, you don't want to see her again?"

The pain traced across her features. "I still love her," she said before hanging her head and crying again.

Farese brought her a tissue and whispered to her. At last, she was dismissed.

Most in the courtroom doubted the wisdom of subjecting Patricia to the trauma of a courtroom appearance in exchange for such minor testimony. As she left the chamber, her sobs echoed in everyone's ears. Even seasoned journalists wiped moisture from their eyes.

CHAPTER 43

Freeland defused the charged atmosphere in the court-room by calling another financial witness, Special Agent Brent Booth with the Tennessee Bureau of Investigation. The agent worked a lot with fraud, lottery schemes and other illegal financial activities, making him the perfect witness to detail the Nigerian check scam, with its many variations, and to explain check-kiting. During direct examination, he admitted that he did see the orange tackle box in the back of Mary's van, but he did not open it.

The cross-examination was conducted by an attorney who had to this point remained silent, Tony Farese, Steve's brother and business partner. Tony Farese attacked Booth's timeline for tracking Mary's check-kiting and argued with the witness about the validity of the TBI policy not to videotape statements.

On re-direct, Booth said that Mary never used the word "accident" in her statement to him. On re-cross, Tony Farese elicited an admission that Mary also never used the word "intentionally" when describing the shooting of her husband.

The final witness of the day was Brandy Jones, a former neighbor in Pegram who lived with Matthew and Mary for a few months. She testified about Mary's insistence that she was happy in Selmer and said that she had never seen any evidence of Mary's physical or emotional abuse.

Leslie Ballin cross-examined this witness, asking her about the time when Matthew had a drug reaction. Brandy said, "I can't say whether or not the medication made Matthew act poorly to Mary 'cause Mary never told me about that, but she was laughing when she came to our door. I didn't get any distress signals from Mary, at all."

At the conclusion of her testimony, the state rested their case.

CHAPTER 44

The defense opened their case by calling Special Agent Donna Nelson, a forensic scientist with the Tennessee Bureau of Investigation. She described the retrieval of evidence from the parsonage and her interaction with other law enforcement officials on the scene. The positioning of the telephone in the home and at the hotel room became an issue with both sides in their questioning of this witness. The prosecution felt it demonstrated Mary's evil intentions; the defense, on the other hand, felt that the similar positions of the phones in two different locations proved that the baby had played with them in both cases. Nelson said that the only difference between the telephones in two rooms was that one of them was only a few feet away from a dead body.

Next to the stand for the defense was Tennessee Highway Patrol Officer Jimmy Jones, who related the story of Matthew Winkler shouting at him about a barking dog while Jimmy's grandmother lay dying inside the house. That run-in caused him to give Matt a nickname—"the Tasmanian Devil."

The defense called two computer forensic experts to the stand next, to testify about images found on the hard drives used by Matthew and Mary Winkler. More than three hundred had been found on the computers, but many, if not all, of them had been deleted at some date prior to the confiscation of the hard drives by law enforcement.

Although no one specified in court to the exact content of these images, the clear allusion was that they were pornographic in nature. Although not revealed in court, the majority were shots of pairs of women engaged in sexual activity or of a woman performing oral sex on a man.

Jonathan Allen, a 21-year-old Freed-Hardeman student, said that he knew Matthew from his time as a youth minister at the Central Church of Christ in McMinnville. Allen considered him a friend, but admitted that Matthew's personality clashed with those of two or three of the teenagers in the youth group.

Rudy Thomsen, who hosted Mary in his home after her release from jail on bond, took the stand. He testified about Mary's black eye and the statement she gave about receiving the injury from one of her daughter's elbows.

"Did you ever observe Matthew interacting with Mary in a way that caused you to rethink what may or may not have caused that black eye?" Farese asked.

Rudy recounted the time in the fellowship hall at church where he saw Mary's demeanor change from bubbly to subdued when Matthew entered the room.

"Did that cause you to make further observations during throughout their tenure there at Central?" Farese asked.

"I noticed that behavior more after that, because I became more aware of it."

After a series of questions about Mary's stay at his house, Rudy said, "I saw a woman who came to my house hurt and hurting. Now she has blossomed into that person I saw in that fellowship hall."

On cross-examination, Freeland elicited testimony that Rudy's son had no problems with Matthew as youth minister at Central Church of Christ. Rudy also admitted that he had once gotten a black eye caused by the elbow of one of his nephews when they were horsing around in the swimming pool.

The next witness was reluctant at best. Lori Boyd, former secretary at Central Church of Christ, did not want to testify. But when officers questioned her after Matthew's death, she told them what she remembered. Now, she'd been served with a subpoena forcing her presence in the courtroom.

She talked about her experience working for Matthew, her objections to the belittling way he treated Mary and his heavy-handed management techniques. She also brought up questionable purchases of history books that Matthew made on church accounts.

The pulpit minister of Central Church of Christ, Timothy Parish, stepped into the hot seat. He claimed that the statement he gave to the Tennessee Bureau of Investigation was documented inaccurately. He said he did not see the report until recently. "Some of it was a little surprising to me. There were things I could not recall ever saying. Things attributed to me that, to the best of my recollection, I did not say."

One of the disputed comments in the written statement was that "Mary looked whipped." Parish said, "I don't use that phrase. But there it is in the statement." He also claimed he never said that Matthew was controlling.

Leslie Ballin pointed out Parish's wife in the back of the courtroom and asked, "Did you have any thoughts about Matthew and Mary's marriage?"

"I tend to compare anybody's marriage to my own. I think that I have an exceptional marriage . . . To that extent, I didn't think it was as good as mine."

CHAPTER 45

Just after 1:30 on the afternoon of April 17, the fifth day of Mary Winkler's trial, the defense called Mary's adopted sister, 26-year-old Tabatha Freeman to the witness stand. She expressed her love for Mary and her adopted family, and in answer to Steve Farese's questions, explained the environment in the Freeman home. "It was a loving household. Daddy was head of the family. He took care of discipline. He made all the family decisions."

"Did you notice any changes in Mary after marrying Matthew?" Farese asked.

"She was happy at first. As time went on, a very bubbly, outgoing sister became subdued, and I didn't get to see her."

Then she testified, "After Mama died, I don't think she [Mary] ever came to Knoxville to see the family."

Farese asked her about the death of her adopted mother, Mary Nell Freeman. Tabatha, crying, responded that when she was a senior in high school, Mary Nell died of cancer.

The defense attorney turned the questioning to Matthew and Mary's relationship. Tabatha said, "Matthew pretty much dictated everything. Mary could not make decisions for herself . . . She always said, 'I'll have to check with Matt' when we invited her to visit, and the answer was usually 'No.'"

Contradicting an earlier statement that she hadn't seen

Mary for the three years prior to Matthew's death, Tabatha said that Mary visited the family in Knoxville for two hours on Christmas 2005. "Matthew, at times, just left family get-togethers and visited other people in the area. He often left angry, but I usually had no idea what he was angry about. I remember one time he was upset about dinner arrangements."

Farese asked again about how often she was able to see her big sister after she married Matthew. "Seeing Mary was normal in the beginning, then it became less. I understood when they lived in Louisiana, but when they moved back to Tennessee, it seemed unusual," Tabatha said.

When asked if she ever visited her sister, Tabatha said that she was never invited there for birthday parties or other occasions and didn't show up for that reason.

After fifteen minutes of gentle questioning from the defense, Tabatha faced the harsher reality of answering questions from prosecutor Walter Freeland.

"How would you describe the relationship between Mary and her father before Matt's death?"

"I know they didn't talk much . . . As an outsider, I would say the relationship didn't exist."

The prosecutor said that the adopted brothers, Eric and Chase, had legal problems, insinuating that Mary would not want them to know where she lived. When he moved on to use the word "criminal," Farese leaped to his feet. "I object, Your Honor."

The attorneys gathered around the judge for a sidebar. At the bench, Farese shouted, "I object. I object," loudly enough to be heard across the courtroom.

When Freeland returned to questioning Tabatha, he asked, "How often did you see Matthew and Mary in the last two years?"

Tabatha said, "At the birth of one of the children and Christmas 2005—the only times in years. I've never seen Breanna." (Since she accompanied Mary on the September visit with the children, it can only been assumed that she was referring to the time before Mary's arrest.)

On re-direct, Farese played on his witness's emotions, bringing out tears, sniffles and tissues. "Prior to her marriage to Matthew, what type of person was Mary?"

"She was my big sister. I wrote Mary a letter when this first occurred, and I told her I didn't understand everything, but I wanted her to know, as a little sister coming from a very bad abusive past, that she was the first person that ever told me that she loved me and I believed her. Because not even my adoptive parents, who mean everything to me, who've given me every opportunity, but it was Mary that changed my life and all of our lives."

When Farese asked her about changes in Mary since Matthew's death, Tabatha said, "Before, the only way I could describe her is, the light had gone out of her eyes. She didn't have any fire in her spirit anymore, and slowly she's come back to be that person I first knew and needed in my life, and still need very much . . .

"She's the best example of a good person I can think of . . . She's in control, and she is a happy person now, she's improved so much, she's so brave, I don't know how she does it."

Farese turned his questions to Mary's lack of contact with her family. "Is the reason she's not seen you is because she's been segregated from her family for years?"

"Yes," Tabatha sobbed.

"Because she'd been beaten by her husband for years?" Farese asked.

Freeland objected and the attorneys again gathered at the bar.

When the testimony resumed, Farese asked, "The fact is, you know why you didn't get to see your sister, don't you?"

"Yes, sir," Tabatha answered, wiping her nose with a tissue. She then was dismissed from the stand.

CHAPTER 46

Mary's probation officer, Donna Dunlap, stepped up next on Mary's behalf. Ballin asked, "Have you found her compliant?"

"Yes."

"Truthful?"

"Yes."

"Honest?"

"Yes."

"Would you believe her under oath in a court of law?"

"Yes."

On cross-examination, Freeland established that she'd only known her for eight months, and seen her only in her office once a week. "Your testimony is that she's been on her good behavior since she's been accused?" Freeland asked.

"Yes."

"Any opinion that you have of Ms. Winkler is based on what she has told you?"

"Yes."

"And based on the thirty-five to forty visits, you have made a judgment about her truthfulness?"

"Yes."

"And she's never lied to you?"

"Not to my knowledge."

Dr. Timothy Fisher entered the box. He was the doctor who treated Mary in McMinnville when she claimed that she had been hit in the jaw by a softball. In answer to Ballin's question, he said that his nurse practitioner characterized the injury by a softball in the medical record as "Mary's story."

Freeland got the doctor to admit that he had no recollection of the visit, but had referred to his medical records for all his information. Ballin, on re-direct, elicited the testimony that the injury was caused by blunt force trauma that could have been from a softball or from a hand or a foot.

Dr. Lynne Zager, a clinical psychologist, established her credentials and was declared an expert by the court. She looked type-cast for the role—long hair, simply styled with a part on the side, a long nose and thin, downturned lips, wearing silver-framed glasses with thick lenses and a tailored suit.

She told the jury about her first few visits with Mary, which included the administration of the MMPI—the Minnesota Multiphasic Personality Inventory—their work with Rorschach cards and the lengthy conversations with Mary that led to her diagnosis of PTSD—post-traumatic stress disorder—dating back to the death of her sister when Mary was 13 years old.

Leslie Ballin asked, "Did Mary share with you any information about the issue of this abuse?"

"Yes, she did. She described situations—it was very hard for her, as she didn't want to speak in a negative light about her husband Matthew. But after we worked together for a time, she described situations where he was verbally inappropriate to her, physically inappropriate to her, sexually inappropriate to her and emotionally inappropriate to her."

"I'm going to have to ask you for specific examples."

"For example, one classic thing that occurs with people who are in a situation—when they are in an abusive situation, when they're a victim of that—one thing that most often occurs is that the person is isolated. Like, they have family, they have friends, they have co-workers, they have classmates, and when a person gets involved in an abusive type of situation, it is very common for the abuser to isolate the person from all the other people who could perhaps be of support or help. And as Mary described her marriage with Matthew Winkler, it appeared as if that is exactly what happened."

Zager described the common situation in which abused people stay with their abusers because the fear of what would happen to them if they left was greater than the fear of remaining in the relationship. She moved on to relate Matthew's habit of nagging Mary and controlling what she ate because of the weight she gained through the births of three children. She added, "She often said that Matthew helped her improve herself."

"You spoke about sexual abuse. Did Mary share with you what she was made to do?"

"Yes," Zager said.

"What's that?" Ballin said.

"Do you want me to talk about that?"

"Absolutely."

"What she described was her husband asking her to do things that she wasn't comfortable with sexually. She described things like putting on wigs and high heels, or clothes that she wasn't comfortable with. She described that he had pornographic pictures or movies that he wanted her to watch with him, and she wasn't comfortable. She'd look at the desk or look down when he wanted her to do that. She shared the times that she didn't care to be sexually intimate at the time, but that was not okay."

"Not an option?" Ballin interjected.

"That was not an option, no. Sometimes she would say she was on her cycle extra to avoid being intimate with her husband. And there were also times where he wanted— and insisted—that they have anal sex, and that was not something that she cared to be involved with, but it was something that occurred."

In the jury box, heads turned downward, faces flushed red and the jurors seemed very preoccupied with taking notes. At the defense table, Mary rested her chin in the palm of her hand, her skin flushed from her scalp to the neckline of her shirt as Steve Farese wrapped a protective arm around her shoulders.

"Did she relate to you that she told him that it hurt, and to stop?"

"Yes, she did."

"Did she relate to you whether or not if he did stop?" Ballin asked.

"Yes, she did. He would not stop and she was concerned that he would hurt her and her body in some way, and he made a comment that she could always have surgery to fix that."

Ballin led her through an explanation of memory in situations like Mary's. Zager said that typically in a dissociative episode, common to people with PTSD, there was ". . . some recollection, but it is not complete." Like Mary, ". . . people remember bits and pieces." On the other hand, she said, "Fakers lose memory completely right before the event and remember nothing until after the arrest."

Zager went on to discuss Matthew's physical abuse, saying that when Mary got out of jail in August, she said that it was the first time she'd been able to wear shorts in years because she didn't have any bruises on her legs, and that Matthew was also the cause of her bruised jaw, not the softball.

She said that Mary also claimed that she ". . . always had to carry a cell phone because she always had to answer when he called. He was very concerned about keeping up with her."

Zager attempted to explain Mary's shooting of Matthew. "My professional opinion is that Mary suffers from PTSD, and at the time this occurred, she was in a dissociative episode and was not able to think or plan in the way she normally would do."

"Was she capable of forming the intent to commit a crime?" Ballin asked.

"I don't believe so."

"On March twenty-second, 2006, do you think she was capable of forming an intent to kill?"

"I don't believe she was."

The prosecution could have sought and perhaps found a psychologist to offer opposing testimony, but it was a gamble. If they tried and failed, they had to inform the defense, who would then have two mental health professionals to bolster their claim. Dunavant had encountered Zager in court before, and believed that she could find "PTSD in an inanimate object." But she'd made finding an expert who would disagree with her opinion more difficult by putting the genesis of Mary's PTSD in her childhood instead of in abuse by her husband. In the end, they decided not to take the risk of another psychological consultation.

Instead, Walt Freeland stood before the psychologist and belittled her profession and her credibility. He argued with her over semantics, and accused her of wanting a platform to speak on the issue of spousal abuse and PTSD. He attacked the mental health profession with its classifications of Caffeine-Induced Disorder, Nicotine-Induced Disorder and Football Widow Syndrome.

He asked, "There is no question in your mind, is there, that at the time of this event, Mary was sane?"

"That is a legal word, not a mental health word."

"Can you say that someone charged with a serious crime has, at least, a motive to malinger?"

"Yes, sir."

Freeland brought out the fact that Mary had no mental health records prior to Matthew's murder, and questioned Zager's assessment that Matthew was in charge of the financial situation. Then he asked, "Where did you get your information that Matthew Winkler isolated Mary Winkler from her family?"

"From Mary."

"You don't recall her saying that she didn't want to be around her father? It was her decision and not Matthew's?"

"I don't recall that, but it doesn't surprise me. In many ways, she described her father as being like Matthew. In many ways, she described her mother as her role model."

On re-direct, Ballin walked Zager through the validity scale in testing that measured people's honesty by determining when they attempted to make themselves appear worse than they are. The psychologist said, "Mary's score is very low—she was doing just the opposite."

Up again, Freeland asked questions centered on the frequency of Mary's visits with her lawyers, in particular about how those sessions related to visits with her psychologist. Zager didn't have answers for him.

On re-cross Ballin popped up, approached the podium, and asked, "Did you do anything unethical in your examination?"

"No, sir."

"Neither did we," Ballin snapped, glaring at the prosecution table. He slammed his legal pad on the podium, then turned back and gave Freeland another dirty look.

CHAPTER 47

The trial opened on Wednesday, April 18, with the most anticipated witness of them all, Mary Winkler. She took her seat looking demure and achingly vulnerable in a white cardigan sweater over a modest black-and-white dress. She personified an innocence and a lack of sophistication so complete, many wanted to believe every word she said even before she opened her mouth.

Steve Farese took her through her childhood, the death of her sister and the adoption of her five siblings. When he asked her if she was raised in a strict household, she agreed. Then he asked, "Strict in what way?"

"My mother and father wanted us to obey our elders, to have good manners and to obey the rules."

In a soft, childlike voice with its laid-back east Tennessee drawl, Mary talked about her brief courtship with Matthew, their marriage, their beginnings in Louisville outside of Knoxville, their return to Henderson and the move to Louisiana. When asked about their life in Louisville, she said that she was surprised when, a short time into their marriage, the screaming and hollering began.

"When you say he screamed and hollered, what did he scream and holler about?"

"He wanted me to quit inviting brothers and sisters over, and staying over there and just us."

"Did you do as he wished?"

"Yes, sir."

About Baton Rouge, she said, "We had good times. We had bad times, too."

"Why did you have bad times, Mary?"

"There's nothing I can tell you that's a particular reason. There was many times that I got hollered at, got on to. One time, Matthew thought I'd done something with the shirts wrong and I felt like it was my fault. But when I look back on pictures now, Matthew had just gained weight when I gained weight having Patricia. I see that now. That wasn't anything for me to be in trouble with. Patricia's elbow was dislocated and I don't know what happened there."

"Let's talk about that. Children get hurt."

"Yes, sir."

"Sometimes they hurt themselves, correct?"

"Yes, sir."

"Sometimes they accidentally get hurt?"

"Yes, sir."

"What happened to Patricia?"

"I don't know."

"Well, were you with her when she got hurt?"

"No, sir."

"Who was with her?"

"Matthew."

"Do you know if he did anything intentionally or unintentionally?"

"No, sir, I don't."

"What were you told?"

"That they were playing."

"How old was she?"

"She was between nine months and a year-and-a-half."

They talked about the death of Mary's mother and about the move to the Nashville area. Mary said the yelling and screaming continued there, too.

"How did he act when he yelled and screamed? What were his movements?"

"He flailed. He was a big guy. He was just all over."

She said that he'd point his fingers inches from her nose.

"Whatever he was upset about, it was my fault. 'Don't do it again.' " She said if she wanted to talk about it, "He would tell me that was just ugly coming out and it needed to be put away."

She said, "Pegram was a hard place . . . a hard place in my life, in my home." Asked why it was so difficult, she said, "Matthew's temperament escalated. He would just be furious about certain things. He went from certain threats to more serious threats."

"When you say 'threats,' what do you mean by 'threats'? Can you be specific to the jury about what you mean by 'threats'?"

"He told me one time he was going to cut the brake lines out of the van."

"Why?"

"I don't know."

"Did he ever get physical with you in Pegram?"

Mary did not respond.

"Mary," Farese said to get her attention.

"Yes, sir?"

"Did he ever get physical with you in Pegram?" he repeated.

"No, sir." She then described the medication incident in Pegram, but indicated that it had nothing to do with a drug reaction. She claimed that she covered up her distress when she spoke to Glenn and Brandy Jones. "Don't know what I told them. I laughed and tried to play it off. I was ashamed. I didn't want them to know how Matthew was acting."

Farese then spoke to her about her husband. "Let me ask you something, during these times, could Matthew be good, too?"

"Yes, sir," she said with a laugh.

"Was Matthew talented?"

"Yes, sir."

"Was he smart?"

"Yes, sir."

"Did he have a way with people?"

She smiled and said, "Yes, sir."

"Could he cause people to believe him?"

"Yes, sir."

"That's part of being a minister, isn't it?"

"Yes, sir."

In the courtroom, a very distressed Clark Freeman hung his head, shaking it back and forth as tears formed in his eyes.

"Is that what Matthew wanted to be—a minister?"

"If he could have his dream job, he'd be a history teacher."

Farese questioned her about their time in McMinnville. "Did you love the town?"

"Yes, sir."

"How was your relationship in McMinnville?"

"It was very bad." Mary hung her head and swayed back and forth.

"Mary? Mary, tell the jury about how your relationship was."

"It was very bad. I asked Matthew to have a divorce. And he absolutely denied it. That would not be allowed."

"That was not an option?"

"No, sir."

"According to who?"

"Matthew."

"Why did you want a divorce?"

"Because it was just so bad. I just wanted out."

"Why was it bad?"

"He just could be so mean."

Mary described the softball injury that she said was made much worse when Matthew kicked her in the face. Farese asked, "Prior to being kicked in the face, had he ever been physical with you before?"

"Yes, sir."

"Tell the jury how he had been physical with you."

Mary did not respond, prompting the attorney to say her name again.

"He pushed me down, used his belt, kick."

"But up until the time you had gotten to Selmer, had he ever actually hit you in the face? Hit you with his hands?"

"No, sir."

"Did he hit you in the face in Selmer?"

"Yes, sir."

"Why?"

"I don't know."

"Mary, there has to be some reason, something he was angry about or something, why can't you tell the jury a reason?"

"I can't remember back to anything, why he was upset."

"Well, did you ever do anything bad to make him mad?"

"No, sir."

"Did you run around on him?"

"No, sir," she said and laughed.

"Did you talk back to him?"

"No, sir."

"Did you not go where he told you to go?"

"No, sir."

"Did you not do what he told you to do?"

"No, sir."

"Were you sneaking around seeing your family?"

"No, sir."

"What did Matthew tell you about your family?"

"Once the girls started getting older, he didn't want them to be around my family. There was something talked [sic] that one of my brothers got into trouble, and we didn't have any facts, and that was just it. He didn't want them anywhere near Patricia and Allie."

She said that Matthew got along with her father in the beginning, but over time, Matthew grew to dislike him. "He just got on his nerves."

Farese asked her about disciplining the children. Mary said, "They could lose privileges or they would get spankings."

"Did any of the spankings ever get out of hand?"

"Yes, sir."

"Tell the jury," Farese urged.

"If Patricia and Allie ever got into trouble, if he was having a bad day, then they would just get some of it, too. And then, they stayed home from school sometimes."

"Why'd they stay home from school?"

"Matthew didn't want anyone to see their legs."

"Why?"

"They were bruised."

After Mary said, "I would just do anything to help him stay happy," there was a long pause. Then Farese approached the witness stand and handed her a bag.

"Mary, would you open that sack, please?"

She complied, glanced inside, scratched her face and closed her eyes.

"What's in that sack, Mary?"

"A shoe and a wig."

"Show me that shoe that's in there."

Mary pulled it from the bag and set it on her lap.

"Put it up on the side there."

Mary set an outrageous white pump with a five-inch flared heel in the back and a three-inch platform in the front. It looked perfect for a striptease act in a gentlemen's club.

"Is that the kind of shoe you would wear to church?"

"No, sir."

"What else is in the sack, Mary?"

"A wig."

"Let me see."

Mary pulled out another plastic bag containing a short brunette wig—not unlike Mary's own hair. She set it down beside the shoe and bent her head, putting one hand in front of her eyes.

"Where did you get that shoe?"

In a muffled voice, she said, "From Matthew."

"Did he buy that?"

"Yes, sir."

"Where'd you get that wig, Mary?"

"From Matthew."

"Who bought that?"

"Matthew."

"Why did you need a shoe like that, Mary?"

"I didn't need it."

"Why was the shoe bought, Mary?"

"Matthew wanted me to wear it."

"What do you mean, he wanted you to wear it, Mary?"

"He just liked to dress up."

" 'Dress up'?"

"Yes, sir."

"Dress up for what purpose, Mary?"

"Sex."

"Sex? Besides the wig and the shoes, what was the—how else were you dressed?

"Just skirts or something slutty," Mary said with her head still facing downward. Prior to the introduction of the shoe, Mary had mostly kept her attention on Farese. Now she didn't seem capable of looking at anything but the hands in her lap.

"How long was the skirt?"

"Very, very short."

"During the course of this, did you ever have the occasion that he asked to look at his computer?"

"Yes, sir."

"What were you asked to look at?"

"Pornography."

"What kind of pornography? Was it still photographs, movies or what?"

"I think they were movies."

"Were any of them stills?"

"They might have been."

"Well, why would you look at them? Did you enjoy that sort of thing?"

"No. He told me to, but I just looked at the back of the desk."

"You wouldn't look at the photographs?"

"No, sir."

Throughout this testimony, Dan and Diane sat rigidly upright, their faces devoid of any expression. Their stoic response concealed the little death they suffered in their hearts, as they believed their son was being victimized again.

"What would occur after he asked you to look at the photographs?"

"We'd go have sex."

"Did he ever ask you to engage in any type of sex you felt was unnatural?"

"Yes, sir."

"Tell the jury what that was."

Mary didn't respond or look up until Farese prompted her by saying her name again. "He just wanted to have sex in my bottom."

"Did that concern you or worry you?"

"Yes, sir."

"Did it hurt you?"

"Yes, sir."

"What were you told when you expressed your concern?"

"He said okay, and then he'd do it again."

"What was his answer for if it did hurt you?"

"He saw some show one time and they said that does happen, but they had surgery that could fix it."

"When he had you dress up, did he have you engage in any other kind of sex that you thought was unnatural?"

"It may not be unnatural, but stuff I didn't want to do."

"Give the jury just one example."

"Oral sex."

During a sidebar, Mary continued to hang her head low. She formed a fist with her hand and leaned her forehead on it. Out in the rows, her sisters looked at her with furrowed brows and compressed lips.

After break, Farese said, "Mary, if it's okay, would you hold your head up? Okay?"

"Yes, sir."

The attorney handed her the exhibit of pornographic images and asked her if she recognized them. A high red blush bloomed on her cheeks as she acknowledged that she'd seen them on the computer at home. He pointed out an image of a shoe retrieved from the hard drive. Mary said that it looked just like her shoe except that the ones in the picture were black. The thick document of the computer analysis was passed to the jurors to review.

Farese's questions about abuse led Mary to testify that Matthew had hit her in the face in Selmer, but when she visited Dr. Eason, she told him that it was from a bee sting. Eason disagreed with that diagnosis and recommended that she see a dentist.

About other acts of violence, Mary said, "He threatened me with a shotgun, many times pointing it in my face . . . He said if I ever talked back to him the way one of my sisters-in-law talked to my brother-in-law, he'd cut me into a million pieces."

Farese asked, "Mary, have you ever shot a shotgun?"

"No, sir."

"Have you ever loaded a shotgun?"

"No, sir."

"Do you know how a pump shotgun works?"

"No, sir."

"Mary, when you were released from jail on bond, did you try to see the children?"

"Yes, sir."

"How hard did you try . . ."

Freeland objected on grounds of relevance. The judge sustained. Farese changed direction. "Why would Matthew point a shotgun at you? For what reason?"

"To reaffirm that he was in control."

"How did that make you feel?"

"Scared."

Farese questioned Mary about incidents when Allie was a baby, and she said, "When she was crying and was supposed to be going to bed, Matthew would suffocate her to get her to go to sleep."

"What do you mean by 'suffocate her'?"

"Pinch her nose and hold her mouth."

"Would you let him do that to your child?"

"I just couldn't stop him."

"Why?"

"I just couldn't physically do anything."

Clark Freeman bent his head down and placed his hand over his face. He rocked forward, sliding his hand up to the top of his head.

Farese questioned her about a large check that came to the house. Mary said that Matthew opened it but her name was on the check. She said that Matthew told her to fill out sweepstakes forms for all kinds of prizes, from cash to televisions and cars. She claimed that although she was skeptical about the check, Matthew believed it was winnings from an entry they mailed.

She also claimed that Matthew directed her every move when she shuffled checks from one account to another. It was also his idea that she open an account in her name in Henderson, saying it would be convenient when she was in school. She said that she transferred the home mail to a post office box on Matthew's instructions. He was concerned that their mail would be tampered with by the neighbors because he had threatened their family dog.

The questions moved to the events of March 21, 2006. Farese asked her about the phone calls she received when she was at school. "I was unable to talk, but I could listen because I was in a classroom."

She said that she talked to Matthew and told him that one of the bankers kept saying that something is illegal. She said that she kept trying to convince him to go to the bank. "He said he would, but he'd been saying that for weeks."

Farese questioned Mary about the early-morning hours of March 22, leading up to the moment of her final confrontation with Matthew. Farese asked, "Did you go back to the bedroom to talk to Matthew?"

A tearful Mary said, "Yes."

"Did you talk to him?"

"No."

Farese asked, "Why?" When he got no response, he said, "Why didn't you talk to him, Mary?"

"I couldn't."

"What do you mean, you 'couldn't'?"

"I was too scared."

"Scared of what?"

"Matthew."

"Do you remember getting a gun?"

"No, sir."

"Do you remember ever having a gun—holding a gun?"

"Yes, sir."

"Do you remember ever pointing a gun?"

"No, sir."

"Do you remember pulling a trigger?"

"No, sir," she sobbed.

"Did you pull the trigger?"

"No, sir."

"How do we know that, Mary?"

"Because I am telling you."

"Do you remember a gun doing anything?"

"Yes."

"What do you remember?"

"Something went off."

"When you said 'Something went off,' what went off?"

"At the time, I didn't know."

"What did it sound like?"

"Ka-boom."

"Did you see, hear or smell anything?"

"Yes, an awful smell."

"What type of smell?"

"Nothing I've ever smelled before or since."

Out on the benches, Diane Winkler maintained her blank expression, but the set of Dan's mouth made his anger apparent.

"Do you remember what you did after the gun went off?"

"I ran to get out of the house."

"Why did you want to get out of the house?"

"Because Matthew would be mad at me. And I didn't know what he would do to me, because he'd think I wanted to do that."

"And where did you run to?"

"I ran outside to the carport."

"Was anyone following you?"

"No." She then told the jury about her return to the bedroom. Farese asked, "How did he look?"

"He looked dead."

"Did you see any blood anywhere?"

"Yes, sir."

"Where?"

"In his nose, in his mouth and in his ears."

She described wiping his mouth, but said she did not remember saying anything to him. She said all she could think about was that "I knew something terrible had happened, I knew no one would believe it was an accident. And I'd lose the girls."

She talked about her flight with her daughters and their ultimate arrival in Orange Beach. After establishing that she hadn't packed or made any reservations or did not remember how the gun got in the van, Farese asked, "Look at the jury, please."

Mary turned her face toward them.

Farese asked, "Did you intentionally, purposefully, kill your husband?"

"No, sir."

"Did you love your husband?"

"Yes, sir."

"Do you still love your husband?"

"Yes, sir," she said choking on her words as tears filled her eyes.

"Even after all that?"

"Yes, sir."

She told her attorney that she didn't tell the whole truth to the police in Alabama because she was ashamed and didn't want them to know about Matthew. Farese asked,

"Have you told this jury to the best of your ability and re-membrance the truth of your marriage and what happened on or about March twenty-second, 2006?"

"Yes, sir."

CHAPTER 48

Now, Mary faced the ordeal of cross-examination. Walt Freeland asked her, "In a statement in Alabama, you stated that Matthew was 'mighty fine,' did you not?"

"Yes, sir."

"You stated that he was 'so, so good,' or something of that nature."

"Yes, sir."

"What did Matthew Winkler ever do to deserve the death penalty?"

She stared hard at him and then said, "I don't understand that question."

"What did Matthew Winkler do to deserve to die?"

"Nothing. Nobody made that decision," Mary said with an edge of sharpness in her tone.

"Matthew Winkler, in fact, did not deserve to die, did he?"

"No," she said strongly with a shake of her head.

"Not for anything he did to you, did he deserve to die?"

"No."

Freeland reviewed the banking situation with Mary, bringing up the last large check she deposited and asking her if she was happy to receive it. Mary said that she wasn't but remembered Matthew saying, "It's not a million dollars, but it's something."

Freeman brought up her testimony about the suspicious dislocation of Patricia's elbow and asked if it had been investigated. Mary said it hadn't and added, "I think that Matthew didn't know his strength. I don't think that he hurt her intentionally."

After questioning some of her allegations of abuse, Freeland asked, "Did the shooting of Matthew give you self-esteem?"

"No."

Freeland went over her testimony about the drug reaction incident in Pegram that caused her to go to Brandy and Glenn Jones' home seeking help. He pointed out that the couple obviously did not realize there was a problem because of your laughter. He asked, "You were able to convince your friends of something that wasn't true?" He moved on to the injury to her jaw and repeated that contention about Dr. Fisher. "You were able to tell him something untrue and he believed you?"

"Yes, sir," she admitted with reluctance.

The prosecutor addressed the injury in Selmer that caused her to seek medical help from Dr. Eason. Mary responded that later that week, she did, in fact, have a root canal at the dentist. Then, Freeland asked her about the spankings that she claimed got out of hand. "Did you mention anything about this to Matthew?"

"Yes, sir."

"Did you mention it to anyone else?"

"No."

He asked her about the computer in their home, establishing that she was able to operate it, was not denied access and used it frequently. He also got into the record that to Mary's knowledge, the three little girls never saw any of the dirty pictures.

"Were there problems in the marital bedroom, as expressed by Matthew?"

"He wanted to change scenarios, looks and try something new."

He asked a few more questions about the pornography of the computer and then asked if she had to engage in anything physically degrading like handcuffs or whips.

That gave Mary the opportunity to mention plastic penises.

"Is it safe to say that Matthew's sexual appetite was more than yours?"

"Yes, sir."

Freeland then set her up for the rebuttal witness he planned to call. "Did Matthew ever take you to the target range to practice using the gun, in case you needed to defend yourself?"

"No, sir."

Freeland asked her about her flight to Alabama. Mary said, "The stupid gun just went off and no one would believe me. They would take my girls away and lock me up. I just wanted to have a little time."

He took her back to the night she was questioned by investigators. "Well, were you in a fog or were you not in a fog, Ms. Winkler?" When Mary did not answer, Freeland continued, "When you were talking to these authorities in Orange Beach, Stan Stabler of the ABI and Chris Carpenter of the TBI, were you in a fog or were you not in a fog?"

"I would say I was. I was trying to do the best I could in the situation I was at, and the surroundings where I was at, and everything that was going on."

"You knew the surroundings where you were at, and you knew what was going on, did you not?"

"Yes, sir."

"Because you, by your testimony, made some sort of conscious decision that you weren't going to smear Matthew, is that true?"

"Yes, sir."

"Well, how in the world, ma'am, would it have smeared Matthew to have said that it was an accident, the gun had gone off accidentally? That would not have smeared him."

"No, sir."

"You were aware of your circumstances in talking to the police. Why did you not tell Chris Carpenter that the gun accidentally went off?"

"When you're so beaten down, you just don't understand

and you don't think you've got a way up. At that time, I was led to feel like I didn't have a family. I never would have imagined that I would have been able to have any kind of attorney. If I got into talking, I'd have to talk about how he was. And I didn't want to get into that."

"Well, why in the world would you have to talk about the way he was if it was an accident? What would that have to do with anything if the gun just accidentally went off?"

"It's what led me to get into that position."

"So something led you into a position of having an accident. Is that what you're saying?"

"Yes, sir."

"What was it that led you into the position of accidentally shooting Matthew Winkler?"

Mary shook her head.

"All this past you've testified?"

"I just wanted to talk to him."

"It wasn't an accident, was it?"

"Yes, sir."

"You just wanted to talk to him and he wouldn't listen, so you just shot Matthew in his back while he was asleep. Now, has that memory come back to you, Ms. Winkler?"

"No, sir."

"You don't have that memory now?"

"I don't have any memory of the way you just said that."

On redirect, the defense asked, "Do you know whether it was an accident or not?"

"Yes."

"How can you know that if you don't remember when the gun went off?"

"Because I didn't want any of this to happen."

Farese asked his final question. "Did you say that you didn't tell anyone because you didn't think they'd believe you?"

"Yes."

Farese made a broad sweep of his arm around the courtroom, bringing his hand to rest where he could point at the prosecution table. "They still don't believe you, today, do they?"

Immediately after a lunch break, Steve Farese got to his feet and said, "Your Honor, may it please the court, the defense rests."

The prosecution called two rebuttal witnesses. The first, former neighbor Brandy Jones made her second visit to the witness stand. She testified that in August of 2005, her family vacationed with Matthew, Mary and the girls. Glenn wanted a gun in the home and Brandy was uncomfortable with it. They discussed the issue with the other couple. "Mary said that I'd probably be more comfortable if I went to a firing range and learned how to use it. She told me that Matthew had taken her to a firing range and taught her how to use the gun."

Leslie Ballin cross-examined the witness, trying to leave the impression in the jury's mind that Brandy fabricated the story. Brandy said that she didn't realize the significance of the information until she listened to Mary's testimony that morning and heard Mary's claim that she did not know how to use a gun.

Not wanting the jury to believe a word of Brandy's testimony, he badgered her about her response to a question about her friendship with the Winklers, asking if she'd said 'he' or 'she' was her best friend. Brandy said, "I know I said *she* was my best friend and *he* was like a brother to me."

Ballin said, "Oh, so now I understand," leaving the scent of innuendo hanging in the air.

Brandy rolled her eyes in response.

The prosecution called Investigator Howard Patterson of the Tennessee Bureau of investigation, who testified that the pornographic images on the computer were down-loaded on two different dates, once in October 2005 and another date in January 2006.

Another member of the defense team, Steven Farese, Jr., cross-examined this final witness, though no revealing testimony was elicited.

CHAPTER 49

Walt Freeland began his closing arguments by impressing upon the jurors the importance of what they had done and thanking them for their service to the state of Tennessee.

"There's been a lot of confusion, I submit. If I have contributed to that, I apologize, because as difficult as your job is, it's really a pretty simple thing that you have to decide."

He displayed a definition of first-degree murder on a screen and discussed each element that the state needed to prove beyond a shadow of doubt and with moral certainty. The first on the list was that the state needed to show that the defendant unlawfully killed the victim. "A determination of whether it was an unlawful killing is: Did he deserve to die? According to Mary Winkler, he did not deserve to die. According to every piece of evidence that you heard from that witness stand, he did not deserve to die. Here was a thirty-one-year-old man, in his own house, in his own bed, with his family, his little girls—two in the next room, one down the hall—asleep, asleep in his own bed. Not a threat to anybody. He was brutally, intentionally, premeditatedly killed. Shot in the middle of his back as he slept. He did not deserve to die."

He moved on to the second element, the desire to kill, or intent. "It would be easy to say you cannot know what is in somebody's mind. Nobody knows what is in somebody's mind, but the person. Well, of course, that's silly, because that would mean that it would require every defendant to testify or give a confession that 'It was in my mind to intentionally kill this person.'

"The question, I submit, is: Was this an accident? Now you have heard . . . that this was abuse on one hand . . . or on the other hand, if it wasn't abuse, it was an accident. I submit to you that these are theories that don't go together . . . This is not an accidental death. It is ludicrous . . . the intention can be concluded by the action . . . It is ridiculous to think that it was an accident. It was not an accident."

He told the jury that the state had to prove intention, but not intelligence. "Murder by definition is not intelligent . . . The question is whether it was intentional . . . It wasn't well thought out, but the question is: Did she mean to do what she did when she aimed that shotgun and pulled the trigger? If she did, then that is an intentional act.

". . . She may have regretted it the second after she did it. She may regret it for the rest of her life. That is not the question. The question at the time of the killing is: What was her mental state? At the time of the killing, not now— if she's remorseful—not one minute after, but at the time of the killing."

He next argued about premeditation, telling the jury that it was not required to be present for a definite amount of time. She had to be ". . . sufficiently free of excitement and passion to form premeditation." He insisted that her knowledge of the banking problems and her retrieval of the shotgun from the top shelf of the closet proved that Mary premeditated the crime.

He reminded the jury that Mary said in Alabama, " 'I always thought it was going to kick hard.' She thought about it? Now this is a lady who claims she doesn't know how to use a shotgun, but she thought about how hard it was going to kick."

He cast doubt on Mary's ability to remember the actual murder while being able to recall that it was " 'a little bang, it wasn't as loud as I thought.' She thought? She was thinking about the sound it was going to make. How long was she thinking about that?"

He drew their attention to another statement made by Mary Winkler, " 'It's crossed minds.' Now, Ms. Winkler can't explain what she meant, because she can't recall saying it. Again, you don't have to abandon your common sense to know what that meant.

"She told Stan Stabler she'd been 'battling not to do it forever' . . . It is impossible to spin that as anything but a confession."

He described the defense case as "sleight-of-hand." He told the jury that the custody case and the wrongful death civil suit had nothing to do with this trial. He reminded the jury that, "Because of the defendant, brothers have lost their brother, a mother and father have lost [their] son, and three precious children have just lost their daddy. That's for your consideration. That's the murder."

Freeland charged that the confusion in the courtroom was created by the defense strategy. All designed with the intention of making you see Mary Winkler as a victim.

"I submit, the only verdict that truth dictates and justice demands is a verdict of first-degree murder. You are not to have sympathy for Matthew Winkler or Patricia Winkler or Allie Winkler or Breanna Winkler. You're not. It doesn't have anything to do with whether or not Mary Winkler is guilty of murder.

"And I submit that you should not have any sympathy for Mary Winkler for the same reason. It has nothing to do with whether or not she's guilty of first-degree murder."

He then argued why the other degrees of offense were inappropriate, and wrapped up his statement. "It's not up for you to decide if Matthew was a good guy or a bad guy, or if he could have been a better husband. Or if she could have been a better wife. That has nothing to do with what you decide. Your attention must be focused on March twenty-second, the instant she pulled that trigger.

". . . Ladies and gentlemen, has the state carried its burden of proof that Matthew Winkler was unlawfully killed? Has the state carried its burden of proof that he was intentionally killed—that it was an intentional act? I submit that it has.

"And has the state of Tennessee carried its burden of proof that this act was premeditated? I believe, ladies and gentlemen of the jury, that the facts that we have presented prove that.

"Truth dictates and justice demands one verdict, and that is guilty of murder in the first degree."

CHAPTER 50

Leslie Ballin stepped up to address the jury. He opened by proclaiming the great responsibility of the defense team to speak up for Mary Winkler. "Lord knows that we are not worthy. A feeling of inadequacy fills my body because the words I am about to share with you, you will use as building blocks to build firm foundation to arrive at a verdict that truth dictates and justice demands."

He then promised to be brief. "Words and facts do not cease to exist simply because they are ignored. It's time to take your blinders off. Open your eyes. Open your eyes to the truth. Open your eyes to the life that Mary Winkler lived that brought her to March twenty-second of 2006.

"Facts do not cease to exist simply because they are ignored." He expounded on the cornerstone of our justice system—the presumption of innocence. "We need facts in this courtroom for you to hear, for you to feel, for you to understand in this case."

He then described the possible charges they had to consider. "Three charges . . . require proof of a culpable state of mind . . . What proof has the state produced to convince you that Mary Winker knowingly or intentionally committed any crime?"

He explained that a conviction based on circumstantial evidence could not be reached unless it was consistent with the theory of guilt, and must exclude every other reasonable explanation. "Where is that proof?

"Facts do not cease to exist because they are ignored."

A premeditated act had be committed when the accused was free from excitement and passion. "Under the facts of this case, her whole life was in a state of excitement—a heightened state of emotions."

He reminded them that they needed to look before the day of Matthew's death and told them, "Do not forsake your eyes and ears that have been with you for the last ten days."

He said there was no proof for the second-degree murder charge or for voluntary manslaughter, since there was no intent. "It's not up to the defense to prove that it was an accident. It is up to the state to prove, beyond all reasonable doubt, that it isn't."

He spoke of the two other possible charges that allowed the jury to decide that, even though the act was not intentional, it still might be criminal. He added, "I do not think that Mary is guilty of anything."

CHAPTER 51

Steve Farese stepped before the podium looking solemn and pained. "There's nothing more dangerous in this world than a sincere ignorance and a conscientious stupidity. Those that can make you believe things with ignorant, sloppy recording, insufficient data, really make you less than human.

"Does the prosecution expect us to leave our life experiences at home? That we put on a juror's cap and we become a robot? You have seen a robot. You've seen Mary Winkler."

He drew an analogy of the Borg on *Star Trek* to the prosecution in their ability to assimilate and defeat all resistance. "If we put a witness up and the witness says, 'I don't know how to shoot that gun' . . . they put up another witness who says, 'You do know how to shoot that gun.' How do you fight that? Well, we fight it with truth.

"Mary Winkler told you the truth. You know that. The truth has, what a professor told me one time, the ring of truth. Unfortunately, Matthew could talk the talk, but could not walk the walk. He couldn't practice what he was preaching. It's not unusual. It happens to a lot of people. He had a problem. His problem was that, as Trooper Jones said, of a bully.

"And what bullies do is, they pick on people that are smaller than them. They talk about people as if they're not human, as if they're second-class citizens—that they're better than they are. Maybe because they're better-looking, maybe because they're smarter, maybe because their status in life is better economically—because that's what bullies are.

"And if you don't believe Mary Winkler was beaten up and subjected to years of abuse, then that's okay. You heard the proof."

Farese evoked the 1968 Democrat convention in Chicago, where the chant was: "The whole world is watching." "I suggest to you, that the whole world *is* watching. This is not just about Mary Winkler. This is not just about Matthew Winkler. This is not just about Patricia and Allie and Breanna, or Dan and Diane Winkler, or Daniel and Jacob Winkler.

"This is about a problem we have in this country, and it's spousal abuse. The whole world is watching.

"Now, they think of us in Tennessee and Mississippi as a bunch of bumbling, redneck know-nothings. We know that. But we're just as smart as anyone else. We care just as much as anybody else. And our family matters to us just as much as anyone else's family does. We're as honest as anybody. We're as good as anybody.

"And I say to you, if you looked up abuse—spousal abuse—in the dictionary, you're gonna see Mary Winkler's picture looking back to you.

"Does that mean that Matthew Winkler *had* to die? No!

"Does that mean Matthew Winkler *deserved* to die? No!

"Does that mean that this family," he continued, pointing to the Winklers, "has to sit through a trial for two weeks and suffer? No!

"Therein lies the sincere ignorance of the prosecution. They say, 'Okay, the defense is accidental. Okay, we'll debunk that. Wait a minute. Did you say the defense was domestic abuse? Okay we'll debunk that.'

"It's like *My Cousin Vinny*, where the prosecutor says, 'Over here we have domestic abuse and over here we have accidental shooting, and they won't meet.' That's ridiculous. *And* insidious. Because that's exactly what the defense is, because the defense is based on truth, not supposition.

"The defense is based on her statement. Now, you haven't heard her statement in closing argument, have you? Because if you hear her statement, you hear her voice. If you hear her voice, you have empathy, because you're hearing the truth and it's painting the picture of someone who's been beaten down. Someone who's been 'nailed . . . in the ground,' according to her statement. Someone who is trying to protect her husband, trying to protect her children, because that is the pattern of an abused spouse."

He talked about Lynne Zager's testimony that Mary had all indicators of an abused spouse. He blasted the prosecution for using the psychologist's statements when it suited them and when it didn't, making fun of her expert opinions. He said that their attitudes toward the issue of domestic abuse and psychology were behind the times, and drew parallels to past discrimination against women and minorities. He accused them of being intellectually dishonest.

He moved on to an analogy about the Wizard of Oz. "Pay no attention to the man behind the screen. Pay no attention to the custody hearing in another court. They have segregated Mary from her children. And I submit to you that segregation is wrong in any circumstance."

He turned to the men who died on Normandy Beach during the D-Day invasion. Their last words, he said, ". . . were never 'Daddy.' They were 'Mother.'" There is a bond between a mother and their children that can never be expunged. These children are part of their mothers. They came from their mothers. They are inextricably twined with their mothers. Daddies can love their children. I love my children. But I guarantee you this: My daughter loves my wife more than she can ever love me. There is something inherent about that relationship. It is unnatural for daughters to be separated from their mothers."

He detailed the birthdays and other special events in the children's lives that Mary has missed since March

2006 and then moved back to that fatal morning. "It is un-controverted that there was any planning, and yet the pros-ecution says there was planning. What? If grabbing a pair of baby socks as you leave the home is planning, then I guess she planned. If not knowing where you're going is planning, then I guess she planned. If using your name everywhere you went is planning, I guess she planned. Planning? Intellectually dishonest."

He pointed out that no evidence was presented to show that Mary went to the closet to retrieve the gun, yet, in closing, the prosecution claimed that was part of the plan-ning. He said it would be easy to have Mary manufacture a convenient story about the location of the gun that morn-ing, but that would be a lie that would undermine our sys-tem of justice.

"It's uncontroverted that there's no criminal intent, be-cause there was no planning, if you throw in Dr. Zager's testimony. And if anyone is honest in this courtroom, it can't be murder one or murder two. It cannot be!"

He spoke of the alienation of the children and said, "Mary was isolated from her natural family when she was married. Now she is isolated from her natural children when she got charges. And the cycle of abuse continues.

". . . It's uncontroverted that the gun could have dis-charged unintentionally. It's uncontroverted because we know that from Steve Scott, who's an expert, who had a gun unintentionally discharge."

"It's uncontroverted—and I've hit on this—that she did not have the state of mind to form intent to commit a crime.

"It is absolutely unconscionable to me that the state of Tennessee can raise the issue of the unplugged phone as a part of the planning of the premeditated murder when they know why that phone is unplugged. They know. You know, too.

"Unfortunately, the ABI, who doesn't know how to search a van and find evidence in a murder case—it's only a murder case, so why be concerned?—the ABI did some-thing right." The photograph of the unplugged phone on the floor of the motel room surrounded by baby toys appeared on the screen. "Impossible that a baby will be playing with the phone in a home and at the motel? Now, what are the chances that we would have this picture? That's scary, isn't it?"

He then took a swing at the prosecution's financial motive. "I spent three days of my life listening to that crap."

He brought out the shoe. "This is not about religion, but, I submit to you, that a Church of Christ's minister's wife does not wear this kind of shoe."

On the sexual abuse, he demanded, "Is it funny that he forced her to have anal sex? Is that funny? Is that funny to you? Is that nothing? How could she even make up a story like 'He told me I could have surgery if it damaged me'? How could you even make that up? You couldn't, because truth is stranger than fiction."

He talked about the pressures on Matthew to follow in his father's footsteps. He pointed out Mary's inability to talk to anyone about her problems, because it would affect Matthew's career and harm her children. "She'd finally gotten the courage to get his attention, but after years of abuse and being a punching bag, of being belittled and have the self-worth of a crippled ant, she shorted out. That's what Dr. Zager said.

"The gun goes off. None of us will ever know how. None of us can ever possibly know if it was intentionally or unintentionally, whether it was accidental. I don't know. I wasn't there. I can't tell you. I cannot set up here and be intellectually dishonest with you. I can't do it.

"Could she have killed him intentionally? Sure, absolutely, positively. Have they proved it? Absolutely, positively *not*! Have they proven any crime? This is hard for me to say, maybe. Maybe she was negligent. Maybe she was negligent. But what I can't get by is what Dr. Zager said: She couldn't form intent.

". . . I don't believe she is guilty of a crime. But I'd be less than honest if I stood here and told you she couldn't have been negligent."

About the children, he said, "Do I think their grandparents love them? Absolutely." He spoke of his empathy for Dan and Diane Winkler and their remaining sons. He said if it was his family, he would be bitter and couldn't let go. "And sometimes it's hard to forgive. And sometimes when you're getting bad information, it's hard to let things go. And if it was me, I couldn't do it.

". . . But you know what? Mary has a family, too. They're out here," he said as he turned to them and pointed, "and they're reunited, but they're missing three.

"Mary never once during this ordeal ever thought of herself—never once. Did she lie to her children? Yes she did. She lied to protect them, to ease them. She wanted to go to the beach with them and have some good days before the bad came. And the bad did come, like a thief in the night.

"Mary Winkler sits before you innocent of any crime. She is covered with a veil of the presumption of innocence. She is protected by the greatest hurdle in the free world when it comes to burden of proof. And that hurdle is reasonable doubt."

He talked to the jurors about how to know if they made the right decision. If you catch a glimpse of yourself in the mirror next week, ". . . would you say to yourself, 'Did I do the right thing in convicting that girl?' If you do say that, you did not do the right thing. To me, that's a pretty simple guide.

"As you all can see, I love what I do. Y'all would rather be home, but I'd rather be right where I am, 'cause I have the chance to represent someone who needed help, and this time it's pure. There's no money involved. It's pure. And I get to represent somebody I can believe in and get to know this person and know her family. And it's real. These are real lives. These are real people," he said, pointing to Mary's family members. "These are real tragedies."

Waving his arm in the direction of Matthew's family, "And it's full on this side of the aisle, too.

"Circumstances are not dependent on men. Men are

dependent on circumstances. And in this case, there was an accumulation of circumstances. Mistakes by both people. Should she have left? Yes, she should've left. But could she leave? No. Should he have acted in the way in which he did? No. But he certainly did not deserve to die.

"Mary loved Matthew. I guess you could say she loved him to death. If you don't believe she loved him, look in her eyes, because they are dead.

"You heard Mary testify that she loves her children. I guess she's just talking," he said, his voice dripping with sarcasm. "I don't guess she really loved them. I don't guess she proved by her actions that she really loved them. And I don't guess that he loved her.

"And I guess over in Iraq or Afghanistan or one of those countries where our young are fighting, one of them is getting shot right now and he's lying on the ground. And you know what he's saying? 'Mama.'

"Thank you."

CHAPTER 52

Since the state carried the burden of proof, Walt Freeland had one last chance to persuade the jury. "I'll let you decide whether improper attempts have been made to direct you by sympathy. I'll lead you back to the facts of the case, which is why we are here."

He argued with Leslie Ballin's statement that this was just a circumstantial case and reminded the jurors that there was direct evidence, too. "As for her mental state, ladies and gentlemen, you take your good walking-around-McNairy-County common sense back in there about determining what that lady's mental state was.

"Now Dr. Zager testified, you heard her testimony. There's an old saying in the South, 'Bless her heart.' Well, bless her heart." He dismissed Zager's diagnosis, saying that the death of Mary's sister twenty years ago and having a bad marriage is not the equivalent of being in combat or being in a hostage situation. "I am in no way diminishing domestic assault. This is not a case of domestic assault. I'm with the state of Tennessee, we prosecute domestic assault."

He reiterated his acceptance that domestic violence was a real problem, but he said, "Is it a defense for shooting your husband while he sleeps? While he's in the middle of the bed? Shoot him in the middle of his back with a twelve-gauge shotgun?"

He referred to the testimony of Dr. Zager again and

said, "I am not alleging this is not PTSD. I'm saying it's not post-traumatic stress disorder. This is Pre-Trial Strategy by the Defense."

He suggested that Mary could have easily figured out what she should say to her mental health expert, and that Dr. Zager was "a true believer." She was hypothesizing about domestic abuse before Mary and the children were even located.

"The whole world is watching, and that makes it difficult. It puts pressure on you that you shouldn't have to have. The question is, Will you do your duty? Will you follow the law? Or will you be swayed by improper arguments? By things that have nothing to do with the murder case?"

He told them that the custody case and the fact that the children went to Disney World had nothing to do with the murder case. "It had nothing to do with determining whether there was an intentional act and whether there was a premeditated act."

He decried the introduction of diversions like the "dirty pictures, the shoe and the wig." He said even if everything she said were true, which he suggested was not probable, "does that mean Matthew deserved to die? It does not. There was no immediacy there.

". . . Matthew Winkler did not die accidentally, and it is insulting to your intelligence to suggest that it was.

". . . At some point before she pulled the trigger, she formed in her mind what she would do.

". . . I want the last two words that I say, and that are in your mind, not to be 'Thank you,' which I do. And I don't want them to be 'Poor Mary.' I want them to be about the fella who's never going to see his daughters graduate or get married or have another Father's Day with him. I want the last two words that you will think about to be: 'Matthew Winkler.' "

CHAPTER 53

The next morning, Thursday, April 19, Judge McCraw read off the names of the alternates and sent them home. He instructed the jury of ten women and two men before leaving them to deliberate the fate of Mary Winkler. The long wait began. Reporters and cameramen chatted in the media room, gave live reports on the air and roamed around aimlessly. The room had a constant flow of traffic. Judge McCraw dropped in, defense attorneys strolled through, law enforcement personnel leaned back and talked. But one arrival took everyone by surprise. His appearance merited an introduction.

Sue Allison got everyone's attention and presented McNairy County General Sessions Court Judge Van McMahan. "This is his courtroom and he graciously allowed the media to use it for the duration of the trial. He moved his offices downtown to the old courthouse, but he needs this room now for just a short while."

Spontaneous applause erupted as the judge apologized for the inconvenience. He took his seat behind the bench, listened to testimony of a uniformed police officer and issued search warrants. Job done, he exited, thanking the reporters for their cooperation.

During the day, there were two verdict false alarms. One was generated by the jurors submitting a question to the judge, the other by the arrival of Matthew's grandmother. Media trailed her into the courtroom like bloodhounds on a scent. But she just returned to pick up an item she had left behind.

The television reporters and their crews were all in front of the courthouse setting up for live shots on the 5 o'clock news when, eight hours after convening, the jury really did arrive at a verdict. The press tripped over one another swarming into the courtroom. They packed tight into the back rows.

An apologetic Sheriff Roten stepped in front of the eager group. The courtroom had to be cleared on orders of Judge McCraw. Everyone would have to be wanded before entry. The reporters plodded out and lined up for the security ritual.

The judge and jury entered at 5:25. Mary Winkler, flanked by her attorneys, walked in a few moments later, followed by Mary's family. As the door to the judge's chamber opened, the bailiff intoned, "All rise."

Judge McCraw stepped up to the bench and took his seat. "Ladies and gentlemen, I understand the jury has reached a verdict. Let's bring them in and hear from them."

The jurors filed into the tense courtroom, their eyes focused on the floor in front of their feet. When they all took their places, the judge asked, "Ladies and gentlemen of the jury, have you reached a verdict?"

"Yes, sir, Your Honor," juror Bill Berry answered.

"Sir, are you the foreperson?"

"Yes, sir."

"Would you please pass the sheriff your verdict, please?"

Sheriff Roten accepted the black notebook containing the documents from the panel and walked them over to the bench. The judge pulled out the papers, glanced at them and said, "Ms. Winkler, if you could stand, please, ma'am."

Mary stood, looking dazed. Her eyes were vacant. Her hair was disordered with stray strands sticking out at odd angles. The cross on her necklace hung off-center. Her mouth was a thin, pale slash across her face.

"All right, ma'am. The verdict reads as follows: 'We, the

jury, find Mary C. Winkler guilty of voluntary manslaughter." This verdict was the least of the three possible felony charges. Mary faced a sentence of 3 to 6 years, with a required 30 percent of that time to be spent behind bars.

The judge polled each individual juror to assure that the verdict delivered was the verdict of all. Mary's expression did not change. She gave no indication that she even knew what was going on. Two rows back, her father Clark looked worried and confused, as if the verdict had no meaning. In the seats behind the prosecutors, Diane Winkler looked lost. Dan tensed and relaxed as he vigorously chewed the gum in his mouth. The silence in the courtroom was eerie. There were no immediate outbursts of joy or dismay in the small room. But, far away, in the studios of Court TV, everyone watching the proceedings let out a collective gasp.

The attorneys had a sidebar with the judge, where he determined that Mary would remain out on bail until the sentencing hearing. Mary swayed on her feet at the defense table. When Steve Farese returned, she whispered, "Does this mean I can get my children back?"

In the deliberation room, Judge McCraw met with the jurors to thank them for their service and answer their questions. He thought they'd want to know about what had happened since they were first cut off from the rest of the world. On the top of his mind was his awareness that the jury knew nothing about Monday's Virginia Tech shooting rampage that left thirty-three dead and many others injured.

With his thoughts on that tragedy, he was taken aback by the first question: "Who's the daddy?" At first, he didn't understand what was being asked. Then, chattering jurors brought the puzzle pieces together. The first thing they wanted to know about was the anticipated DNA results determining the paternity of Anna Nicole-Smith's baby.

Outside of the courthouse, Dan and Diane Winkler stepped up to a bank of microphones. Holding Diane's hand, Dan said, "We wish to say thank you to our God and Father. He has been our rock and our shield."

A reporter asked him about Matthew. Dan's eyes twinkled with repressed tears. "We're very grateful for the privilege and honor that was ours to be the parents of Matthew Brian Winkler, and we treasure the memory of the love that he had for his family, for his Lord, for his Church, for us as parents, for his brothers and for all of his extended family and for his friends."

THE REVERBERATIONS

"For a woman which hath an husband is bound by the law to her husband so long as he liveth; but if the husband be dead, she is loosed from the law of her husband."

—*Romans* 7:2

CHAPTER 54

One juror expressed his displeasure with the verdict just two days after the trial. Jury foreman Billy Berry said he was surprised when the first vote was taken and he learned that many of the women wanted Mary to walk. He went into the jury room believing she was guilty of first-degree murder.

With those divergent points of view, the deliberations were stressful and often got very argumentative. He felt that the panel, to be fair to the victim, should have had more male jurors. He also said that he was not convinced that Mary's claims of abuse were even true.

Mary returned to McMinnville to await her sentencing. There, she dated Darrell Pillow, brother of one of her employers, whom she had been seeing since February. Now rumors emerged that Mary would soon marry again.

Her criminal attorneys filed for diversion. If granted, it would allow Mary to serve her entire sentence outside of prison on probation. At the end of the probationary period, it would then be possible for her to get her criminal record expunged—as if the crime never happened.

Between the time of the verdict and the sentencing, the child custody case raged in a number of different courtrooms. Dan and Diane Winkler filed for a termination of Mary's parental rights. After Patricia confessed her fear that, since her mother shot her daddy, maybe she'd shoot her, too, Dan and Diane were even more staunchly opposed to any contact. Mary did not get a visit with her children.

On June 1, Mary's attorneys filed a motion seeking a new trial on the criminal charges. Many were stunned by their audacity—it was hard to believe they really wanted to challenge the verdict of the first trial.

One week later, everyone returned to court for the sentencing hearing. Mary sat in a chair at the defense table with downcast eyes and an expressionless face.

Walt Freeland first addressed the court citing the enhancing factors he'd filed for the judge's consideration: the victim was particularly vulnerable because of physical disability—meaning he was shot in bed while asleep; Mary Winkler used a firearm; she had no hesitation to commit a crime when the risk to human life was high; and she abused a position of private trust.

He called two witnesses to the stand. The first was Daniel Winkler. Although his face was fuller and his hair clipped shorter, he bore an eerie resemblance to his deceased brother. He said, "I have sat quietly for the last year and more, and watched. I watched the life of my brother be turned into a circus. The character of my brother be intentionally murdered just as his body was intentionally murdered. He has torn me, my family—and, Mary, your family—apart. And I think it is time for us to hear what Matthew has to say."

"Do you feel qualified to speak for Matthew?" Freeland asked.

"Obviously, you can't hear Matthew's voice, because it's no longer here. Matt can't tell you what and who he really was. He doesn't have a voice anymore, so I'm going to do the best I can to tell who Matthew was.

"Matthew was a wonderful father teaching his kids how to play sports . . . played with them, read with them. Matt was a wonderful father.

" . . . Nothing hurts, to me, more than to see how much this hurts these little girls. After the funeral, Patricia was in the back seat of my car and she was crying. She said, 'Daddy won't be at any more of my birthdays. He won't come anymore to my softball games. I don't even want to marry if Daddy won't be there. I'm afraid I'll forget what my Daddy looks like.' That broke my heart."

Daniel talked about a weekend he spent at his parents' home when Allie was the first one to get out of bed. "She sat in my lap, rubbed my face and said, 'Your face feels like Daddy's. I miss my daddy.' Matt was a great father, and you can see it in the eyes of his children and how deeply they miss him.

"But they'll never see him again in this lifetime, because of your intentional act," he said, looking at Mary.

He told the judge that Matthew was a wonderful brother, his best friend—the one constant in his life. "Matthew was a servant. He put others before himself. You could see that through all the lives he's touched, all the people he's helped, all the teenagers and children he helped do better and had a positive impact on their lives. Matt was a wonderful servant."

He spoke of the pain of only being able to visit his brother at the cold cemetery. He told of his experience of comforting a friend at a family funeral and how that gave him a new outlook. Now when he looked at the grave marker, he focused on the dash between the dates of Matthew's birth and death, and knew that was what mattered, because it represented Matthew's life.

Then he turned to his brother's wife. "You have spent the last month and year, Mary, writing letters to people asking them to respond about you, to say something nice about you, something good about you. I never received a letter. I never received a letter of apology for taking away my constant, my best friend. So I don't see any remorse in your behavior. I don't see the love that you have so carefully explained. No matter how long you live, your dash will never equal the dash of Matthew Winkler."

Diane Winkler took the stand next. She read an open

letter from her sister to Mary. In it, the harshest words focused on the lives of the three girls.

> *"Will Patricia, Allie and Breanna think it's okay to take a life when life is hard or challenging? Their mother did.*
>
> *"As they get older will they wonder if they will follow in your footsteps? When they become teenagers and want to date, will there be anyone to date them or will the shadow of their mother's poor choice hang over their heads?*
>
> *"Will any parent want their sons to marry your daughters, for fear they might follow your example? What legacy are you leaving your daughters?*
>
> *"You alone will have to bear this burden while your children suffer for your bad choice. They lost a father. And a mother, too. How sad and devastating for all."*

After finishing the letter, Diane voiced her own thoughts. "You've destroyed Matthew's memory. You accused him of being a monster. But of everything you accused him of, there is no proof.

"I wonder, Mary, how it is you want your children to remember their father? Your daughters loved their daddy and they loved you, Mary. They do not understand.

". . . Your girls have nightmares at night. They dream of someone breaking into their home. They dream of someone with a gun. I don't know that you truly understand, Mary, the impact you've had on your children.

". . . You know, Mary, this is a serious thing. You took another's life. And you had a choice . . . And you made it, didn't you? And it's a choice that you'll have to live with the rest of your life . . . You took his life. You took something from your children: their father. You took a son from us. You took a brother. You took an uncle. You took a best friend. And for there to be no remorse, no remorse ever shown to your girls, never written in a letter to your girls—you never told your girls you're sorry. Don't you think you, at least, owe them that?

"You've never told us you're sorry. I think you, at least, owe us that. I think we are owed the truth."

Steve Farese questioned Diane about the filing to terminate Mary's parental rights. Walt Freeland immediately objected to that line of questioning. Judge McCraw said he didn't need that kind of information to make his decision. The state closed its case.

After a short break, Steve Farese called Tabatha Freeman to the stand. Much of what she said was a rehash of her testimony at the trial—including the tearful delivery. In her plea for leniency, she told the court that she still needed her sister in her life—"she is the world to me."

She also evoked the children. "She needs them and they need her. She's not complete without them, and they aren't without her."

Paul Pillow, manager of Cleaners Express spoke highly of Mary as an employee. "She's done more than she's been asked to do." He also talked of his fondness of her as a person. "Mary has a way of making you feel comfortable when you are around her . . . Mary is merry all the time."

Rudy Thomsen said that Mary was "a very compassionate, very loving person."

On cross-examination, Freeland asked, "You're not worried about Mary killing or harming anyone if she gets out?"

"No, sir."

"You didn't have any concerns that Matthew would be hurt, did you?"

"No."

Donna Dunlap, Mary's probation officer, spoke once again of Mary's good behavior. Arlington Church of Christ pulpit minister Wayne Cantrell spoke of her truthfulness, but admitted to the prosecutor that he had not known her long, and his judgment of her honesty was based on the fact that he never caught her in a lie.

Dr. Lynne Zager testified that Mary would need more psychological help, but she was not a danger to herself or thers.

Mary read a statement asking for mercy. She acknowledged the pain she'd caused and hoped her case would encourage others to reach out to those in abusive situations. She said she prayed for the Winkler family every night. She still did not tell them she was sorry for shooting Matthew, but she did say, "Any sentence you give me will not punish me enough."

The judge prepared a twenty-four-page document outlining the reasoning behind his sentencing decision. His first words crushed the defense. "The court finds that the defendant is not a suitable candidate for judicial diversion, nor an appropriate candidate for full probation."

Their worries lessened, however, when he granted her partial probation. He said he reached his decision by balancing the verdict of guilt on the charge of the lower class-C felony and Mary's lack of criminal record with the "especially violent, horrifying, offensive" circumstances of the crime.

He awarded Mary a 3-year sentence, ordering that she spend 210 days of that time in strict confinement. But, even that was softened. He allowed her credit for time served, and gave her the option of spending up to 60 days of that incarceration in a mental health facility approved by the court. When her days behind bars—from the time of her arrest in March 2006 to the day she was released on bond in August of that year—were subtracted from her 210-day sentence, there was a balance of sixty-seven days. The defense team was overjoyed.

If Mary's attorneys moved quickly to place her in a psychiatric facility, the most time Mary faced in an actual jail was seven more days—one week and nothing more.

CHAPTER 55

On June 13, Mary's attorneys withdrew their motion for a new trial. Under the circumstances, facing a new judge and jury extended the ordeal for Mary, and posed an unacceptable risk of a greater sentence. It was better to bring it all to a quick conclusion.

In Selmer, whether angered or pleased by the verdict, the residents were relieved. The circus had left town. The national spotlight shined down on them no more. Then, just eight days after Mary's sentencing, another tragedy struck, drawing the media back to the small Southern town.

During a fundraising race, a driver lost control of his car and veered off the roadway into a crowd of spectators. Six people died—all under the age of 30. Eighteen others, including a 5-year-old, were injured seriously enough to require hospital treatment.

Photographer Robert King, indicted by a McNairy County Grand Jury for impersonating a licensed professional when he entered the jail to photograph Mary, still awaited final disposition of his case. His lawyers had filed for judicial diversion.

After nine days in the McNairy County jail, Mary was transferred to an undisclosed, locked-down mental health facility in central Tennessee. She was released from there on August 15, 2007—one year to the day that she walked out of the county lock-up on bond.

She bounced through the doors of Cleaners Express as soon as she returned to town that morning. Smiling and laughing, she kidded around with manager Paul Pillow. Then she paid a visit to her probation officer, Donna Dunlap. She would be supervised by that office until 2010.

For reasons Darrell Pillow did not understand, Mary terminated their six-month relationship upon her release. The reasons Mary gave made no sense to him—he thought their involvement was serious.

Mary continued to make repeated appearances in court over visitation and custody of her children. Every time, she loaded up the three car seats in the optimistic belief that she would come home to McMinnville with her girls.

She filed for full custody in mid-September. On September 19, she appeared at a hearing before Carroll County Chancellor Ron Harmon.

Dan and Diane's custody attorney, James Adams, grilled her. "You have in fact begun another relationship since you got out of prison, haven't you? Or since you got out of your mental health treatment?"

"Ah, no, not," Mary stammered.

"It's your testimony here today that you have not dated anyone or had a relationship with anyone since you got out of your mental health treatment?"

"I have not."

"Did you or did you not have a relationship with Darrell Ray Pillow?"

"Yes," Mary admitted.

"You did?"

"Uh-huh," she said with a nod.

"And are you still dating him?"

"No."

"When did that stop?"

"Sometime in August."

"When did it begin?"

"Springtime."

"Were you ever close to getting married?"

"No."

"You never discussed marriage?" he pressed.

"Light discussions, but nothing serious."

"You don't think there's any problem with getting in a new relationship this shortly after you murdered another man who you had a relationship with?"

"I don't think that's appropriate terminology," Mary objected.

"I'm sorry, was 'murder' an inappropriate terminology?"

When Kay Farese Turner complained that the line of questioning was not relevant, Chancellor Harmon said it was relevant to him.

Mary answered, "We talked and got to know each other, and then, I just came to a point where I wanted to be single, and all I want is my girls."

At the end of the hearing, Harmon issued a court order allowing Mary a supervised visit with her daughters on September 30. But the day before, in the state Court of Appeals, a response was issued on Dan and Diane's emergency filing. The court stayed all visitation activities until the claims of "irreparable harm" alleged by the Winklers could be fully explored.

Months after the criminal trial, District Attorney General Michael Dunavant added fuel to the custody fire, when he spoke to Tonya Smith-King of *The Jackson Sun* about Mary's flight after Matthew's death. "She drove hundreds of miles to Jackson, Mississippi, spent one night, and then to Orange Beach, Alabama, and was in a hotel the next night. She was running out of money. How was she going to feed her children? How was she going to get back to Tennessee?

"You know what she was going to do? She was going to kill her children, and herself, and she was just going to do it at the beach instead of in Selmer, Tennessee. Now, that's my own personal observation and opinion, which she never came out and admitted that. But that's our speculation. We couldn't prove it at trial."

Mary continued to receive media attention. She was featured on *Snapped*, airing on the Oxygen channel and on the syndicated *Montel Williams Show*.

And she achieved the ultimate in the talk-show circuit— an appearance on *The Oprah Winfrey Show*. The courts blocked her travel to Chicago, but an interview in her lawyer's office was telecast to millions.

As the summer of 2008 approached, Mary no longer lived with her loyal friend, Rudy Thomsen. She no longer worked for Paul Pillow and Matt Hash at Cleaner's Express. And the battle for the custody of the girls raged into its third year.

Surprisingly, it all came to an abrupt end on August 1, 2008. That afternoon, Mary Winkler picked up her girls and took them to her home in McMinnville. Matthew's parents and Mary reached an out-of-court agreement allowing the children to live with their mother. No formal custody papers were filed at that time.

Mary has begun her life anew.

Matthew's parents will never again see their son's smile.

And three little girls struggle to find meaning, healing and understanding in a world turned upside down.

AFTERWORD

Was justice done in the courthouse in McNairy County, Tennessee? It's a difficult question to answer. This case has no black and white, no sharp defining edges delineating the truth. The bottom line for me, though, is that the ultimate act of domestic violence is homicide. Mary committed that act and Matthew was its victim.

But what of Mary's alleged years of victimization at Matthew's hand? If you believe every word she said, it still comes down to one cold, hard fact: Mary was not in fear of her life when she pulled that trigger. She could not possibly feel as if she were in imminent danger—Matthew was asleep when she shot him in the back.

Can you believe Mary's entire story? There appears to be enough corroboration to indicate that Matthew was controlling and did have a quick temper. But beyond that, so many stories were changed between the time of Matthew's death and now, that it's difficult to ascertain the truth.

Mary's father Clark Freeman originally said that he had no idea that his daughter was being abused; a month later, he suspected, but did nothing; and in the spring, he told of the many times he begged her to leave.

Her attorneys alleged that she was sexually abused. Mary testified that she'd been forced to perform anal and oral sex, and dress up in "slutty" clothes. But she also said that if she told Matthew to stop, he would. On *The Oprah*

Winfrey Show, she said that Matthew would stop what he was doing if she made the slightest involuntary flinch. Perhaps Mary should have spoken up more often in the bedroom, but didn't. And since she didn't, he had no way of knowing in the heat of passion that she was unhappy with their sexual activity.

There are other things that don't have "the ring of truth" Steve Farese mentioned in his closing. Mary testified that in February 2006, she forwarded all of the family mail to a post office box at Matthew's instruction because he'd threatened the neighbors' dog and feared they would tamper with his mail. But that run-in with Sharyn Everitt had been many months before.

The shoe—something about it was off. I was amazed that no one searching the home in the aftermath of Matthew's death ever saw it. When I listened to Special Agent Brent Booth's admission that he saw the orange tackle box but did not look inside it or collect it as evidence, that excuse sounded sensible. However, when the shoe was revealed in the courtroom, no one on the prosecution side had seen it before. Steve Farese argued that it was not a typical shoe for a preacher's wife, and he was right. If any one of the investigators had seen it, surely it would have stood out enough to be remembered.

And why just one shoe? And how did the defense obtain it? No one testified to that. Every visit Mary's attorneys made to the home on Mollie Drive was monitored by law enforcement. They would have known if the lawyers removed anything.

The wig is confusing me, too. Typically, a man who wants his spouse to wear a wig selects one that is strikingly different from his wife's usual style to add to the fantasy. Long blonde tresses, for instance, would have made more sense than that short brunette hank of hair that was revealed.

Then, there was a story circulating in September 2007 that cast doubt on Mary's credibility. According to

McMinnville friends, Mary rented a U-Haul and a friend volunteered his cattle truck so that she could retrieve her furniture from the Selmer home. But they later claimed that Mary told them as she prepared to leave, she learned that Dan and Diane Winkler had obtained a court order forbidding it.

In Selmer, though, it's believed that the church is eager to get the Winklers' belongings out of the parsonage, and people were in the house that day waiting for Mary's arrival to do just that. But Mary never came.

A search of jurisdictions uncovered no court order. If the McMinnville tale were true, there would be a document in evidence somewhere. Why, though, would Mary even fabricate a story like that?

If Mary is a liar, as the prosecution alleged, what was her motive for shooting Matthew? Was it really over the mess at the bank? That logic does not hold. She would not be afraid of Matthew unless she was abused. And if she didn't genuinely fear him, why would she react that way over a financial problem?

That brings us full circle and, in my mind, proves that Mary's story cannot be total fabrication. But "Why?" still lingers in the air.

Some place a mountain of blame on the churches of Christ. Is such a condemnation really fair? As in other conservative walks of faith, the churches of Christ do not acknowledge that there is a difference between the laws God set down to govern our lives in perpetuity and the prohibitions in the Bible that are merely reflections of that social reality. In biblical times, women *were* second-class citizens, less educated, less powerful, more vulnerable. In that context, the gender distinctions seem a concession to the times. But to adherents of the churches of Christ, it is immutable, timeless law.

Matthew and Mary were both raised in that faith and accepted its tenets. They observed the authority of the man in their birth homes. It was only logical that they brought it to their marriage. Mary accepted her secondary role as a matter of course, just as her mother did. She continued the habit of obedience, and paid the emotional price required by submission to another human being and by the suppression of her aspirations to the desires of someone else. The corrupting influence of holding a dominant position can distort reasoning and warp behavior—as it may have done to Matthew. It definitely created a gulf between them that only equality could fill.

Where is the truth about their relationship? In Dr. Zager's testimony? Zager only knew what Mary told her, and what she could discern with psychological evaluation tools. The analysis of those tests, however, is part science, part art.

We are left with no corroborating police or medical reports that indisputably point to domestic violence toward Mary or the children. No one but Mary claimed to see Matthew cutting off the baby's breath to make her stop crying. There are those who saw evidence of Matthew's dominance in Mary's life, but no unassailable eyewitnesses to spousal abuse.

Unfortunately, this is all too often the case when a marriage ends in a violent loss of life. Red flags are often not seen or warning signs are ignored.

One truth stands firm. Abuse within the home is a lethal force in our society. Tear down the walls and throw open the doors. Shine light on the darkness that destroys lives. Look at your family members and friends. Watch out for the subtle indicators of emotional, verbal and physical abuse—the isolation, the lowered self-esteem, the bouts of depression, the frequent injuries. When you see them, reach out and don't let go.

Ministers' wives are particularly vulnerable to isolation because of their position in life. If you are active in your church, advocate for the pastor's wife to be given opportunities to network with other women married to clergy. There are organizations designed for just that purpose. She needs a safe place to voice her concerns, laugh at problems and share secrets without concern of harming her husband's career. Help her find one.

One unresolved issue remained in this case: the custody of the now fatherless Patricia, Allie and Breanna. Who should raise these girls? What is in their best interests? Many vilify Dan and Diane Winkler, and do not want them to keep the children. They receive criticism for their religious beliefs from those who insist that if the children live with them, it will perpetuate the cycle of submission and destruction. But if that is true, does it matter where they go? Mary, too, is still an active adherent of the churches of Christ.

Others criticize the Winklers, saying that they are vengeful and vindictive. Why such harsh criticism for family members of the victim? Their choice in the courtroom to conceal their pain behind a mask of stoicism does not negate their suffering. They are victims, too. They have lost a loved one to an act of violence at Mary's hand. Even Steve Farese, in his closing, empathized with the sorrow they undoubtedly feel.

The other alternative is to return the girls to Mary. Do I believe Mary loves them? Absolutely. Do I think she will do the best she can for them? Without a doubt. Mary cherished those girls, and, like most every mother, wants to protect them from physical and emotional harm. I understand that.

Yet, I still have questions. Was there really any danger to Breanna that morning? Or did Mary think there was? Did she lash out in a fury of enflamed maternal instincts? Was it over the alleged "suffocation," or did Mary finally realize that by leading a life as a second-class citizen, she was a poor role model for her daughters—that she did not want them to follow in her footsteps as she followed her mother's? I can understand how that would stir up maternal rage. I can feel the intensity of that emotion.

But I am still left with a concern about what else Mary's actions say about her. She demonstrated poor impulse control—to say the least—on March 22, 2006, when she pulled a gun on her husband while her children slept just feet away. She was not thinking of her girls when she took that action. Does she have the necessary skills and psychological stability to successfully guide those girls to adulthood? It is unclear.

Regardless of whether or not it is in the best interests of the children, Mary now has custody of them. The dominant focus of the law in the state of Tennessee is the superior rights of the parent. A few years ago, it was the pre-eminent consideration in the neighboring state of Virginia, too. It took the death of a little girl at the hand of her parents to change the legislative priority to the best interests of the child.

After closely considering the circumstances of the case, one can't help but wonder: Where's the justice?

Is it justice when Dan and Diane Winkler watch the person responsible for their son's death walk free to begin her life anew less than a year-and-a-half after that fatal confrontation? It doesn't feel like it.

Is it justice when a battered woman, driven to a violent act in a moment of desperation, is deprived of her freedom for the rest of her life? Hardly.

But *was* Mary a victim, too? Only she and Matthew could have known with certainty.

Often the truth evades us all. It shimmers in the corner of our eye but when we turn to capture its image, it is gone. Make it your mission to search for the light of truth every day and to use it to expose the deeds done in darkness.

Justice can exist only where truth prevails.